Reason and God

REASON AND GOD

Encounters of Philosophy with Religion

by JOHN E. SMITH

New Haven and London: Yale University Press, 1961

BL 51
S64 2

To M. S. S.

Contents

Introduction

RELIGIOUS FAITH and philosophical thought, the most fundamental spiritual forms in human life, have always found themselves in the peculiar position of not being able to get along with each other and of not being able to remain permanently apart. Their overlap of interest, as shown in their common concern for such matters as the ultimate nature of things, the form of the good life, the destiny of man and his status in the universe, has led to their mutual involvement. At times the two have developed together in fruitful cooperation and mutual support, at times they have eyed each other with infinite suspicion born of the fear that each seeks to supplant the other. As regards their cooperation, it has been shown that religious thought can develop most successfully through the medium of concepts and categories furnished by philosophical investigation, and that philosophy proves to be most original and vital when it is directed toward those ultimate questions about the universe and human life which religion keeps continually before us. The tradition of Christian Platonism, for example, and the great synthesis achieved by Thomas Aquinas show the power and depth of theology when it has philosophical form and self-consciousness; the great philosophers, on the other hand, have been those who concerned themselves with the most fundamental metaphysical questions that have always bordered on the religious concern.

Though the two forms may work together, we must not forget that their relations have also been marked by serious tensions. Philosophical minds have often regarded religion as superstition and as an easy road to conclusions about nature, man, and God which, if justified at all, can be attained only as a result of long and painstaking argument. Religious thinkers have sometimes looked upon philosophy as a blasphemous exaltation of human reason which leads man to venture into regions reserved exclusively for revelation. Every form of philosophical nihilism, materialism, and positivism expresses the suspicion from the philosophical side. Pietism, ecclesiastical dogmatism, and fideism give voice to the suspicion from the religious side. Where either side has prevailed, the inevitable result has been some form of fanaticism and the sealing off of the different aspects of human experience from interchange with one another.

It has been characteristic of the Western tradition that one or the other of these basic outlooks has dominated at a given time. We think, for example, of the Greco–Roman world as a time when the ideas of the great philosophers prevailed and of the Middle Ages as a period under the sway of religion. This seesaw relationship has given rise to the impression that the connections between them belong to the accidents of history and that there is no inner truth of the matter. Nothing could be more erroneous. Our experience of the long interplay between the philosophical traditions initiated by the thinkers of the ancient world and the schools of Christian theology shows that there is an intrinsic connection between the philosophical enterprise and religious faith. This connection, paradoxically enough, becomes most clearly apparent when attempts are made to hold the two entirely apart. Experience has taught us that religion is in constant danger of falling into superstition, dogmatism, and obscurantism unless it encounters philosophical criticism and becomes related to other facets of cultural life. Whether this criticism comes from without, in the form of a philosophy that seeks to interpret religious affirmations in critical terms, or from within, in the form of a theology sensitive to philosophical considerations, it remains true that religion, left to its own internal devices, tends to be self-indulgent and to insulate itself from critical contact with culture and knowledge gained from so-called secular sources.

Philosophy, on the other hand, is not free from complacency. Without the goad of religion and its focus on the ultimate problems of human existence, philosophers tend to retire into technical corners of their own and to concentrate exclusively on questions of methodology and formal expression. Discussion about how one *would* go about dealing with a given issue, or prescriptions concerning the form that the results *would* take, have an endless fascination for philosophical minds, especially when they are free from concern for the urgency of the concrete problems themselves. Religious experience and insight highlight concrete problems of human existence and continually draw thoughtful men to their consideration. The religious dimension of human life provides philosophy with endless material for its own speculation. When philosophy loses touch with religion, there is the great risk of formalization, so that ultimate questions are postponed and preliminary questions gradually come to occupy the whole ground.

For many reasons intimately connected with the far-reaching social and cultural developments of the past two hundred years, philosophy and religious thought have grown steadily apart. As a result of the critical examination of reason and the skeptical conclusions that followed, philosophy was forced to renounce its competence and then its right to deal with classical metaphysical problems and the related issues posed by religious belief. Religion became for many a wholly practical affair, to be allied with morality or art but separated from philosophy and science. The divorce has had the most deep-seated consequences for both sides, and the present intellectual situation presents us with a clear picture of the end result. The scale of philosophy has been greatly reduced; direct confrontation of speculative questions has given way to largely technical questions of procedure and to the formalization of previous results; the search for new philosophical ideas has often been abandoned in favor of attempts to find clearer ways of stating old conclusions. From the other side, religion has found itself separated from rational justification; it has been tempted to retreat within the confines of its own community, to reject all critical discussion with the cultural forms in which it exists, and to base itself so completely upon "commitment" that it appears devoid of all rational compulsion. Some spokesmen for religion speak as though religious doctrines become suspect just to the extent to which it appears possible to give rational justification for them.

Another factor leading to the present situation has been the phenomenal development of the natural sciences. At the same time that philosophers were abandoning their classical province of metaphysics, the natural sciences were establishing themselves as the final arbiters of all questions of fact and existence. Philosophers themselves were fascinated by this development, and many sought to become part of it through the reconstruction of philosophy with science as a basis. Various forms of scientific philosophy developed, and the important total outcome was the exclusive rooting of philosophical thought in the highly abstract conclusions of the sciences. Quite apart from the many issues raised by this turn of affairs, philosophy slipped into a one-sided dependence on science to the *exclusion* of other aspects of man's total experience such as religion and art.

Of vital importance to the cultural life of the present time is a renewal of the ancient encounter between philosophy and religion. The essays that follow are aimed at bringing about such a renewal by focusing on crucial questions that arise when religion and philosophy meet— the relations between Christianity and philosophy, the possibility of natural theology and the relation of religion to experience, the problem of a morality completely separated from religious foundations, the nature of religious symbolism and the bearing of a sacramental conception of the universe upon the expression of a poetic vision. Over and above specific issues, there is the matter of a basic self-understanding; the true nature of religion and philosophy is most clearly revealed in mutual encounter, and aspects of each that are often hidden or thrust into the background become manifest.

Religion is instituted by and continues to draw its life from the initial certainties arising from the experiences of its founders and heroes. Consequently, to proceed from the religious side means not so much the seeking after a truth yet undiscovered as the proclaiming of the meaning and importance of a truth already found. Philosophy, on the other hand, is born from wonder and from the quest of reason to find a pattern, a wisdom in things which is still to be disclosed. One side sets out from certainties; the other seeks to arrive at them. Viewed immediately, each side has its own distinctive and dominant character. This character, however, is not exhaustive; each side has within itself, as a kind of recessive element, the distinctive characteristic of the other, a similarity that becomes fully realized only when the two encounter each other; genuine encounter means that each enterprise is forced to a new level of self-consciousness. Religion discovers that its life is not exclusively a matter of certainties which exclude doubt and the rational quest; philosophy discovers that its life is not exclusively a search, because the rational quest itself must be carried out against a background of truths taken for granted and never fully justified in the course of any inquiry. Philosophy, moreover, comes to its own certainties when it comes to express its constructive results.

Religion becomes a stagnant, lifeless affair if all doubt and questing are removed from it. In the encounter with philosophy the meaning of faith as a continual incorporation and overcoming of doubt is revealed. Philosophy, in turn, becomes a sterile formalism when it takes itself to be no more than a way of attacking problems, a method for conducting an inquiry. The encounter with religion forces an acknowledgment of the certainties which all philosophies harbor in themselves, even if their proponents claim that they have no fixed conclusions and are merely humble seekers after truth. No philosopher has been able to avoid assumptions and no one has ever succeeded in doubting everything consistently. The encounter of philosophy with religion shows, in short, that religion cannot be all finding and that philosophy cannot be all seeking.

The following essays were written at various times and for various occasions. They all point to a common theme: the encounter of philosophy with religion, the interplay between philosophical thinking and the religious questions. The essay on Rousseau appeared in *Yale French Studies* (spring, 1954) as part of an issue devoted to Romanticism. "Nietzsche: The Conquest of the Tragic through Art" was part of a volume dedicated to the memory of David E. Roberts and entitled *The Tragic Vision and the Christian Faith* (ed. Nathan A. Scott, Jr., New York, Haddam House, 1957). The essay on Peirce's philosophy of religion was included in a cooperative volume initiated by the Charles Peirce Society, *Studies in the Philosophy of Charles Sanders Peirce* (ed. Philip Wiener and Frederic Young, Cambridge, Mass., Harvard University Press, 1952). "John Dewey: Philosopher of Experience" was one of four lectures delivered at Yale University in 1959 in honor of the one-hundredth anniversary of Dewey's birth. It has previously appeared in the *Review of Metaphysics (13, 1959)* and in *Dewey and the Experimental Spirit in Philosophy* (ed. Charles W. Hendel, New York, Liberal Arts Press, 1959). "Is Existence a Valid Philosophical Concept?" appeared in the *Journal of Philosophy* (*47*, 1950). "Christianity and Philosophy" was the opening address at a conference on the relation of philosophy to theology held at Denison University in 1955; it appeared in the *Christian Scholar* (*39*, 1956). "The Experiential Foundations of Religion" and "The Present Status of Natural Theology" both appeared in the *Journal of Philosophy* (*55*, 1958). "Religion and Morality" was delivered as an address at Vassar College and was published in the *Journal of Religion* (*29*, 1949). "Poetry, Religion, and Theology" appeared in the *Review of Metaphysics* (*9*, 1955). "The Individual, the Religious Community, and the Symbol" was presented to the Conference on Science, Philosophy, and Religion sponsored by the Institute for Religious and Social Studies of the Jewish Theological Seminary in New York; it appeared in the Conference volume, *Symbols and Values* (ed. Bryson, MacIver, and McKeon, New York, Harper, 1954). "The Permanent Truth in the Idea of Natural Religion" was the Dudleian Lecture for 1960 at Harvard University; it appeared in the *Harvard Theological Review* (January 1961). I take this opportunity to express my gratitude for the honor bestowed and for the kind hospitality extended to me by the faculty and students of the Harvard Divinity School.

J. E. S.

New Haven, Connecticut
April 1961

I. The Past

1. The Religious Implications of Kant's Philosophy

IF OUR ACQUAINTANCE with Kant's philosophy is neither broad nor deep, we shall be apt to think of him primarily as a thinker who set forth a most intricate theory of empirical knowledge and at the same time rejected the classic arguments for God's existence by citing the decisive difference between entertaining the concept of one hundred dollars and actually possessing the cash. To think of his philosophy in this way is to view it as no more than an epistemology which leads to an ultimate skepticism in metaphysics and theology. But such a view is woefully inadequate. Regardless of our final acceptance or rejection of his principal theses, it is essential that we come to some understanding of the depth of his struggle with the nature of perennial philosophical problems, especially their bearing upon the religious concern.

That Kant approached these issues in an entirely new way and that he at times overestimated the force of his critical method cannot be denied. It is essential, however, that we understand why Kant entered upon the analysis of reason and experience in the first place. We have filled our heads with arguments about forms of intuition and categories, and reams of paper have been consumed in discussions of the things in themselves, but we invariably fail to understand the dominant reasons and motives behind the critical philosophy as such. We consistently fail to understand Kant's philosophy as a whole.

Kant appeared at a critical point in the development of two distinct, and at many points opposed, streams of thought. He was sensitive to the metaphysical concerns of the rationalist tradition on the one side and to the empiricist criticism of reason on the other. The main aim of his first *Critique,* as he so often repeated, was to carry out a critical examination of man's rational faculties, to estimate their nature and powers, and to come to some conclusions about the extent or limits of human reason, especially with regard to the metaphysical problems. In the light of rationalist claims in behalf of reason and empiricist attempts to curtail its powers, Kant asked: How much can reason achieve when it seeks to pass beyond the confines of experience? The resulting theory of knowledge was no critical exercise for its own sake; it was intended to show to what extent we might solve those problems concerning the self, the cosmos, and God which form the substance of the Dialectic or third part of the *Critique.* This fact has been obscured by many decades of discussion focused upon the epistemology as an end in itself. But this it decidedly was not, as the first sentence of the preface to the first edition makes clear: "Human reason has this peculiar fate that in one species of its knowledge it is burdened by questions which, as prescribed by the very nature of reason itself, it is not able to ignore, but which as transcending all its powers, it is also not able to answer" (A vii). Here we have Kant's real concern: What are we to make of a situation in which human reason comes inevitably to raise questions which it cannot answer in a definitive way? These unavoidable questions are one and all metaphysical questions, problems concerning what is, from Kant's standpoint, the sphere of the transcendent.

My main purpose is to point out the influence exercised by Kant's general philosophical outlook upon contemporary religious thought; I shall not attempt a survey of Kant's philosophy of religion. There are, however, some pertinent facts about his thinking prior to the period of the great *Critiques* which help us to understand the underlying motives of his thought. Much as he was interested in the natural sciences and in attacking the adequacy of British empiricism as a foundation for scientific knowledge, he was even more concerned over the status of metaphysical questions and the ultimate interests of human reason. Although Kant criticized traditional arguments for the existence of God, the problem of God's reality and relation both to man and to the world never ceased to occupy his attention.

In 1755 he published his *General Natural History and Theory of the Heavens,* a cosmological theory which still has value for modern thinkers. In this work he aimed at harmonizing the idea of God as ground of the universe with the conception of nature as a system developing according to natural laws. He denied that the infinite universe of Newtonian mechanics is in any way incompatible with God's reality, and he especially defended, as the most perfect expression of divine purpose, a universe which does not stand in need of the intervention of a "strange hand" for its operation. In the same year he also published a little known work on metaphysics, the *Nova Dilucidatio,* in which he maintained the reality of God as the ground of all possibility, a position he was to reaffirm some years later in his essay, *The Only Possible Rational Ground for a Demonstration of God's Existence* (1763). In these pre-critical writings there emerges a problem which in many aspects forms the main theme of the first *Critique:* What is the meaning of the concept of *existence* and how is existence known? The problem was first raised by him in connection with the distinction between God and the world. An existing world is more than a system of essences in God, because it has a certain exteriority in space and time. In the course of time Kant came to see the existence problem exhibited par excellence in the case of divine existence. In either case it was fundamental to Kant's thought.

In moving toward his critical or transcendental idealism and the doctrine of empirical grounds for all knowledge, Kant became increasingly critical of the tendency of rationalist thinkers to move from purely logical or rational criteria to a world of existing things. In attacking the principle of contradiction as a sufficient criterion for actuality or existence, Kant was already on the road to his later empiricism. The logical possibility of concepts is not the same, he argued, as the actuality (or even the real possibility) of things. Existence means a real positing and it does not follow from logical principles alone.

Existence troubled Kant more and more. It is no accident that when he later came to formulate the task of pure reason proper in the *Critique,* he described it as the complete determining of the concept of God on the one side and the deduction of his existence on the other. The apex of reason's power, could it only be realized, would consist in reaching existence from rational activity alone. That existence cannot be reached in this way is one of Kant's mature teachings; the impossibility to which the criticism points coincides with the limitation of reason.

The doctrine that knowledge of existence requires more than rational thought and that God's existence cannot be reached by theoretical argument has been the decisive one in its influence upon subsequent religious thought. For it has meant that if God and the transcendent retain their meaning while at the same time remaining outside the sphere of theoretical knowledge, some other avenue of approach to this domain must be found. The main problem of the theologian working within the Kantian framework has been to discover this other approach. Like Moses, the Kantian is allowed to survey the promised land of the transcendent from afar, but he is prevented from possessing it in the form of secure knowledge because of the limitations of the same theoretical reason which first brought it into view. To this topic we shall return; for the present it will be helpful to have before us a compact statement of Kant's fundamental philosophical outlook, what Richard Kroner has called "Kant's Weltanschauung." I shall single out *five foci* in Kant's total view and in them we shall see the influence he has had upon such molders of current religious opinion as Kierkegaard, Berdyaev, Jaspers, Bultmann, Heidegger, and Tillich. There is no intention of making Kant out to be either a theologian or an existentialist, but rather to show the outworking of his ideas. When a thinker opens as many doors as Kant did, there can be no grounds for surprise over the variety of ideas that may finally crowd through.

THE FIVE FOCI

1. The Primacy of the Subject; the Copernican Revolution

Quite apart from learned discussions about ambiguities in Kant's figure of the Copernican Revolution, the principal point is clear. Instead of starting with the object as something already fully given to which the subject or knower must conform, we reverse the order and view the object as in some determinate respects constituted by the a priori contributions of the knowing subject. In thus emphasizing the contribution of the knower, Kant was attacking the received opinion that experience means the passive reception or observation of what is given. According to Kant's normative conception of experience, the contribution of the experiencer, both in intuition and in judgment, is given the status of a necessary condition. Experience requires judgment and judgment is impossible without spontaneity in combining concepts. And even if Kant himself did not use the concept of *freedom* in describing theoretical knowledge, the spontaneity which plays so large a part in the Analytic of the first *Critique* can scarcely be viewed in any other light. Experience demands the ability to synthesize and subsume; the spontaneous activity required is actually a form of freedom. And indeed Kant might have expressed the matter this way himself had he not taken freedom in so exclusively a moral sense.

Kant traced out the consequences of the primacy of subjectivity, not only in his interpretation of empirical cognition, but in morality, art, and religion. In every case the pattern is the same: The structure of subjectivity is shown to be a necessary condition for the possibility of some actuality taken for granted. Reality thus appears as reflected in and interpreted from various human standpoints, and in each case the contribution of the subject is well defined and taken to be universally valid. If, therefore, we describe the Kantian idealism as a subjective philosophy, it becomes necessary to add that the subject in question has a structure which is universal; in other language, Kant's subject is not "subjective."

2. *The Reflective or Critical Standpoint*

Kant did not inaugurate what I would call the "reflexive turn" in modern philosophy, but he gave to it a new precision and a place of such importance that many later thinkers came to regard it as the whole of philosophy rather than as a propaedeutic aimed at resolving questions falling beyond the scope of critical philosophy itself. Historically speaking the reflective approach to knowledge had been well established in the Platonic–Augustinian tradition, and it came to the fore once again in Cartesian thought. Kant, however, established it in a new and refined sense when he maintained that the reflecting subject is able to make his own reason the object of a critical analysis. Kant's method of transcendental deduction appeared as a new philosophical approach, distinct from the older rationalism with its reliance upon deduction but also from the generalizing of repeated instances characteristic of the British philosophical tradition since Bacon.

The results of this critical approach are well known: Objective knowledge is always bound to a sensible basis; the categories of human understanding are confined to the domain of possible experience and, though our reason has the power to *think* more than we can objectively *know*, it cannot by itself produce theoretical cognition of a transcendent object. The singularity of Kant's approach at this point is that the Idea of the Unconditioned is said to arise inevitably within human reason, but understanding in its empirical employment is unable to fulfill the demand which that same reason makes upon it to know the unconditioned reality. God as the absolutely unconditioned cannot be reached by theoretical reason, because he is not an object appropriate to any form of intuition possessed by us. This conclusion, from the standpoint of critical philosophy, is reached via the analysis of human reason. It thus purports to be no less than the view which reason takes of itself.

3. *The Concept of Existence*

If we were to express Kant's doctrine of existence in more classical language, we would say that he denied the validity of placing *existentia* on the same level as *essentia*. The "that" is not merely a part of the "what," and consequently it cannot be known as such through conceptual apparatus alone. The upshot of the matter is that knowledge of existence must be a matter of encounter or confrontation. Secondly, if we attend to the meaning assigned by Kant to existence as a modal category and also to its schematization in the "Postulates of Empirical Thought," we see that existence and intuition of some sort always go together. Existence can be reached only via the constructive process of pure intuition (as in mathematics) or through the givenness of sensible material (as in the general science of nature). Our inability to arrive at knowledge of existence in the absence of these two types of intuition cannot be compensated for by any rational argument. Thirdly, the consequence of Kant's position is that the existence of God, considered from the standpoint of theoretical cognition, would require the one sort of intuition which we do not possess, namely *intellectual* intuition. This lack is, from Kant's critical position, the heart of human finitude.

4. The Denial That We Can Approach God through Proof

Kant's doctrine here has two sides: first, it asserts that no proof of God's existence from theoretical reason can withstand criticism, and secondly, it asserts that a God who could be reached in this way would have to be conceived as a finite, conditioned object and thus not as the God of the Western religious tradition. The first point has been much discussed, whereas the second has frequently been neglected. Kant was raising the question of the place of *proof* in religion, along with the ancient question of the adequacy of human reason for grasping and expressing the nature of God. Kant's contention is that to conceive God through the categories of the understanding is to conceive him as a finite object besides others. The question is raised specifically with regard to existence. Can the existence thought in relation to God mean the same as the existence thought in relation to finite empirical objects? In other words, if we argue that God necessarily exists, does "exists" mean just what it means in the case of tigers or tables, or must we not have another concept of existence? It would appear that we require the concept of *necessary existence,* where the "necessary" aspect is not that of a purely logical determination attached to the finite and ordinary conception of existence, but where the necessity belongs to the nature of the subject concept, God. A necessary existence is one in which there is no separation of the "that" and the "what," and this is not to be confused with a necessity which arises out of the logical character of a deduction (i.e. that existence "necessarily follows"). Kant did not join these issues, for to have done so would have been to pass beyond critical philosophy into the sphere of constructive metaphysics.

Kant's questioning of the approach to God's existence through demonstrative proof brings the issue of God's existence into focus, but in view of the fact that he confined the meaning of existence to that of the schematized category, legitimate within finite existence alone, he was prevented from exploring the problem further. The claim, nevertheless, that theoretical proof is inadequate opens up the possibility that God may be reached or become related to the self in some other way. This remains a genuine possibility in Kant's philosophy because his rejection of the way of proof is not a rejection of God. On the contrary, Kant often claimed that it is of the utmost importance for us to be convinced of God's reality, but not so vital that we be able to prove it.

5. *Primacy of Freedom and Practical Reason*

In addition to his status as a part beside other parts in a system of nature, man is also a subject capable of acting in accordance with the conception of a law. This capacity exercised in accordance with reason's own autonomous imperative serves to mark out the moral dimension of life and the sphere of freedom. When Kant wrote at the beginning of the *Critique* (B xxx) of the need to deny *knowledge* of God, freedom, and immortality in order to make way for faith, it was moral or practical faith which he had in mind. The doctrine of reason's limitation was aimed at showing not only the reality of the moral dimension but the possibilities it harbors for reaching the sphere of the transcendent. For in Kant's later development of the idea, man's awareness of the unconditioned in the form of a categorical imperative represents a *practical* transition to the supersensible. The absolutely unconditioned remains effectively beyond the synthesizing activity of theoretical reason, but man can still be related to it in a moral form. Kant was less inclined than many of his nineteenth-century followers to transform this moral relationship into another *theoretical* argument. His so-called moral argument is to be interpreted in the transcendental sense of finding the conditions for the intelligibility of morality rather than as a new theistic argument in which morality is used as an empirical fact from which to deduce God's existence by theoretical reason.

If there are any doubts about the validity of placing the moral above the theoretical in describing Kant's view, they can be stilled by pointing to his assertions about freedom in the *Critique of Judgment*. There Kant twice states (trans. Bernard, appendix, sec. 91, pp. 406, 413) that freedom is the only one of the ideas to be regarded as a thing of fact and as belonging to the *scibilia*. The implication is clear: Reason is able to complete itself and obtain satisfaction in the practical sphere, whereas in all others it falls short of its projected goal. The completion is, however, moral in character; reason *ought* to reach its goal of determining an existence solely from its own resources, and it does so only when we have the act which flows from the good will.

Some Current Consequences

Neither the philosophy of existence, particularly in its religious form and bearing, nor a considerable amount of recent theological thought would have been possible without the foregoing ideas. Most important of all has been the concentration upon and at the same time the transformation of the concept of existence. It has been at the foundation of all philosophies of existence, and it appears in current theological discussion as well through the thought of Kierkegaard and Schelling. Kierkegaard was the forerunner; he fastened upon the idea of existence and was the first to bring about the change from "existence" in Kant's sense of the givenness of a thing through intuition, into *Existenz,* the direct experience or shock received by an actual individual being when he becomes aware of himself as "there"—as occupying a "place"—in a contingent world. As a direct experience, Existenz points to a vivid realization by the self of its own situation. Since existence is no longer viewed as a modal category in a system of categories but the individual's experience of himself as an actual being somewhere and somewhen, the approach to it is radically altered. For Kierkegaard existence becomes "what thought cannot think"; his whole point is that you do not think existence as an appropriate topic for theoretical analysis, but you embody it, experience it, and wrestle with it. Being an individual self carries with it all of the problems attached to the achievement of happiness and self-realization. In attacking Hegel's resolution of Kant's problems by means of an absolute reason, Kierkegaard tried to go back in his own way to Kant's strictures on speculative knowledge. Against Hegel, Kierkegaard says: "To answer Kant within the fantastic shadow-play of pure thought is precisely not to answer him. The only thing-in-itself which cannot be thought is existence, and this does not come within the province of thought to think" (*Postscript,* 292). The view here expressed is not exactly that of Kant as we understand him, but he paved the way for it by his doctrine that existence can never be reached by thought alone. Moreover, Kant's doctrine of the thing-in-itself transcending thought now becomes identified with human existence itself, especially as ethically understood, and it is declared to be outside the province of thought. Again, this is not precisely Kant's view, but he prepared the way for it by his own emphasis upon the primacy of the moral subject and the claim that the moral subject stands related by his moral capacity to what transcends speculative or theoretical reason.

Kierkegaard goes well beyond Kant at many points. In his view it is not so much that we aim at thinking and determining existence and fail but rather that existence in the sense of Existenz is not the proper object of theoretical thought at all. Existence is, instead, the human self actually participating in all the problems of retaining selfhood in a precarious world and of seeking to find a mode of life which excludes falsehood, deception, and pretension.

Although Kierkegaard's existential dialectic of human life embraces a threefold movement from the immediate or aesthetic through the ethical to the religious, the hand of Kant is to be seen in the insistence that being human and becoming ethical are one and the same. Man appears not so much in his classical role as the rational animal as in the form of a being who is capable of moral responsibility and concern for his own destiny. Kierkegaard does not, as has sometimes been supposed, deny human rationality, but rather stresses the point that man is not to be distinguished primarily in this way. The proper differentia of man is his subjectivity or awareness of individuality and its ethical demands.

If Kierkegaard seized upon the concept of existence, Berdyaev made Kant's doctrine of freedom basic in his philosophical and theological writings. In his book *The Beginning and the End* we find Berdyaev lamenting our failure to understand Kant because of the tendency to regard him as the destroyer of all metaphysics. On the contrary, Berdyaev insists, Kant was the founder of a new metaphysics, a metaphysics of freedom and of becoming. An essentialist metaphysics he regards as no longer possible, but an existential metaphysics based on the self and its freedom is not only possible but imperative.

The most fruitful suggestion made by this transformation and development of Kant—it can be seen also in Tillich and Hartshorne—is that a metaphysics rooted in experience makes possible some dialogue between philosophy and theology. The current intellectual scene is one of contrast and deep chasms. The ancient dialogue between philosophers and theologians has all but ceased; between the two there is often little more than mutual abuse flung across an infinite space. And this is mainly because both philosophy and theology have given way to the temptation to positivize themselves, to retreat behind the brute fact. And since the sources of fact for the two are vastly different, there seems to be no point of contact that would make discussion possible. The empirical metaphysic represented by Berdyaev, however, contains resources for keeping the lines of communication open. Unlike Karl Barth, Berdyaev will have nothing to do with a theology which scorns philosophy. One of the most important of Berdyaev's doctrines concerns the need for an existential type metaphysics which would enable us to interpret theological ideas from a critical or theological perspective. And there can be no doubt that Berdyaev would be the first to acknowledge the influence of Kant in the formation of his view.

The philosophical work of Jaspers and Heidegger represents another recurrence of the Kantian philosophy. Each emphasizes in his own characteristic way the finite or human character of man and his reason. But in so doing each allows for the element of self-transcendence which critical philosophy requires. Man appears to them as the being who raises the question of the meaning of his being. To be engaged in a quest and to be involved in the putting of a question are marks of incompleteness and finitude. The limitation of man, expressed by Kant as the finitude of theoretical reason, is here reinterpreted in a more directly experiential way. Man comes up against his finitude in the experience or shock of care and concern. These disclose an imperfect being. Once again, the interpretations offered are not precisely what Kant would have said, but it is clear that he opened the door to these possibilities.

Although we cannot but acknowledge the religious aspect of much existential thought stemming from Kant, we must not overlook the direct Kantian influence upon more properly religious and theological developments of recent years. There is no question that the most influential part of Kant's doctrine for Protestant theology has been his strictures upon the approach to God through proof sustained by theoretical reason. It is impossible to overestimate the extent to which the acceptance of these strictures has led theologians to seek other approaches to God. The tradition of the past hundred years which would have theology more concerned with value than with fact, represents an offshoot of the Kantian criticism. More recently we have seen other proposals for theological construction, and each represents a way of construing theology which makes it something other than speculative knowledge. We have been offered the *historical* approach as opposed to the *metaphysical; personal encounter* has been set against *knowledge about* God; the *revelational* has been contrasted with the *speculative;* and the *linguistic* often takes the place of the *cognitive.* It is not that these possibilities can be derived from Kant nor is it suggested that he would have approved such alternatives since he had his own moral continuation for theology, but it is significant that they have been developed by thinkers decidedly under Kantian influence. Many have set out from his conception of the limitation of human reason and then searched for some other avenue of approach. The dominant view has been that if God can no longer be understood as an object to be reached through demonstration, he must be reached, if at all, either in direct encounter, in moral obligation, or as implicit in the experience of finitude itself. The use made of these ideas by such thinkers as Buber, Bultmann, and Tillich is known to every student of contemporary religious thought.

Kant's assertion, moreover, of the limitations attached to human rational categories has given rise to the doctrine that myth and symbol are the most adequate forms of expression for the shaping and communication of religious ideas. The underlying problem is not new; Christian theologians since the third century have been aware of the problem of discovering adequate and critical forms of expression for religious meaning. The development of the doctrine of analogy in the medieval philosophers and theologians testifies to the same concern. Kant focused the problem anew through his radical epistemological criticism of the metaphysical sphere. With the criticism and curtailment of the older metaphysics, theology was deprived of a powerful and extensive set of concepts and principles through which to express itself. Consequently, the task of finding a new and critical form of expression for religious meaning has been before us ever since. Kant's limitation of the scope of concepts has further aggravated the problem and increased the need for symbolic forms and language not wholly conceptual in character.

We could continue the process of pointing out the reappearance of Kant's focal points in contemporary discussion; it will, however, be more illuminating if we can summarize the religious implications of his position in a more direct way. For those who saw only the negative side of Kant —his quasi-phenomenalism and rejection of metaphysics as knowledge—the only consistent development was in the direction of positivism or a scientific empiricism remaining within the boundaries of methodology or the theory of knowledge. From this perspective, God and the transcendent became meaningless and arguments for God lost all standing, even the right to be called wrong! It is, however, interesting to note that many who adopted this extreme position often expressed in a private and personal way their nonofficial understanding of many things spoken of by religious thinkers. And a response of this sort is consistent, because all is permissible in the personal or practical sphere as long as there is no invasion of the sacred domain of cognitive meaning by anything like religion advancing cognitive claims of its own. The divorce has come to be complete; the cognitive sphere contracts, and more and more matters of concern and import are forced into the irrational. We must not overlook the fact that antiphilosophical theologians very much welcome this type of philosophy as the perfect ally; they suppose that, while the position is irrelevant to their own claims which are all based beyond reason, it can be safely used to eliminate metaphysical rivals who come with philosophical ideas of God.

At the other pole there are many who, while accepting the main outlines of Kantian criticism, did not regard it as destroying God and the transcendent but only as sweeping away a certain deistic and speculative approach to the religious reality. The door was thus left open for new approaches. These thinkers, including many theologians, have taken note of Kant's doctrine that we can *think* more than we can legitimately *know*. The thought guarantees the possibility of God, the actuality must be reached in some way which does not contravene the Kantian limits. Kant did, of course, point the way himself; he left us with the moral pathway as the only possibility, but whether it was broad enough to do justice to the religious dimension may well be questioned. Important as the moral aspect is, we cannot hope to fit all of religion into it. Many basic theological concepts, though they undoubtedly have relevance for morality, cannot be interpreted adequately within the limits of morality alone.

If we survey the development of religious thought since

Kant, we cannot escape one fact: Most thinkers who have taken Kant as a point of departure have accepted without question the validity of the analysis through which he arrived at his conclusions regarding the limitation of reason. Few philosophers or theologians have gone again into the heart of Kant's analysis of the mathematical and general empirical knowledge in order to discover for themselves its own validity. The common and less arduous tendency has been to accept the conclusions Kant reached—the confining of reason to the materials of intuition—without repossessing the arguments by which they were established. Had they attempted to do so, they might have been led to raise questions about the sufficiency of the critical approach itself. Did Kant really treat reason in its full scope and capacities or did he rather, as Hegel always maintained, assume the validity of understanding at the outset and then use it as a sole criterion for judgment? A peculiar fact about Kant's entire first *Critique* is that nowhere does it have any place within itself for the type of knowledge it purports to be. And, on Kant's own grounds, we are entitled to ask why we should accept as true any doctrine which cannot itself be shown to be knowledge in its own terms. Perhaps the *Critique* itself shows powers for reason which the official conclusions of that work rule out. The whole question of the nature and scope of reason must be reopened so that we may reconsider some of the dichotomies introduced by Kant in the light of their subsequent effects. We need to ask whether there is any rational way out of the impasse in the present philosophical and religious situation: On one side stands the domain of "factual" knowledge represented by science and positivistic philosophies and on the other stands "value" represented by existential philosophies and theology. The existence of this split in the modern intellectual situation points back to the ultimate dualism in Kant's own thought between Nature and Freedom.

That dualism stands in need of radical re-examination. But though we may find reasons for amending some Kantian conclusions, we cannot ignore the power of Kant's influence in raising and discussing questions of this sort. The history of religious thought since Kant illustrates, better than that of any other sphere, the truth of the oft-cited thesis that you can philosophize with Kant or against him but not without him.

2. Rousseau, Romanticism, and the Philosophy of Existence

"CONTRAST," said Royce, "is the mother of clearness." This is a truth which any man can verify simply by recalling the way in which he is most likely to grasp the nature of any of his own experiences. It is virtually impossible to describe a writer, a work of art, a friend, an occupation without doing so by means of comparison and contrast. The writer we have in mind is important because he is more adept than others at expressing the temporal character of life; our art form is meaningful to us because it is closer to our concrete experience than any other form; our friend is dear to us because he is dependable, whereas many of our casual acquaintances are not; our occupation stands out with clarity as soon as we know that it is more demanding or less rewarding in certain respects than some others. Human attitudes, outlooks, and temperaments can best be understood when set off in contrast to each other and to their surroundings, just as mountains reveal themselves vividly and clearly because of the valleys and plains in between.

Romanticism, both as an individual temper of mind and as a comprehensive outlook on the world, and the philosophy of existence as a philosophical response characteristic of the individual in the modern world can be viewed together and understood through just this sort of contrast-effect. In some respects the two are similar, and in others they are very different; but however this may be, each will be better understood if we can succeed in getting them both into view at the same time in order to compare certain of their significant features.

It may safely be assumed that Romanticism is accepted as the name of a broad cultural movement of the late eighteenth and early nineteenth centuries, even though what is to be meant by the term will depend to a large extent on the particular individuals chosen to represent the movement. The philosophy of existence, or "existentialism" as it has come to be known, presents its own problems for the interpreter: first, because we are at present in the midst of its development, and second, because many of those who might legitimately be called "existentialists" are inclined to deny not only their own membership in the movement but even that there is any such thing as a movement at all. The first problem is always a formidable one for any effort of contemporary understanding; the second can be resolved by bearing in mind that those actively engaged in elaborating a form of thought are not the best interpreters of what it all means. Despite the disclaimers, there is a very definite main drift of thought which stems from Kierkegaard and can legitimately be regarded as existential philosophy.

Confronted with two complex outlooks on the world, it is clearly impossible to follow either through the details of their many representatives. It is possible, however, to consider each as an example of what Whitehead called a "climate of opinion," a cast or temper of mind appearing at a definite historical period and possessing sufficient identity and continuity throughout a variety of thinkers to justify our taking it as a single entity. In order to hold any discussion of such climate to the concrete, it is necessary to introduce one or more representatives and to ask them to do double duty. On the one hand they must appear as typical of the movement, and on the other they must be able to

stand as individual thinkers in their own right, differing
in this or that particular from the general climate which
they exemplify. For Romanticism we may conveniently
choose Rousseau and for the philosophy of existence, Kierkegaard and Jaspers,[1] relying here and there on others of a
similar bent who might also have been chosen to be the
main representatives. All that it is necessary to bear clearly
in mind is that whatever is said about a representative
thinker points beyond itself as revelatory of the general
climate of opinion. Moreover, it will be necessary to select
from all the possible aspects of these movements which
might be considered three concepts—the individual, freedom, and reason—employing them as reference points for
comparison.

The most obvious meeting point is the primacy of the individual. There can be little question that Romanticism
in all its forms expressed a high regard for the individual,
and the Romantics waged an incessant war against whatever
tended to hinder the free development of individual talents
and capacities. Speaking of the English Romantic poets,
Bowra says: "The Romantic movement was a prodigious
attempt to discover the world of spirit through the unaided
efforts of the solitary soul. It was a special manifestation of
that belief in the worth of the individual which philosophers and politicians had recently preached to the world."[2]
In Rousseau this concern for the individual took the form
of a stress on all that is most intimately personal in life:
inclination, desire, feeling, and will. Indeed one might say

1. To attempt within a brief chapter to justify the selection of these as
representative would be disastrous; the reader is free to choose his own representatives.

2. C. M. Bowra, *The Romantic Imagination* (Cambridge, Mass., Harvard
University Press, 1949), p. 23.

that whatever misplaced reputation Rousseau has earned
for being a "sentimentalist" stems from his insistence on the
importance of the intensely personal features of individual
life. A concern for the status and ultimate destiny of the
individual is likewise a common theme for the philosophy
of existence; for all of them without exception, existence
means something individual or it means nothing at all.
"The whole development of the world," said Kierkegaard,
"tends to the importance of the individual,"[3] and it is clear
that the aim of all his writing (especially the works "indirectly communicated") is to call the individual back to
what is unique in himself and away from exclusive concern
with what is common to the species. Kierkegaard saved
some of his bitterest irony for the "comical" man, the man
of much knowledge and erudition, the man who is learned
even about himself and human affairs, but who has man-
aged to overlook his own self, the fact of his existence, and
the problems connected with the working out of his own
destiny. A similar emphasis is found in Jaspers in his distinction between the truths which the individual counts
as part of his knowledge and the truths by which the existing individual actually lives, truths so intimately bound up
with his individual self that he is ready to die for them if
necessary.

Granted that these two types of thought have a common
concern for the individual, it must be asked whether they
both understand the individual in the same way. For many
Romantics and for Rousseau in particular, the contrast
between the individual and civilized society was a contrast
between the natural and the artificial, between an original

3. *The Journals of S. Kierkegaard,* trans. Dru (London, Oxford University
Press, 1938), no. 632 (1847); cf. no. 1050: "In the animal world 'the individual' is always less important than the race. But it is the peculiarity of the
human race that just because the individual is created in the image of God
'the individual' is above the race."

nature and a highly organized and contrived set of institutions.[4] In seeking to recover the individual from a maze of social relationships and structures and to set him free again, Rousseau was trying to make it possible for an original individual nature to come forth and express itself frankly without false restraint.[5] It is important to bear in mind, however, that he clearly presupposes the existence of this individual nature which needs only to be provided with a proper environment in order to flourish. "Oh man," he says, "live your own life and you will no longer be wretched. Keep to your appointed place in the order of nature and nothing can tear you from it."[6]

With existentialism, however, the protest in the name of the individual is not made in behalf of an original nature taken as a norm in Rousseau's sense; it is rather an attempt to bring the individual face to face with the fact of his own unique existence. Despite criticism of the anonymity of the mass man in society, society is not looked upon simply as an artifice through which something natural has been distorted. For Kierkegaard and Jaspers the individual finds himself set down in the midst of a bewildering and threatening environment, and, starting with a full recognition of this fact, he must find his meaning and fulfillment in the relatively short time allotted to him. For existentialism there is no conception of an original nature which provides a norm for man, a nature to which man may turn and return

---

4. This is not to say that the contrast between "individual" and "society" corresponds in every respect to that between "natural" and "artificial." If this were the case it would be impossible for Rousseau to speak as he does of the "natural society." Cf. *Emile*, V, "ce qui est naturel a l'état naturel et ce qui est naturel a l'état civil." See H. Hoffding, *Rousseau and His Philosophy* (New Haven, Yale University Press, 1930), p. 116.

5. Notice in this connection Rousseau's remark: "There is no one in the world less able to conceal his feelings than Emile." *Emile*, V, trans. Barbara Foxley (Everyman Edition), pp. 377–78.

6. Ibid., II, p. 47.

in confidence.[7] On the contrary, almost all of the existential philosophers stress the precarious foothold which man has in the world; he is the being who asks what it means to be and, discovering that he cannot lay hold of his own nature (let alone his ideal fulfillment) with certainty, he is anxious, concerned, and driven. In Jaspers and Heidegger particularly there looms large the idea of Kant that man has no fixed "nature" like other things but possesses instead freedom, something which is his by "nature" but which is at the same time a task to be completed, an achievement rather than a fixed endowment. It is almost as if the individual were to give his own nature to himself in the design and prosecution of the projects which manifest his freedom. Man is existence and his existence is prior to all essential nature, to all essence, which is precisely why, for the existentialists, the individual cannot be interpreted as an original nature waiting for its development upon the removal of artificial restraints.

It is important to notice in this regard that a great deal of Romanticism, despite its criticism of the eighteenth-century world of Reason, could still presuppose this world as a stable background for individual development. In short, for all of their criticism of their own immediate past, most Romantics, and Rousseau particularly, still believed in the idea of Nature as a norm and as a guide. Were this not true, Rousseau would not have been able to say to Emile, "You must follow nature's guidance if you would walk aright." In contrast, the philosophy of existence does not have the objective world of Reason and Nature upon which to fall. Between the age of Romanticism and the contemporary world falls the second half of the nineteenth century and the shaping of the historical consciousness. In a sense the

7. See Rousseau, *Contrat Social*, II, chap. 9: "Comme la nature a donné des termes à la stature d'un homme bien conformé, passé lesquels elle ne fait plus que des géants ou des nains. . . . "

individual of Romanticism still lived in a relatively stable world; the individual of Kierkegaard, of Heidegger does not. He lives in a world of temporality, of historical acts and movements. It is impossible to overestimate the difference. The world of Rousseau was one of boundless space, of remote places, fascinating and attractive. The setting of the individual for the philosophers of existence is not space, but time and history. Space no longer enjoys its power to overawe man, nor its supremacy over his will.

Time, we say, is of the essence, and it is in time that the individual of Kierkegaard and Jaspers must dwell. History, however, is almost endlessly plastic and forms not so much a stable background against which and from which the individual develops as a fluid medium of change demanding decision and action. Such a medium carries with it the possibility of individual fulfillment, but it also harbors the possibility of frustration and nothingness, the possibility that man's time will run out before his goal is reached. The individual of existentialism is prospective in his outlook and is forever attempting to create; he does not look, like the man of Rousseau, to an original nature or to a system of universal forms to be unfolded as soon as the artifices of social organization are done away with. The individual for Rousseau is continuous with nature and becomes alienated only through a distorted society; the individual of existentialism has no fixed nature and he is not at home in the world; consequently he must find his way by plumbing the depth both of his freedom and the possibilities of history.

The second reference point, the concept of freedom, provides another meeting ground between Rousseau and the philosophers of existence. Kierkegaard, Jaspers, and Sartre have outdone all other philosophers in maintaining that man not only has freedom but that he *is* freedom, that

freedom defines his nature, and that only as a free being can
he be understood. "There are," says Jaspers, "two ways of
looking at man: either as an object of inquiry, or as freedom."[8] It is clear throughout the entire range of his work
that it is man as freedom who is decisive; man as object of
knowledge, as one thing to be studied besides other things,
is not man as he really exists. For Rousseau also, man finds
his proper dignity in and through the freedom he possesses.
Man shares self-love and sympathy, the two primary senti-
ments, with the animals, and although he possesses a distinguishing characteristic in his reason, what *essentially*
distinguishes man is his freedom.[9]

Freedom includes the possibility of moral perfection
(vertu), a perfection which goes beyond the attainment of
happiness or well-being *(bonté).* For Rousseau freedom has
a threefold character: It is in the first instance *independence,* the immediate conviction of being in possession of
sufficient power to initiate acts. The Savoyard Vicar says:
"No material creature is in itself active, and I am active. In
vain do you argue this point with me; I feel it, and it is this
feeling which speaks to me more forcibly than the reason
which disputes it."[10] But independence by no means exhausts the nature of man's freedom. It expresses itself further, as *civil liberty* which, as E. H. Wright remarks, "begins
as soon as any group of us engages in a conscious common
aim."[11] When independence enters into the community it
sacrifices its unboundedness in return for the security of
mutual rights and duties. The third feature is the ideal

8. *Der philosophische Glaube* (Artemis Edition, Zurich, 1948), p. 50;
trans. Ralph Manheim, *The Perennial Scope of Philosophy* (New York, Philosophical Library, 1949), p. 54.

9. See *Contrat Social,* I, chap. 2, where "common liberty" is said to be a
"result of the nature of man"; *une conséquence de la nature de l'homme.*

10. *Emile,* IV, trans. Foxley (Everyman Edition), p. 242.

11. E. H. Wright, *The Meaning of Rousseau* (London, Oxford University
Press, 1929), p. 27.

completion of freedom (what Hegel would call "concrete freedom") in the attainment of *virtue*. Virtue is the realization of freedom as having a certain quality; virtue is freedom which realizes itself as moral good. In asking the question, "What is meant by a virtuous man?" Rousseau answers, once again through the mask of the Savoyard Vicar,[12] "He who can conquer his affections; for then he follows his reason, his conscience: he does his duty."[13]

Freedom is thus essentially the realization of the true nature of man as reason and as conscience. Such freedom has form and structure; it is no lawless self-indulgence, for nature always supplies the norm, and the mastery of life for the individual consists first in discovering this standard and then in conforming to it.

Freedom is in the background of Kierkegaard's thought despite the fact that he does not make it an object of extravagant praise as, say, Berdyaev does; Heidegger presupposes it in the elaboration of his doctrine of man; Sartre makes his entire intricate and subtle analysis of man in the world turn on the essentiality of freedom. "Freedom," says Jaspers, "is the path of man through time," and he regards it as the goal of all human endeavor. Freedom in existence, for Jaspers, is principally a matter of overcoming what threatens us from without and within, and reaching out to include the fullness of life by bringing together in a fruitful way the inescapable *polarities* of life: "Along with every position, the counterposition unfolds . . . freedom is lost where the polarities are sacrificed to a limitation—whether it is in an order which forgets its own limits or

12. The interesting suggestion is made by Pierre Burgelin in his *La Philosophie de l'Existence de J. J. Rousseau* (Paris, Presses Universitaires de France, 1952), that Rousseau, like Kierkegaard with his pseudonyms and Nietzsche with Zarathustra, employed the technique of "indirect communication." Julie and the Savoyard Vicar are cited as examples (p. 4).

13. *Emile*, V, p. 408.

in extremes which partially contradict the order."[14] Freedom is the encompassing of many possibilities, but it also
holds out the possibility of failure and despair, for only a
being who is free can fail to attain his goal. "Freedom," says
Jaspers, "arouses enthusiasm, but freedom also causes anxiety."[15] It is stress upon this "dark side" of freedom which
is characteristic of the philosophies of existence. Freedom
for them is anxious; it is precarious and is always bound up
with risk and uncertainty, just because freedom is empty
unless it is realized in accordance with some order—some
true meaning—which may be past finding out. Man cannot
turn to any fixed nature for guidance because, as a creature
of freedom in existence, he is a creature of time and change.
If he is to find the truth of his existence at all, it can only
be in history.

The precariousness of existence as freedom in the existentialists may be even more vividly expressed through the
idea of *estrangement*. Heidegger makes much of the idea
that man is the one who is "thrown into the world"; Sartre
frequently stresses the absence of signs in the world, signs
which might indicate the way for man, and he even thinks
of man's freedom as guaranteed simply because there are
no signs and the real world is a desert. Perhaps the best illustration of this is provided by Kierkegaard when he says:
"One sticks one's finger into the soil to tell by the smell in
what land one is: I stick my finger into existence—it smells
of nothing. Where am I? How came I here? . . . How did
I come into the world? Why was I not consulted?"[16]

Surely this points to a more radical feeling of homeless-
ness on the part of man than is to be found in Rousseau, or

14. *Vom Ursprung und Ziel der Geschichte,* p. 199; translation mine.
15. Ibid., p. 196.
16. From Kierkegaard's *Repetition.* See Helmut Kuhn, *Encounter with
Nothingness* (London, Methuen, 1951), pp. 30–31.

even in those of the Romantics who were far less at home in the world than he. Despite their undoubted feeling of estrangement in the Newtonian world of physical reality, or in its eighteenth-century counterpart, the Romantics had a confidence in their own free creative power, in their own feeling, imagination, and will. Above and beyond this uneasiness was a strong conviction that there really is a natural man underneath, and that his development only awaits the setting aside of artificial restraints. The tone with which Rousseau appeals to the individual to realize himself, presupposes a confident belief that each individual has an essential nature and that it can be brought to full expression through courage and the exercise of will.

Existentialism stresses more the peril of freedom than the promise. Its individual has no such confidence; he is estranged from the world and his life is filled with all the concern and anxiety which flows from an awareness that he is free and perhaps the bearer of a destiny denied to those who have no freedom—and at the same time he is in great danger of losing the prize and of failing to find the desired fulfillment. The incongruity between the possibilities inherent in freedom and the risk which accompanies what is merely possible and thus may fail to come to pass, leads to uneasiness and to an experience of the radical contingency of individual human existence.

The last concept singled out for attention is the most difficult to discuss. Both opponents and sympathizers alike have interpreted Romanticism, and particularly the work of Rousseau, as expressing an outlook thoroughly opposed to reason and devoted to the undisciplined indulgence of feeling and sentiment. Irving Babbitt, it should be noted, was not alone in adopting such a view. Likewise, a good deal has been written which brands existentialism as "irrationalism" and as "enemy of reason." Actually the situation is far

more complex in the case of both movements than is generally supposed. A full discussion would require, in addition to a considerable acquaintance with the works of many
writers, a clear view as to the nature and scope of reason,
for it is obvious that you cannot decide the relation of a
type of thought to reason unless you know what you mean
by the term.

Perhaps for our present purpose it would be best to confine attention to a basic similarity on the one hand and a
striking difference on the other. There can be no doubt that
Rousseau, Kierkegaard, and Jaspers are at one in their opposition to making objective knowledge and discursive
thought primary in individual life. These thinkers, not to
mention others on both sides, reject *rationalism* and refuse
to accept the thesis that the concrete self is identical with
the knowing self. Each in his own way calls attention to the
gap between the idea and the reality and to the possibility
that thought instead of uniting the knower with his world
sets him instead at a distance. "By nature," says Rousseau,
"man thinks but seldom," or again, "the most virtuous
woman in the world is probably she who knows least about
virtue."[17] Here the exercise of thought, particularly of
speculative thought which directs attention away from the
concrete social and political duties of man, is regarded as
unnatural. The man of thought is not identical with the
natural man, because the natural man is the concrete self,
embracing a range of experience which no thought can
adequately encompass. For Rousseau instinct, feeling, and
inclination have their rights and are closer to man's essential
nature than is discursive thought. These aspects of man's
life are to be trusted and, when exercised in accordance
with conscience, they express man in his perfection. It is
not that Rousseau rejected reason but that he wanted it to

17. *Emile,* V, p. 371.

be set in proper relation to other aspects of human life.[18] There can be no doubt that he did look upon the reflected power of man as a power which enters into and breaks up the spontaneity and continuity of life. The needs and demands of concrete life determine the place and the importance of reason, and not the other way around. Subtleties of distinction and argument consequently must justify themselves to the individual by their direct relevance to his own life and personal situation. In this regard there is a genuine and important tie between Rousseau and Romanticism generally and the *Lebensphilosophie* of the later nineteenth century.

The attitude of Kierkegaard and Jaspers toward reason is more radical and more intimately connected with the development of problems in the tradition of Western metaphysics and theology. The contrast envisaged by them between thought and individual life is not, as in Rousseau, a contrast between the spontaneous or self-forgetful expression of one's own nature on the one hand and the studied precision of reflection and argument on the other. It is not a contrast merely between what one thinks and what one feels. It is a contrast which is infinitely more complex and ultimately stems from the problem of finding the proper relation between *essence* and *existence*, the two poles of concrete being in classical metaphysics. For Kierkegaard and for Jaspers reason is fitted to grasp the *what*, essence, universal nature and structure, but existence, the *that*, escapes and even defies rational apprehension. The individual, in existence, both exists and thinks, and self-realization consists in his ability to bring thought into fruitful relation to that particular existence which is his alone. Reason, in-

18. See the excellent remarks about Romanticism in this regard in James Gutmann's introduction to Schelling's *Of Human Freedom* (Chicago, Open Court, 1936), p. xxvii.

stead of being regarded as an unambiguous source of light and guidance for the life of the particular existent, is looked upon as a power which, because it enables him to abstract from existence, leads him away from the contingency, which is actual life, into the domain of the necessary, which is thought. Kierkegaard, who invariably thought of reason and philosophy as being what Hegel conceived them to be, was more radical than any of the other existentialists in contrasting reason, which sees *sub specie aeternitatis*, with existence, which is *hic et nunc*. For all existentialists, however, regardless of their differences in other respects, the gap between thought and existence is not to be bridged by more thought, but only by something, an acting, a believing, a deciding which transcends thought. One may say that it is more the proper relation between thought and existence within the life of the individual existent that concerns existentialism, than any ultimate interest in keeping them forever apart.

The relation of thought to existence must always appear as paradoxical from this viewpoint. Man is, among all beings, the only one endowed with reason and freedom, and he is thus the only being able to *exist* in the proper sense of the term. But curiously enough, it is just his power of thought and his freedom which enable the individual to abstract from his own existence and, as Kierkegaard says, to "abscond to the realm of pure being." From such a vantage point, thought is regarded as being more radically at variance with individual selfhood than it was for Rousseau and other Romantics. This is a conclusion which can be maintained for the main drift of existentialism, although it would have to be qualified according to the particular thinker in question. For this reason further comparison of a general sort is not fruitful. A more detailed account would require not only the consideration of Heidegger, Sartre, and others individually, but it would also have to include careful distinction between the various senses of "thought," i.e. as science, philosophy, etc.

It seems especially important, in the case of provocative movements of thought like the two we have been considering, to understand them thoroughly before getting on to criticism and evaluation. A larger part of such understanding depends on a grasp of what these movements were reacting against. Romanticism sought to recover the individual from a world of overweening rationalism and a nature which had come to be regarded as a gigantic machine. Existentalism seeks to recover the individual from the universal anonymous knowledge of science and from the cultural machine, the modern technological mass organization. The former sought for the natural man; the latter seeks for the man of history. The two quests illumine each other both in the points at which they come together and in those where they are far apart.

3. Nietzsche: The Conquest of the Tragic through Art

WHEREAS most philosophers have been eager to communicate their visions and to proclaim the results of their thinking, Nietzsche was a philosopher who liked to hide. Not only was he capable of producing pages filled with a not inconsiderable obscurity but, like Kierkegaard and even Rousseau, he employed the device of a mask for purposes at once of communication and self-concealment. Moreover, Nietzsche's use of irony adds to the general difficulty of understanding his thought, which has very often been misconstrued in the past by a too literal interpretation of essentially ironical utterances. These difficulties are not lessened but rather increased when we approach *The Birth of Tragedy*, which is the book that will be at the center of our attention in this study. The work introduces many subjects in its course, including an historical account of Greek tragedy, a theory of tragic pessimism, a metaphysic of tragedy and of art, and, not least of all, a criticism of late nineteenth-century German culture. And since these themes interpenetrate each other, the consequence is that *The Birth of Tragedy* is by no means an easy work to comprehend.

In order to achieve the greatest possible clarity, the discussion has been arranged in such a way as to move consecutively through a consideration of the following topics: the setting of *The Birth of Tragedy* in the pattern of Nietzsche's development; his special concern for Greek life of the late sixth century and the pessimism he attributed to it; his view of tragedy and the accompanying philosophy of Dionysus; his doctrine of art as metaphysics; the conquest of tragedy through art and the special sense in which pessimism is the truth about human existence; and, finally, the comparison with Christianity, the last topic representing the purpose of the entire study.

The Birth of Tragedy, the first published product of Nietzsche's peculiar and erratic genius, "was begun," as he tells us in *Ecce Homo,* "in the thunder of the battle of Wörth" during the Franco–Prussian War. And, he continues, "I thought out these problems on cold September nights beneath the walls of Metz, in the midst of my duties as nurse to the wounded."[1] Thus, while the main ideas expressed in the work grew out of his studies and lectures on ancient Greek civilization, Nietzsche's own personal experience of pain and suffering must also be kept in full view in any attempt to understand and estimate what he then called the philosophy of pessimism. It is possible to go further and show, as perhaps cannot be done to the same degree for any other significant philosopher, that Nietzsche's entire thought can be correlated with and interpreted by means of a minute account of the course of his life. Finding the man behind and in the thought has been attempted many times in the past, and not always with justifiable results, since the temptation to view his philosophical position from the perspective furnished by the tragic end of his life has always been great and few have been able to resist it. There is, however, no need to follow the biographical interpretation here; the presentation of Nietzsche's position with regard to the meaning and nature of tragedy can and must be accomplished in systematic fashion, for only if we can break

1. *Ecce Homo,* in *The Complete Works of Friedrich Nietzsche,* ed. O. Levy (New York, Macmillan, 1924), *17, 69.*

through and grasp his doctrine in this way will it be possible to discover exactly how the tragic becomes an object of conquest by art and how this solution is finally to be estimated from a Christian perspective.

In 1869 Nietzsche accepted a call to be professor of classical philology at the University of Basel, and *The Birth of Tragedy*, published several years later, was his first and most ambitious effort in the field of classical studies. Unfortunately, it did not meet with a warm and cordial reception in the academic world, and this fact had its own tragic influence upon the course of Nietzsche's later life and thought.[2] His view of scholarship and of science was that such learning is without aim and direction of itself and that consequently it must be guided either by a theory of art or by the exigencies of life.[3] His small work *The Use and Abuse of History* makes clear enough his rejection of a detached scholarship which is without some clear relationship to the actual problems of human life. In accordance with this conviction it was impossible for him to pursue classical studies after the fashion of the reigning academic philology. A. H. J. Knight, in his instructive and measured work on Nietzsche, has expressed the point very well in

2. Nietzsche's creative and vigorous attempt to project himself into the life of classical Greece and to animate it through his own spirit was too much for the classical philologists of his time. Wilamovitz-Möllendorff, the authoritative classicist of the period, set out at once to destroy Nietzsche's speculative approach in a monograph, *Zukunftsphilologie!* (Berlin, 1872). He paid no attention whatever to Nietzsche's efforts to understand the philosophical and religious significance of the tragic form, and consequently he missed all that was important in the work; instead, he confined himself to historical details and inaccuracies of which there were admittedly many. E. Rohde, Nietzsche's lifelong friend and author of the brilliant work *Psyche*, came to his defense, only to be met with a second monograph of the same title further aimed at discrediting *The Birth of Tragedy*.

3. See, for example, *The Genealogy of Morals*. All citations from this work are to be found in the new translation of *Die Geburt der Tragödie* by Francis Golffing, *The Birth of Tragedy* and *The Genealogy of Morals* (New York, Anchor Books, 1956).

saying, "It appears . . . that Nietzsche considered Greek literature, Greek life, and Greek thought from the unusual and unphilological standpoint of a Greek born out of time, not from the standpoint of a normal critic."[4] Curiously enough, what makes *The Birth of Tragedy* significant is the "unscholarly" and unusual thesis it contains concerning the rise of the tragic art form as a means of expressing the pessimistic view of life, and the no less unexpected view that by the Attic period tragedy had run its course, being finally laid to rest by the approach of Euripides and the Socratic spirit.

It has often been pointed out, and with good reason, that in *The Birth of Tragedy* Nietzsche's outlook was profoundly influenced by Schopenhauer, particularly his doctrine of pessimism and his theory of music as the immediate language of the Will, the reality behind all phenomena. It would, however, be an error to suppose that he had just taken over Schopenhauer's philosophy and thus overlook the extent to which Nietzsche believed that he had discovered tragic pessimism for himself in his study of that portion of Greek history that most interested him. And, since his unorthodox interpretation of the Greek development was another instance of Nietzsche the thinker "out of season," it is necessary for us to turn to a brief consideration of the period he regarded as the embodiment of the tragic sense of life.

Nietzsche's view of the origin of tragedy was not the only novel result of his classical studies. Whereas most classical scholars since Goethe had identified "the glory that was Greece" with the achievements of the Attic period—the heart of the fifth century—Nietzsche instead looked upon

---

4. A. H. J. Knight, *Some Aspects of the Life and Work of Nietzsche* (London, Cambridge University Press, 1933), p. 9.

that period as one of decadence and insisted that "the summit" of Greek life was to be found in the preceding century and a half, the period beginning after Hesiod and ending with Aeschylus, which he called "the tragic age." For him this was a time of profound participation in the mysterious depths of life; he saw it as the great age of lyric or dithyrambic poetry and, above all, as the time of Dionysus, the god after whom Nietzsche named his philosophy.[5] His later attack upon Euripides and Socrates as destroyers of tragedy through their optimism and rationalism must be understood against this background of the tragic age.[6] Nietzsche's characterization of the Greek attitude toward life as one of pessimism sounds strange if we are accustomed to deriving that outlook from the thinkers of the Socratic period, where all the emphasis falls upon rationality, optimism, and the moderation of the rational soul. But Nietzsche looked elsewhere for the foundation of his view, and consequently he emphasized the "dark side" of human existence in the period of the pre-Socratics. He was deeply impressed by the Greek's concern for the consequences when man oversteps the limits set to his life—the consequences of *hybris*—and by his sensitivity to the pain in life which often amounted to a cosmic sense of guilt at being alive at all. Immediately prior to the writing of *The Birth of Tragedy,* he had been making a study of Theognis of Megara, the elegiac poet, and he was fond of his line, "For mortals

5. See especially Section II of *The Birth of Tragedy.*

6. Of great importance for a fuller understanding of Nietzsche's outlook in *The Birth of Tragedy* are his lectures on the pre-Socratic philosophy, entitled, appropriately enough, "Philosophy during the Tragic Age of the Greeks" (1873), to be found in *The Complete Works of Friedrich Nietzsche,* ed. O. Levy, 2, 71–170. See also Knight, pp. 22 ff., for the suggestive idea that Nietzsche viewed the history of Greece itself as a great tragic drama, once again reversing received opinion by regarding the triumph over the Persians in 470 B.C. not as the beginning of an ancient glory but as the start of the tragic decline.

not to be born is better than to be born." Nor was he any less attracted by the belief expressed by Sophocles in lines that might be duplicated from the works of many others, "Not to be born is the best fate: but if a man be born, then it is much the next best thing that he should return whence he came as quickly as he can."

In addition to a grasp of the pessimistic outlook gained through his study of antiquity, Nietzsche, from the very outset, saw in the speculations of the pre-Socratic philosophers another idea, and it is one which stands in the center of his vision—the idea of the aesthetic man who has learned from the artist how to contemplate the plurality of human life and to envisage it as the *play* of a poet who has no other end in view but that of the play itself. This idea stands out clearly in his interpretation of the fragments of Heraclitus and Anaxagoras, and we shall have occasion to see its importance for the view expressed in *The Birth of Tragedy* that man can triumph over pessimism only by capturing the standpoint of the creative artist.

We will now turn directly to Nietzsche's theory of tragedy as presented in *The Birth of Tragedy*,[7] particularly to the philosophy of Dionysus and the redemption of the self through participation in the cosmic Will. Central to Nietzsche's interpretation is the initial contrast between Apollo and Dionysus and the two points of view which they symbolize or the two forms of art over which they preside. For from the contrast between the two, and their effective combination, comes the form of tragedy. Apollo, the god of

7. Limitations of space preclude a treatment based upon all of Nietzsche's writings. It is true that in *Ecce Homo* and in the Preface added to *The Birth of Tragedy* in 1886 he tried to give a somewhat different emphasis to his earlier views (e.g. he later distinguished sharply between pessimism and tragedy and contended that, for the Greeks, the latter was the means of overcoming the former), but this need not destroy the authoritativeness of the position that he first expressed.

plastic art, was for Nietzsche the symbol of rational form and moderation, distance from the phenomenon which characterizes the role of spectator or detached observer, and of high individualization of the self against both society and the system of nature. Dionysus, on the other hand, was interpreted by Nietzsche as the god of music,[8] the symbol of enthusiasm and ecstasy, of participation by the self in an overwhelming unity having the power to destroy the isolation of individual life. It is important to notice that Nietzsche first presented the contrast as one between "formative forces arising directly from nature without the mediation of the human artist,"[9] and this would seem to suggest that he understood the two aspects in a metaphysical as well as in an aesthetic sense. This is true, but it is only part of the truth, since the impulses or forces of which he speaks are themselves taken as "artistic urges" on the part of nature.[10] Nietzsche offers illustrations for the two principles wherein the Apollonian is said to be represented by the *dream* and the Dionysiac by the state of *intoxication* or ecstasy, although in his discussion it is difficult to know where to draw the line between the two impulses, as belonging to life in a more extended sense or as belonging exclusively to art. One thing at least is clear: the Apollonian and Dionysiac are taken as expressing distinct attitudes toward life, and, as such, the contrast is revealing because it gives us an insight into Nietzsche's Weltanschauung at the time. In the dream, reality is endowed with the definiteness of form and the sharpness of individuality; the Apollonian

8. The clue to the importance attached by Nietzsche to the music of Wagner is to be found in Nietzsche's identification of Wagner's music with the spirit of Dionysus. See Knight, pp. 9–10.

9. *The Birth of Tragedy*, p. 11.

10. Ibid., p. 24. Unfortunately Golffing's translation misses this point and does not make clear that the "artistic urges" *belong to nature,* as the German text requires—"*ihre Kunsttriebe.*" We have here Nietzsche's idea that nature represents the free play of an artistic impulse.

man faces the world with the confidence that he is an individual capable of understanding both himself and that world by reference to a perfection not exhibited by the everyday world itself. Implicit in this interpretation is the idea that the followers of Apollo derive their security in life from a beauty, a wisdom, and a truth that have the status of "illusion," just because they are not exhibited in the world as it actually exists.[11]

At the other pole (and here we have Nietzsche's peculiar philosophy of power beginning to make itself felt) stands the Dionysiac rapture in which the self puts aside its ordinary hold upon both the world and itself—"the individual forgets himself completely"—and experiences the oneness of all things, and especially his bond with the life and power coursing through the whole of nature. The philosophy of Dionysus means the breaking through all that individuates a self and sets it off from other selves and from nature. Nietzsche's way of expressing this underlines the contrast between the Dionysiac principle and the Apollonian principle at the same time that it reveals the hand of Schopenhauer: "Each individual becomes not only reconciled to his fellow but actually at one with him—as though the veil of Maya had been torn apart and there remained only shreds floating before the vision of mystical Oneness."[12]

Nietzsche thus set himself at this time on the side of all those philosophers for whom the movement toward reality is a movement not toward individuality and specification but toward the ultimate unity of the undifferentiated. Consequently, he always viewed the Dionysiac principle as involving direct participation by the self in the stuff of existence, as identification of the self with the "primal Unity" and as a sort of individual redemption from life through transcendence of the Apollonian individuality.

11. *The Birth of Tragedy,* p. 22.
12. Ibid., p. 26.

Nietzsche was still thinking of Schopenhauer's idea that the aim of life is to transcend the will and to tranquilize desire through an identification of the self with the Oneness of things, but Nietzsche's own voluntarism and tragic sense stood in the way of his acceptance of Schopenhauer's quietistic solution. Nietzsche's view of the primordial unity is not of something static, but is the conception of *a surging power filled with pain and contradiction,* and yet also filled with a fierce joy in all the creativities of life. Dionysiac intoxication not only points the way to the conquest of tragic life, but it is also, in the first instance, an avenue of illumination and the means whereby the tragic character of life is disclosed.

Following another lead pointed out by Schopenhauer, Nietzsche took the ancient lyric, the Dionysiac art, as the one *direct* expression of the pain at the heart of things, and he contrasted it anew with the Apollonian expression of experience through images which, because they *reflect* reality as through a mirror, do not *immediately express* it. Music, on the other hand, is the very language of the Will or primordial power, and, in considering it, we come upon the clear idea behind the obscurity of Nietzsche's analysis. Tragedy was born from the Dionysiac lyric (Nietzsche identified the chorus with the followers of Dionysus), because music expresses directly the terrible truth about existence —that it is pain and sorrow—whereas the plastic arts always interpose between man and his life the images of form which lead to the contemplation of individuality and thus provide a place of standing that is safe from the ravages of existence. From this it is possible to see more clearly why Nietzsche was more inclined to describe the Apollonian world, but not the Dionysiac, as one of "illusion." The lyrical poet does not project anything but rather participates directly in life and is expressive of the ultimate will. He writes: "The lyrical poet . . . himself becomes his im-

ages, his images are objectified versions of *himself*. Being
the active center of that world he may boldly speak in the
first person, only his 'I' is not that of the actual waking
man, but the 'I' dwelling, truly and eternally, in the
ground of being."[13] Yet despite the priority given to the
Dionysiac element in this account (even the full title asserts
that tragedy is born from "the spirit of music"), we must
not forget that only from the cooperation of *both* impulses
can tragedy arise. Thus, for example, the tragedy of Aeschylus, so much admired by Nietzsche, would have been impossible without the utterly Apollonian metaphysical justice
standing in the background.

We must add to this entire picture a further notion, the
full import of which will be clarified in the succeeding section. In addition to his description of the Apollonian and
Dionysiac as two forces in existence which later are expressed in art, Nietzsche also came to view the world, including human beings, as itself a great work of art; at this
point insight into life and into the meaning of the aesthetic
aspect of life become indistinguishable. In a comment more
revealing of his ultimate position than he was perhaps
aware of at the time, Nietzsche maintained that "we have
every right to view ourselves as esthetic projections of the
veritable creator and derive such dignity as we possess from
our status as art works. Only as an *esthetic product* can the
world be *justified* to all eternity."[14] Moreover, the discussion continues by emphasizing the idea that life and art are
a "comedy" prepared by the "primordial artist" for his own
"edification," and that only the creative artist himself—
the man of genius—is really in a position to understand
what this means.

13. Ibid., p. 39. "Himself" is italicized in the original.
14. Ibid., pp. 41–42. Unfortunately, the translation misses the connective
"because" between the last sentence and what precedes it; the italics are in
the original.

The curious fact about Nietzsche's analysis is that he was so eager to grasp and to express the cosmic forces which spawned tragedy that he almost neglected to give a clear account of tragedy itself. The tragic material, the stuff of tragic existence, appeared to Nietzsche primarily as *destructiveness* and *divisiveness;* the world seemed to him a scene of strife leading to untimely death, a realm of loneliness and human isolation. In many ways the latter was more important because it pointed up Nietzsche's sense of the gulfs separating man from man in late nineteenth-century technical society, and, even more, the isolation of man from nature in a culture dominated by what he took to be the Socratic or rationalistic spirit. Tragedy, however, is a more complex and subtle affair in Nietzsche's thought than the mere description of these more or less prevalent evils of life. Tragedy was attached in his mind to a concept of sin and necessity in man's situation. Man must understand, he says, "that everything that is generated must be prepared to face its painful dissolution."[15] And this outcome is bound up with the conflict between different spheres of existence (for example, the human and the divine), each of which harbors a claim that cannot be set aside as long as the spheres maintain their separate natures.

His view can best be presented through the contrast between the Greek (he called it the "Aryan") and the Hebraic concepts of the tragic flaw or sin. He compared the classic myth of Prometheus (who was an eternal type for Nietzsche and not an "individual character" in a play) with the story of the Fall, and in the former he saw sin as *active,* as the transgression and guilt necessarily bound up with the fact that "man's highest good must be bought with a crime and paid for by the flood of grief and suffering which the offended divinities visit upon the human race in its noble ambi-

15. Ibid., p. 102.

tion."[16] He took this myth and its power over the Greek imagination as evidence of the capacity of the Greeks to sense and to bear suffering in the world; to him it meant that the Greeks really felt the deep offense given by man to the gods. And from this offense *inexorable* punishment follows no less than the sense of guilt. Nietzsche was deeply attracted by the idea of an *active* sinning—that is, by the circumstance that in the exercise of his powers of art and artifice man should incur his guilt, and he even compares this Promethean view with the "passive" *hybris* of Oedipus who "unwittingly" brought about his downfall. Oedipus was regarded by Nietzsche as a genuinely tragic figure, but he was less attracted by him than by Prometheus, whose downfall was brought about through a tremendous display of power and daring adventure.

At the other extreme in Nietzsche's description stands the Hebraic conception of sin which he is content to characterize simply as weakness in the face of temptation. Concentrating all of his attention upon the motif of disobedience in the story, Nietzsche could see in it only "feminine frailties," and consequently he was unable to see the point of the myth as the misuse of freedom. No doubt it appeared as a moralistic conception to him, but it is ironic that, having always been a voluntarist at heart, he should have missed the fact that the biblical tradition found the flaw of man in the interiority of his will, understood as the seat of decision and of the self's basic orientation. Failure at this point may have been due to Nietzsche's different conception of the will, as power and as restless creativity, but the fact remains that the peculiar voluntarism of the Judeo–Christian tradition—as Augustine showed, without counterpart

16. Ibid., pp. 63–64; cf. *The Genealogy of Morals*, p. 228, where Nietzsche holds that in Greek life it is *folly* which leads to suffering, whereas in the Judeo–Christian tradition it is *sin*. Folly is, presumably, more admissible because it is not a "moral" category.

in the classical world—was lost upon him in its fundamental significance.

Nietzsche's choice of the downfall of Prometheus as the model of tragic existence enables us to see how the concept of individuation is related to suffering in the world and how Dionysiac art can provide a resolution. The heroically striving individual seeks to break through the limits of his individuality and to approach the universal unity,[17] but in so doing he commits the crime of injustice which leads to pain and suffering and ultimately to the tragic end. The Apollonian impulse, according to Nietzsche, does not fully comprehend the tragic necessity involved and is content to seek a resolution by drawing more sharply the lines of individual existence through self-knowledge and control. Nietzsche's solution is to condemn the individuality at the root of the problem by declaring it to be merely phenomenal—an appearance of separation which does not actually exist from the vantage point of the universal Will. Behind the phenomena of individual life stands the one primordial unity, ever self-sufficient and exulting in the production of the greatest spectacle of all—the cosmos and its raging life. The redemption of existence is the discovery, not as a piece of mere information or knowledge but in the form of ecstatic participation, that the real self is united with all selves and with the power of nature in the one genuine reality. The transitory nature of the phenomenal world of

17. Nietzsche failed to see a matter of the greatest importance at precisely this point: Since he had already given himself over to the influence of Schopenhauer, he was bound to regard the activity of Prometheus as a drive toward the universal Will and *away* from his limited individuality, and consequently, he could not see that the activity of Prometheus is essentially *toward* and not away from higher and higher individualization. The more man has the conditions of existence at the command of his own will, the more is he individuated through high culture and the further is he removed from the source of his being. Nietzsche did not see Prometheus in this light, but instead saw in his heroic activity only an attempt to break through the narrow limits of his individuality.

individuality revealed in the eternality of the world of Dionysus represents the triumph of that "eternal life" which, as Nietzsche says, tragedy affirms.[18] The manner in which Dionysus conquers tragedy can best be understood through two ideas, the "metaphysical comfort" provided by art and the *necessity* of suffering which is the essence of the pessimistic outlook.

There is implicit in Nietzsche's view of both the form of tragedy and of tragic existence itself a means of resolution or of overcoming the tragic dissonance. And the centrality of Dionysus appears most clearly in the fact that the god not only cooperates with the Apollonian principle in bringing about the birth of tragedy, but he points the way beyond tragedy at the same time. Through art and the aesthetic standpoint there comes what Nietzsche called a "metaphysical comfort," and it is this which justifies and redeems existence. The essence of this solace resides in the assurance that "life flows on, indestructibly, beneath the whirlpool of appearances."[19] Further clarification of the meaning of this function of art is to be found in the contrast drawn by Nietzsche between the Old tragedy and the New, or between the earlier "metaphysical" and the later "earthly" solution to the tragic problem. It must be noted that *The Birth of Tragedy* contains, in addition to the theory announced in the title, a theory of the *death* of tragedy as well, and the opposition between the Old (Aeschylus) and the New (Euripides) tragedy is the best way of making clear what the metaphysical solution means.

Nietzsche found the purest example of tragedy in Aeschylean drama, in which problems of cosmic proportions are raised and an effort made to resolve them against a meta-

18. *The Birth of Tragedy,* XVI. This entire section is essential.
19. Ibid., p. 108.

physical background.[20] He did not, however, believe that this original level had been sustained throughout the entire development of the form, and after Aeschylus he saw a steady decline. He traced the death—he called it the "suicide"—of tragedy to the two spirits represented by Socrates and Euripides. The former is said to have destroyed the world in which tragedy can exist by removing its mystery, by identifying virtue with knowledge (so that a morality of individual reflection replaces the aesthetic standpoint), and by optimistically minimizing the darker side of human life. Euripides, working within the tragic form itself, is accused of eliminating Dionysiac music and of substituting the *deus ex machina* solution to tragedy—which is an earthly solution regarded by Nietzsche as theatrically conceived and lacking in metaphysical explanatory power. The most serious aspect of the charge is that the Euripidean answer no longer has "metaphysical comfort" in it; it no longer unites us with the primordial unity beyond the pain and loneliness of individual existence, and it no longer makes us feel, as Nietzsche thought genuine tragedy should, that we directly participate in "the abiding phenomenon of Dionysiac art, which expresses the omnipotent will behind individuation, eternal life continuing beyond all appearance and in spite of destruction."[21] He summed up his understanding of the type of tragedy in which the form met its end in the following words:

> It opposes Dionysiac wisdom and art; tries to dissolve the power of myth; puts in place of metaphysical comfort a terrestrial consonance and a special *deus ex machina*—the god of engines and crucibles; forces of nature put in the service of a higher type of egotism.

20. See especially pp. 62–63.
21. *The Birth of Tragedy,* pp. 101–02; cf. pp. 108–09.

It believes that the world can be corrected through knowledge and that life should be guided by science; that it is actually in a position to confine man within the narrow circle of soluble tasks, where he can say cheerfully to life: "I want you. You are worth knowing."[22]

When it is said, however, that Old tragedy furnishes what Nietzsche has been calling a metaphysical comfort or solace, we must be careful not to mistake his solution for one of a very different kind. It does not mean that in Old tragedy there is a metaphysical theory which is presented in "artistic" dress, for, were this the case, art would be merely a means for the expression of knowledge. On the contrary, although there is a theory behind the resolution (for the Apollonian principle also exists in genuine tragedy), the main point is that the self must *experience* and directly *participate* in the primal unity which knows no division and exults in its power to create; and only through tragic art can this be accomplished. In this Nietzsche is the true follower of Dionysus: Experience and participation have the priority over comprehension at a distance. And this point is not at all undercut by his idea that tragedy incorporates *both* Dionysiac and Apollonian features. That is, the importance of direct participation is not lost just because the element of Apollonian "illusion" intervenes and transforms our participation into a vicarious experience.[23] The self,

22. Ibid., p. 108.
23. Ibid., p. 140. It is important to notice that tragedy represents a genuine cooperation of both principles. In the earlier part of his theory where Nietzsche is intent on explaining the birth of the tragic form, there is an overemphasis upon the Dionysiac contribution, but in the latter part of the work (especially Section XXIV) the function of the Apollonian image is further explained. Tragedy, nevertheless, is impossible without both, and Nietzsche even asserted that the union of the two represents "the final consummation of both the Apollonian and Dionysiac tendencies."

confronted with the drama of high tragedy, must directly experience the loss or exchange of itself in the state of ecstasy, and in so doing it finds a solace which is something more than the communication of an idea. It is thus that the resolution is presented as one that only art and the aesthetic viewpoint can achieve.[24]

Now, in order fully to grasp what is involved in Nietzsche's effort to conquer the tragic through art, we must be attentive to what is meant by the *necessity* of suffering and especially to the sense in which pessimism is said to express the truth about human existence. When he referred to all the terrors of human life as the "terrible truth" about the world, he meant, among other things, to attack the idea that there is a *moral* order behind the world or that there is a *divine* justice beyond the phenomena. Thus at the outset he set himself against both the classic Christian view and the moral idealism of Kant and Leibniz. He seems to have been obsessed with the belief that only if life is surveyed in the first instance without the "illusion" of morality is it possible to grasp its true character and to make this truth a starting point from which to cope with the human predicament. As a result both of his own experience and his study of the classical world, Nietzsche came to believe that the pessimistic view is the only true one and that life must be regarded as essentially pain and destruction and suffering. Yet though he accepted this verdict as the initial truth about existence, he was very far from being content with it, and in the end he refused to admit pessimism as the final word about life. Indeed, even if we do not take without qualifica-

24. When Nietzsche came to review his works in *Ecce Homo*, he had occasion to re-emphasize the fundamentally aesthetic standpoint of his first work. In criticizing Christianity, he said: "It denies all aesthetic values; which are the only values that *The Birth of Tragedy* recognizes." *The Complete Works of Friedrich Nietzsche, 17,* 70.

tion his later description of *The Birth of Tragedy*,[25] it is still true that he was from the outset seeking some resolution of the problem presented by pessimism. And what most attracted Nietzsche in Aeschylean tragedy was its drive beyond the tragic facts themselves to the cosmic background of mystery. We long, he said, for something transcending the symbolic picture of the drama, for some transfiguration of tragic existence itself. And what in fact he intended to do was to conquer tragic pessimism by starting with it, by admitting its truth, and then by passing beyond it, all the while avoiding every solution that refused to begin with an acknowledgment of the tragic facts. The aesthetic expression of the pessimistic view in Aeschylean tragedy may, in other words, become the means whereby pessimism itself can be transcended, for in providing us with an insight into the nature of tragic life, it helps us to admit it and to bear it without "being turned to stone" by the vision. But the question then is: How shall this be accomplished?

The key to Nietzsche's solution is to be found in the concept of *necessity*, for his contention is that, when the inevitability of suffering is grasped, the dark side of our life must appear to us as transfigured and permeated by a new meaning. He asks us to look upon the world as it might appear to a cosmic artist who expresses himself freely and creatively and, in so doing, produces just the world we see. Such an artist cannot but create, and he can do so, in satisfaction of his own unbounded will, only in superabundant fashion. For Nietzsche, we must remember, there is no transcendent idea of the good or of justice present to the artist: There is

---

25. *Ecce Homo*, "The Birth of Tragedy": ". . . the book contains the first attempt to show how the Greeks succeeded in disposing of pessimism—how they overcame it." *The Complete Works of Friedrich Nietzsche, 17,* 68. Nietzsche's account here makes a sharper distinction between the pessimistic outlook and tragedy as a solution to it than is made in the original discussion.

only the sense of restless power and joy in self-expression. It is clear from his early lectures on Greek philosophy that he was fascinated by the idea that a cosmic artist would *play* with the materials of creation[26]—and that the very superabundance of this creativity would *inevitably* lead to conflict and to suffering. And his point was that beings who owe their existence to such a creator must, in the very nature of the case, exceed their limits, this being a consequence of the creative abundance. As he says:

> For a brief moment we become, ourselves, the primal Being, and we experience its insatiable hunger for existence. Now we see the struggle, the pain, the destruction of appearances, as necessary, because of the constant proliferation of forms pushing into life, because of the extravagant fecundity of the world will.[27]

What is arresting in this theory is the peculiar manner in which man is made to know the truth through the medium of the art of tragedy. It is presented not merely as a theory to be understood and considered but as direct participation and experience. The power of tragic myth is that it brings us, after the fashion of Dionysus, into the presence of the one Will expressing itself in the world, and it makes it possible for us to share in the joy of superabundant creation. From this vantage point we are to understand the whole spectacle of life as deriving its pattern from art. "At this point," said Nietzsche,

> we must take a leap into the metaphysics of art by reiterating our earlier contention that this world can be justified only as an aesthetic phenomenon. On this

26. See the striking expression of this point in *The Genealogy of Morals*, pp. 218–19; man is said to be in the center of the spectacle which is the "game of dice" played by "Zeus or Chance."

27. *The Birth of Tragedy*, pp. 102–03.

> view, tragic myth has convinced us that even the ugly
> and discordant are merely an aesthetic game which the
> will, in its utter exuberance, plays with itself.[28]

Nor did he shrink from describing this view itself as a kind
of "illusion" which makes life bearable for "nobler natures"
who are more sensitive to the wounds inflicted by life. Such
natures must, nevertheless, be strong and daring; they must
not only accept the tragic facts, but they must also affirm
life as it is and not merely after it has been coated over by
a moral or religious ideal. Once the tragic truth has been
admitted, however, only an aesthetic view of the world will
suffice to conquer tragedy.

With Nietzsche's view before us, we must now consider
the relation of this essentially aesthetic solution to the religious and moral faith of the Christian tradition. It may seem
strange to set his view in this comparison, for after all did
he not crucify Christianity in virtually every writing and
describe himself through the mask of Zarathustra as the anti-
Christ? Moreover, is it not clear that the aesthetic orientation of his proposed solution of the tragic problem exists in
another world from that of biblical religion? All this is true,
but it does not alter the fact that he was endeavoring to
find some interpretation of tragic existence, and his understanding of the human situation is sufficiently similar to
that of Christianity to make comparison both possible and
instructive.

An opening word about Nietzsche's personal relation to
Christianity is not without its importance. Both his father
and grandfather were Lutheran pastors, and he seems to
have regarded himself as standing in some special, even if
not very clear, relationship to the Christian faith. In *Zara-*

28. Ibid., p. 143.

thustra Nietzsche said: "Here are priests: but although they are mine enemies pass them quietly and with sleeping swords! . . . my blood is related to theirs; and I want withal to see my blood honored in theirs."[29] This sense of not being entirely dissociated from Christianity, at the same time that he rejected it, helped to create in Nietzsche an attitude that can only be described as ambivalent. There are passages in his writings (and they are in the majority) in which Christianity is opposed with a savage violence, but here and there one can find a hint of the reformer who criticizes distortions and aberrations chiefly for the purpose of purifying and restoring. Underneath, however, there can be no doubt concerning Nietzsche's position: His is an aesthetic resolution, and he constantly opposed it to a moral and religious faith. This is not to say that art and religion are necessarily at war with one another or that they cannot dwell together in peace and harmony, but it does mean that they come to stand in opposition to each other in the moment when art is transformed into a substitute for religion. And this is exactly what art was made to be in Nietzsche's thought.

The first point to be noticed is that Nietzsche had no flat view of human life such as was characteristic of late nineteenth-century moralism, naturalism, and positivism. To be sure, he had his own type of genetic reductionism, as is shown by his interpretation of the "bad conscience" as a mere disease in *The Genealogy of Morals,* but this should not be allowed to obscure the fact that he did understand the meaning of tragedy and knew at the same time that no

29. *Thus Spake Zarathustra*, II, xxvi, *The Complete Works of Friedrich Nietzsche, 2,* 105–06. See also the following from a letter to Peter Gast of July 21, 1881: "From childhood on I have pursued it [Christianity] into many corners, and I believe that I have never in my heart been disrespectful to it. After all I am the descendant of a whole tribe of Christian ministers. . . ." *Friedrich Nietzsches Briefe an Peter Gast,* herausgegeben von Peter Gast (Leipzig, Insel, 1908), p. 69; see also No. 66 (*Gesammelte Briefe, 4*).

mere moralism would suffice to conquer it. It is most revealing in this connection that he should have grasped the religious significance of the concept of salvation, even if he rejected its specifically Christian form. Describing redemption in *The Genealogy of Morals,* Nietzsche wrote:

> Neither the Hindu nor the Christian believes that such redemption can be reached by the path of virtue, or moral improvement, no matter how highly both regard the hypnotic value of virtue. The fact that they have been staunchly realistic in this regard is much to the credit of the three greatest religions, otherwise so thoroughly riddled with moralizing.[30]

It is clear, in other words, that while Nietzsche sought for his own solution to the problem of salvation, he could not accept any of the solutions offered in the optimistic progressivism, the scientism, or the social meliorism of his age. And his rejection of later tragedy in favor of the metaphysical approach of Aeschylus shows the reason why. So there can be no question, then, that he knew the metaphysical, even if not the full religious, depth of man and of the cosmos in which he lives.

But since every solution should be internally related to the problem from which it emerges, it is necessary to recall Nietzsche's understanding of the circumstances that give rise to the tragic situation. As we have noted, suffering in his view stems from superabundance of life on the one hand and from the crime committed by man in exceeding the limits of individual existence on the other. In both aspects tragedy stems from the nature of existence itself and from the necessity of conflicting claims—between man and the gods and between man and man—neither of which can finally and simply be subordinated to the other. At least

---

30. *The Genealogy of Morals,* p. 269.

part of the tragic conflict is to be attributed to the fact that the universe is the expression of no single plan or idea, with the result that the terrifying fruitfulness of the cosmic Will ultimately produces a chaos of incompatible claims. The superabundance alone, however, is not sufficient to explain tragic existence, because it leaves out Nietzsche's estimate of the status of individuality and of the tragic possibilities inherent in it. If we take his own interpretation of the Prometheus myth literally, we must suppose that *being individual* and thus limited *is itself the root of tragedy.* That is to say, Nietzsche saw in the *hybris* of Prometheus a move away from individuality itself and a symbol of man's inevitable exceeding of the bounds of individual existence in a drive "towards universality, de-individuation."[31]

This overstepping of the limits represents man's basic crime which, in its encroachment upon the legitimate claims of both the gods and other men, inevitably leads to the prevalence of pain and suffering in human life. And it is just here that we find a point of greatest contrast with Christianity and indeed with the whole of biblical religion. For Nietzsche found the flaw in individuality itself, whereas the Bible views it as bound up with the basic orientation of the self in relation to God. The idea of a rebellion against or a disobedience in the face of a divine command, while not itself excluding the notion of a limit overstepped, is not adequately interpreted in terms merely of a flaw in the nature of individuality. It posits instead the notion of the individual self making a particular decision, and this in turn involves not a movement away from individual existence but away from complete dependence upon God. The biblical story of the Fall of man, while not to be taken as an account of the origin of individual existence, must, nev-

31. *The Birth of Tragedy*, p. 64.

ertheless, be understood in terms of a drive from the side of man to enhance his status as an individual self. The separation from God occurs at the point where man wants to have his own individuality solely within his own hands and at the command of his own will.

Nietzsche, on the other hand, looked upon the individual character of things, the fact of their finitude and limitation, as itself the cause of tragedy. And this is precisely why he sought for a solution not in a higher type of individuality but in the transcendence of individual being.[32] Man is driven by his restless will to *create*—the artist was never far from the center of Nietzsche's thought—and in so doing he violates the rights of others. Such creativity is, however, a form of triumphant self-affirmation and, as Nietzsche frequently expressed it, it is at most a display of *folly* when it leads inevitably to tragic consequences. By contrast, Christianity understands man's tragic situation as related to something more internal to the center of the self; it is seen as bound up with man's will and purpose in life, and especially with his orientation as a total self. The cause of the tragic Fall is seen as coming from a decision within individuality and not from the fact of individuality itself. Moreover, in describing the tragic self-affirmation as *sin*, Christianity means to indicate the self-willed separation of man from God and not merely the defect of man as subject to folly and error. Nietzsche, at least in so far as he followed in the footsteps of Schopenhauer, had an essentially Buddhist conception of the resolution: Since the suffering follows from separateness, the supreme aim of life must be to overcome such individual separation. This is achieved by an ecstatic and enthusiastic identification of the self with the source of life, the cosmic and creative Will. Lyrical

32. Nietzsche's later philosophy of the *Übermensch* was, of course, quite different; it was a summons to the courageous *individual* to abandon conventional existence and heed the call of Zarathustra.

poetry or music makes this identification possible, and in this sense his resolution is an aesthetic one. And Nietzsche was emphatic in his insistence that aesthetic values be recognized as such and that art not be taken merely as an external form in which doctrines either of ethics or theology are expressed. He was, in other words, most deeply earnest in his conviction that the function of art is a metaphysical one and that it is ultimately for the purpose of conquering tragedy.

Now, throughout our study, emphasis has been placed upon the importance of art as a means of overcoming tragic existence. But the question now is: How are we to assess this general approach from a Christian perspective? In Nietzsche's view the aesthetic standpoint provides us not only with an insight into the necessity of suffering which makes life bearable, but it also holds forth the means of attaining a sense of oneness with and participation in the cosmic creativity behind the world of individual phenomena. The solution is essentially one in which the eye of the beholder is changed, and the manner in which the world is viewed or contemplated becomes uppermost in importance. The world that stands over against man is left exactly where it was before, only the light in which it is seen is now different. The solution is typically Oriental: Change the eye, and the reality that is beheld is transformed. From a Christian standpoint there are at least two difficulties with this solution: first, in finding redemption only in the change of viewpoint, the moral and religious aspects of the self are neglected; and, secondly, the tragic character of reality is in no way affected beyond the change in the viewpoint of the beholder.

It is a far-reaching defect in Nietzsche's thought that his criticism of conventional morality and religion, incisive and justified as it was in many particulars, left him without a positive replacement for what he had destroyed. He could not hope to deal with the moral defects in the human will, because his transvaluation of values had gone so far in the elimination of the ethical dimension altogether. Nor is the case different with regard to religion. There the genetic reduction of religious concepts to the status of ideology made it impossible for him to consider man's religious problems except as manifesting a form of disease.

The second difficulty is more important. Christianity cannot find itself in accord with any view of tragic existence in which the proposed resolution leaves existence exactly where it was before, while merely changing the viewpoint of the self. For Christianity something new must enter the objective situation as a leaven which must eventually transform the character of existence itself and not only the standpoint from which it is viewed. In a passage from *The Birth of Tragedy* which has not attracted much attention, Nietzsche saw a solution that he did not develop but which, ironically enough, is very close to the Christian view. "The gods," he said, speaking of Greek mythology, "justified human life by living it themselves—the only satisfactory theodicy ever invented."[33] And indeed for Christianity it is God himself who takes tragic existence upon himself in order to break through the tragic circle: Man, being in need of wholeness, cannot, in virtue of that very need, perform the task of himself alone. The idea that tragedy can be conquered by a type of life willing and able to take suffering upon itself, without at the same time being destroyed by it, is implicit in Nietzsche's suggestive remark. But he had no genuinely transcendent element capable of assuming the tragic burden, and consequently he was forced to retreat to a solution essentially aesthetic and contemplative in character.

33. *The Birth of Tragedy*, p. 30.

4. Religion and Theology in Peirce

SURVEYED in its wholeness, the philosophy of C. S. Peirce is at best an enigma. When, for example, he was supposed to be writing on logic, he wrote about religion, and when he set out to explore the religious consciousness, he was soon deep in a disquisition on the nature of reasoning. It is not that such diverse subjects should be kept exclusive; on the contrary they have, as Peirce saw, important relations to one another, but for one interested in getting at his thought on a particular subject Peirce's manner of relating diverse subject matters is more than a little disconcerting. Yet his philosophy is all the more fascinating on this account and uncommonly interesting as a challenge to the reader to penetrate its depths and capture the core of truth in it. Peirce was not a systematic writer after the fashion of Hegel, although he planned but never completed many enterprises which were to result in full-blown systems of philosophy. This lack of systematic presentation adds to the difficulty of understanding his thought as does also the disjointed form in which most of his writings are available to us.[1] Despite these obstacles, there is much to be found that is of real value, both in itself and in its suggestiveness for further thought on the subject of religion and theology. Peirce was

1. *Collected Papers of Charles Sanders Peirce,* Cambridge, Mass., Harvard University Press (Vols. 1–6 ed. C. Hartshorne and P. Weiss, 1931; Vols. 7–8 ed. A. Burks, 1958).

always frank, and there is a certain charm about the directness, almost naïveté, with which he discoursed about many
of the most debated doctrines of the Western Christian tradition, both in his analysis of the substance of religion and
in the formulation of his credo. He not only exhibited a vast
learning in the field of Christian thought, ancient and medieval, but he spoke about the religious concern with a sympathy not often encountered in philosophers of Peirce's
scientific persuasion. Hartshorne in his article "A Critique
of Peirce's Idea of God"[2] is absolutely correct in calling
attention to Peirce's concern with religion as indicative
of the broadness of his mind and the range of his interest.
He is justified, moreover, in pointing to the fact that others
have been mistaken in supposing this interest to be incon-
sistent with the trend of Peirce's thought. For certainly
the truly empirical temper of mind which Peirce undoubtedly had cannot consistently overlook any aspect of that
wide and varied reality which philosophers are wont to call
experience.

   In an attempt to present and criticize Peirce's thoughts
on religion the following analysis will be divided into two
parts: philosophy of religion[3] and theology.

---

   2. *Philosophical Review, 50* (1941), 516–23.
   3. The expression "philosophy of religion" is used vaguely at present.
Indeed it was used rather loosely by Peirce himself. I prefer to reserve the
term for the philosophical analysis of the religious concern as it manifests
itself historically, in an attempt to disengage the defining characteristics
of religion. As such, a philosophy of religion would be analogous to a philosophy of science or of art. Philosophy of religion would consequently be
distinct from religion, theology, and "religious philosophy" (whatever that
is). Peirce (1.659) used the expressions "philosophy of religion" and "religious philosophy" interchangeably and referred to the works of Aquinas and
Occam as "religious philosophy." In the following analysis I shall use "philosophy of religion" in the above-defined sense, for Peirce, despite his own
usage, had a philosophy of religion in this sense. I shall use the term "theology" for what Peirce referred to as "religious philosophy."

PHILOSOPHY OF RELIGION

Nowhere in Peirce's thought is the distinction between theory and practice more marked than in his view of the basis of religion. In his view strictly theoretical questions, the questions posed by pure science and philosophy, although they may have an ultimate and largely indirect bearing on human life and conduct, are radically different from questions of "vital concern" and consequently must be treated in a different way. These latter have to do with life in its wholeness, with the structure of society, with the deliberate conduct of life, and finally with the character and ultimate destiny of the individual. Vitally important questions,[4] unlike the "useless" pursuits and questions of science which can only be dealt with by reason and empirical evidence, are dependent on instinct and traditional experience for their solution, and concerning them reason has at best a place of only secondary importance. Such, briefly stated, is Peirce's view of the matter. He never ceased to insist on the primacy of instinct and of those considerations generally called "practical" in religious affairs. From the earlier remarks on religion (1878) to the puzzling Neglected Argument, instinct, custom, habit, and the like are definitely judged to be superior to reasoning in the consideration of problems in religion and morality. It is not, as can readily be shown, that reasoning or analysis has no place here at all;

4. The much worked-over lectures, "On Detached Ideas in General and on Vitally Important Topics," 1898 (1.616 ff.), have a marked ironical character. There Peirce overstated his case and made a sharper separation between reasoning (theory) and instinct (practice) than he ultimately wished to maintain. See 1.648, where he attempted to overcome the separation by the suggestion that instinct is capable of a development which "chiefly takes place through the instrumentality of cognition." Cf. 6.457, where Peirce referred to the Neglected Argument as "applicable to the conduct of life," and also 6.497.

such a suggestion would be false, for Peirce himself has reasoned acutely on such perplexing questions as miracle, immortality, etc., but the fact remains that he was so impressed both by the intensely personal character of religion and by the fact that people, including philosophers, generally do not reason carefully and accurately about religious faith, that he consistently accorded reason only secondary importance. No better illustration of this can be offered than the following paragraph from the lectures of 1898:

> Among the advantages which our humble cousins whom it pleases us to refer to as "the lower animals" enjoy over some of our own family is that they *never* reason about vitally important topics, and never have to lecture nor to listen to lectures about them. Docilely allowing themselves to be guided by their instincts into almost every detail of life they live exactly as their Maker intended them to live. The result is, that they very rarely fall into error of any kind, and *never* into a vital one. What a contrast to our lives! Truly, that reason upon which we so plume ourselves, though it may answer for little things, yet for great decisions is hardly surer than a toss-up.   [1.649]

Yet it would be a great error simply to identify Peirce's position with that of many modern philosophers who make a radical distinction between "factual" and "emotional" statements and confine discussion of religion and morality to the latter category, regarding both as expressions or projections of our feelings and emotions and nothing more. Peirce did not believe that religion has to do primarily with emotion but rather that it is based on instinct, and this is entirely different.[5] His metaphysical interest led him to look for an ontological and ultimately purposeful foun-

5. See 6.500.

dation for the characteristics exhibited by the universes, as is shown by the second argument in what he called the Neglected Argument.[6] Since man is a member of that totality constituted by the three universes of the external, the internal, and the logical worlds, whatever instincts and actually revealed tendencies he exhibits must themselves ultimately be traced back to the creator of the universes. As such they are no mere projections of fancy or wish.[7]

The instinct at the root of religion, though it may have a superficial resemblance to what is currently called "emotional," possesses an ontological foundation which distinguishes it from the subjectivism of that modern positivism which interprets religion as nothing but a projection of human feelings or wishes. According to Peirce, the man who puts aside all serious purpose and who, at a level of the soul deeper than the cognitive, instinctively opens his heart to the purposive character of the three universes (both in themselves and in their relations to one another), that man is the religious man and the one who acts as the creator intended him to act. It is precisely this reference to the creator which distinguishes Peirce's emphasis on instinct and immediate experience from much in modern thought which is akin but ultimately lacks the ontological support which he maintained. Although his last appeal is to what are generally regarded as the "subjective" aspects of human experience ("subjective" because "non-rational"), this instinct is not "subjective" in the sense that it is a mere human wish or fancy. The instinct at the root of religion is well founded, first because it is found in all men,[8] and second because

6. See 6.487.

7. See 6.452; also 6.466, 6.467.

8. See 6.467. There Peirce said that "any normal man" who follows the lead of that instinctive consideration of the universes which he calls "musement" will come to know and to love God. See also 6.496; yet 6.162 states the main difficulty faced by his view.

its very existence points to that purposive character in the universes which leads, through *musement*,[9] to the hypothesis of God's reality.[10]

If the question now be raised as to what Peirce believed constitutes the essence[11] of religion, it must be admitted that this is difficult indeed because Peirce's pronouncements are few and far from clear. In the short paper "The Marriage of Religion and Science" (1893),[12] Peirce defined religion as "a sort of sentiment, or obscure perception, a deep recognition of a something in the circumambient All" (6.429) which the individual is said to acknowledge, "the first and last, the A and Ω, as a relation to that absolute of the individual's self, as a relative being" (ibid.). The recognition that one stands in such a relation as a finite being, along with the direct perception of God as the reality to which one is thus related, constituted the very center of religion for Peirce at this juncture of his thought. In another place (1.676)[13] the cognitive aspect of this direct perception came to the surface, and Peirce called religion the complete and perfect generalization of this sentiment which causes us to look beyond finite duties, differences, and discontinuities to a harmonious resolution of all discord and a completion of individual personality "by melting it into the neighboring parts of the universal cosmos" (1.673).

One point is clear, however: religion is always dependent on immediacy of some sort, and the relevant idea of "direct perception" so much stressed by Peirce throws further light

9. The idea of musement is one of Peirce's original insights; it is unfortunate he did not develop it further. See 6.458; cf. 2.266 ff.

10. See 6.157, where the element of purpose in human personality is said to lead directly to the idea of a personal creator.

11. I am using this term in Plato's sense as, for example, in the analysis of piety in the *Euthyphro*.

12. See 6.428 ff.

13. Cf. 1.673.

on this feature of his view. He was fond of tracing the development of religion from its vital roots in immediate experience through all the stages of doubt and decay (usually marked, as he thought, by bad apologetic pretending to be rational) to its eventual death in metaphysical assertions about the nature of the Godhead which have lost their vital spark.[14] "Where would such an idea, say as that of God, come from," Peirce asked, "if not from direct experience?" (6.493) and after putting this question he went on to show that the idea of God is not born of reasoning, whether good or bad, but is rather the result of some direct confrontation in experience. "As to God, open your eyes—and your heart, which is also a perceptive organ—and you see him" (6.493).[15] He conceived such confrontation and direct perception to be related so intimately to the heart and soul of the person confronted that he did not care to use the term "belief" for this, because to him belief implied reasoning and a type of mediation that is inappropriate to characterize the deliverances of instinct and sentiment:[16] "It is absurd to say that religion is a mere belief. You might as well call society a belief, or politics a belief, or civilization a belief. Religion is a life, and can be identified with a belief only provided that belief be a living belief—a thing to be lived rather than said or thought" (6.439).[17]

Peirce confidently defended direct perception against the charge of its being illusory by appealing, in much the same way as Royce did, to its social character. Common sense, taken as the resultant of the traditional experience of mankind, testifies that the heart is more than the head,

14. See 6.438.

15. See also 6.435, 436, where Peirce said that all belief in God sets out from a "stirring of the spirit" in the absence of which, as a starting point, all reasoning about the content of religious faith is idle and vain.

16. See especially the striking analogy in 1.655.

17. See below, n. 31 for a somewhat different view with respect to belief.

and "those persons who think that sentiment has no part in common sense forget that the dicta of common sense are objective facts, not the way some dyspeptic may feel, but what the healthy, natural, normal democracy thinks" (1.654). If these remarks be interpreted in the light of his repeated contention that in matters of vital importance not only is the heart to be followed rather than the head, but also that the "head" can prove this to be true from the actual facts of man's existence, it becomes clear why Peirce was willing to regard religion as ultimately founded on such grounds as might appear to many minds of a scientific bent to be very dubious indeed.

Peirce's appeal to the continuing experience of mankind as this is preserved in the community touches on a highly significant aspect of his philosophy of religion. Like Royce, and unlike James, Peirce believed that religion is essentially social in character. Not that this limited in the slightest his regard for what is sometimes called a personal religion or piety, but in so far as he held that man's most important accomplishments are social, he put considerable stress on the social expression of religion. In short, Peirce believed in both the significance and the necessity of some form of the church. "Religion," he declared, "though it begins in a seminal individual inspiration, only comes to great flower in a great church coextensive with a civilization" (6.443).[18]

It is striking indeed to find that one who, because of his marked interest in the pure sciences and his belief in the centrality of mathematical logic is often considered to be an "emancipated" mind, not only took the religious concern seriously but even upheld the indispensable character of the church. No doubt Peirce's recognition of the social factor in this context stems largely from his theory of the

18. Cf. 6.429, "But religion cannot reside in its totality in a single individual. Like every species of reality, it is essentially a social, a public affair."

relation between reality and the community[19] and from his
theory of dynamic love, which he somewhat clumsily termed
agapism.[20]

There was another reason behind his concern for the
church, one which should not be overlooked since it lay
at the very foundation of Peirce's thought, namely, his
fundamental *empiricism*. Since this empiricism was genuine
(Peirce really tried to discover the facts and to think in the
light of them) and not at all like so much contemporary
"empiricism," which is really a dogmatism that legislates
concerning reality a priori on the basis of some nonempir-
ical preconceptions about what "experience" must necessarily reveal, Peirce recognized the importance of the
church or religious community in all religions, and particularly the actual historical role of the Christian Church in
Western civilization. The following paragraph from a fragment on "Religion and Politics" (c. 1895) expresses this
forcefully:

> Many a scientific man and student of philosophy recog-
> nizes that it is the Christian Church which has made
> him a man among men. To it he owes consolations,
> enjoyments, escapes from great perils, and whatever
> rectitude of heart and purpose may be his. To the
> monks of the medieval church he owes the preserva-
> tion of ancient literature; and without the revival of
> learning he can hardly see how the revival of science
> would have been possible. To them he owes the frame-
> work of his intellectual system; and if he speaks Eng-
> lish, a most important part of his daily speech. The
> law of love which, however little it be obeyed, he holds

19. See 5.311, where Peirce stated the relation between the *real* and that
which is accepted by the *community* of thinkers as true in the long run. It
may be noted that this conception of the relation between reality and community formed the background of Royce's interpretation of Christianity.

20. See 6.302.

to be the soul of civilization, came to Europe through Christianity. Besides, religion is a great, perhaps the greatest, factor of that social life which extends beyond one's own circle of personal friends. That life is everything for elevated, and humane, and democratic civilization; and if one renounces the Church, in what other way can one as satisfactorily exercise the faculty of fraternizing with all one's neighbours? [6.449]

Clearly Peirce's understanding of the function of the church can in large measure be traced back to a perfectly simple consideration: a regard for the facts. As has been pointed out already, he was directly acquainted with the history and doctrines of Western Christianity, and he knew well enough the part which the Christian church has played, both for good and for ill, in the development of Western society. As a good empiricist he took the facts seriously and developed his ideas concerning the social character of religion accordingly.

With respect to the nature of the church, Peirce held what might be regarded by modern Protestants as an ecumenical view. He believed that a narrow and exclusive church is inadequate to express a religion of love, especially in the case of Christianity which is the religion of love par excellence.[21] Consequently, Peirce looked for a truly universal Christian church which would not exclude certain portions of mankind because of differences largely creedal in character.[22] That the church must be both founded on

21. For Peirce's view of the essence of Christianity, see his discussion of the question, "What is Christian Faith?" (1893), 6.435 ff.

22. See 6.447, where Peirce exhorted scientific men not to leave the church, but to help cleanse it from *within*. However, he contended, if a new church must be set up for the scientifically educated, the problem of exclusiveness would still be a pressing one. Consequently, he urged any who would set up such a church not to "go and draw lines so as to exclude such as believe a little less—or, still worse, to exclude such as believe a little more—than yourselves."

love and committed to the task of making love triumphant in the world, Peirce was convinced. For this reason he was, like many others of a liberal stamp in these matters, fond of contrasting what he took to be the lifeless creeds of the historic branches of the Christian church with the vital and dynamic power of redeeming love. "The central doctrine of love," he said, referring to the historic creeds, "is not to be found in any one of them" (6.450). In his view the church is not primarily a community consisting of those committed to some saving theory or formula; it is rather the saving community which leads men out of their petty, self-centered existence to a larger life of love and devotion both to God and to the neighbor. Furthermore the church must not spend too much of its time producing official theology, precisely because it has work to do in the world, practical tasks to be accomplished, and these must be forever in the foreground, as the following passage makes clear enough: "A religious organization is a somewhat idle affair unless it be sworn in as a regiment of that great army that takes life in hand, with all its delights, in grimmest fight to put down the principle of self-seeking, and to make the principle of love triumphant. It has something more serious to think about than the phraseology of the articles of war" (6.448).[23]

What now of a critical nature is to be said concerning those features of Peirce's philosophy of religion briefly touched upon above? There can be little doubt, in the light of the facts known through the history and psychology of religion, that Peirce was correct in stressing the importance of immediate experience for religion, precisely because the religious concern is the most fundamental in human experience and the one most intimately related to the unity and

23. "The articles of war" are of course the creeds and theological statements of the faith which have arisen during the development of the Christian church.

identity of the individual personality. Rationalism in all its forms, whether it be scientific or fundamentalistic in character, is always mistaken when it tries to substitute the logos of theology for the subject's own experience of being grasped by the ultimate reality. It is as little possible in religion to begin with reflection and pass to immediacy as it is to construct the actual continuum of a moving object given any number, however large, of static positions occupied by that object. Peirce, therefore, was correct in saying that religion must take rise in direct perception and that it is "instinctive" in character, welling up from the direct experience of the sensitive soul rather than from the conscious reasoning of the mind which sets out to convince itself of the reality of God.

On the other hand, and this focuses attention on the decided limitation of all attempts to remain entirely within immediacy in religion, the exclusion of reasoning from the religious life leads inevitably to conservatism, stagnation, and an uncritical appeal to convention.[24] The result of a radical separation between theory and practice such as Peirce in fact developed, in which the former is supposed to depend on unalloyed reason and the latter on some exclusively nonrational factor in human experience, will always be skepticism and a final appeal to convention in matters of practice, matters of "vital importance." Such an outcome is an unfortunate one indeed, since all history shows that in affairs like religion, morality, and politics the most significant advances have been made by those who have dared to challenge custom and convention from the standpoint of new insights gained from reflection on fresh experience. While it is certainly true that the first impulse of the religious consciousness is not stirred by rea-

24. Peirce recognized this (1.661) but he thought that a "true" conservatism was possible. The rational element enters at once, of course, in the reference to a "true" as distinct from some other kind of conservatism.

soning, still the exclusive founding of religion on instinct, sentiment, and custom leads to consequences which are far from desirable.

A corollary of the attempt to root religion in features of experience exclusively nonrational is that from there it is an easy step to the position that religion can have no standards of truth or falsity whatsoever, since within that domain reason will have been denied any legitimate place. The outcome is that in situations where rational or considered judgment is required, the issue is left to be decided on purely conventional grounds, or on the vague and dubious grounds of "usefulness" or "success" which in large measure means the meeting of needs solely immediate in character. Such a position finally sacrifices the claim of truth, a claim which should be binding at all moments, to the needs and expediencies of one moment, and all possibility of objective standards in meeting religious issues is given up. Such abandonment plays into the hands of both those who interpret religion as subjective wish or fancy and the religious obscurantists who welcome all strictures on rational criticism. Peirce, of course, did not draw these conclusions in his own thought, but such dangers are necessarily inherent in any view which separates theory and practice, reason and instinct, to so great an extent as he did.

Concerning Peirce's discussion of the social character of religion, it must be said that the history of religion shows that he was on the very soundest ground. As Royce pointed out many years ago, it is lamentable that America's most renowned philosopher and psychologist of religion, William James, should have confined his attention solely to what he regarded as personal religion simply because he believed the social expression of religion in the church to be conventional and to be religion at "second hand." Peirce, like Royce, did not make the mistake of setting the social dimension to one side. In his view religion is everywhere a social phenomenon and the religious community is its most prevalent expression. The Christian ideal for all mankind is, as it was in the highest expressions of the Old Testament tradition, a social goal, a *kingdom* of God, an ideal which Christianity believes is foreshadowed in the church as the body of Christ. Peirce saw the importance of all this and consequently stressed the indispensability of the church as the creator of community among men as well as the locus of the most perfect expression of religion.

When Peirce faced the problem of the tremendous differences between the historical churches, however, his view was not a little naïve. What he overlooked, just as do all thinkers who interpret religion as entirely practical, is that ecclesiastical differences in theology, liturgy, social organization, etc. are not in fact easily overcome by spirited exhortations to emphasize practical tasks or to forget doctrinal differences through a return to the "simple gospel of Jesus,"[25] or the like. The multifarious differences between churches, petty though many of them undoubtedly are, generally have a profound religious basis. Such a basis is not easily or even profitably to be ignored. The religious significance of these differences seems not to have been grasped by Peirce, just as he seems not to have been sufficiently aware of the enormous immediate obstacles facing all efforts to eliminate parochialism from Christianity and institute a truly ecumenical or universal church which would not be based on authoritarian methods and practices clearly inimical to both religious freedom and the pursuit of truth. Nevertheless, despite these oversights, Peirce's thought about the church moved in the right direction, as all those who deplore narrow sectarianism in religion will recognize. "Without a church," said Peirce, "the religion of love can

25. The reason that such an appeal is naïve is that most divisions among the churches stem from various interpretations of what this "simple gospel" is and means.

have but a rudimentary existence; and a narrow, little exclusive church is almost worse than none. A great catholic
church is wanted" (6.443).[26]

THEOLOGY

No complete discussion of all that may legitimately fall
under this head is possible here, because it would lead inevitably to a consideration of Peirce's general metaphysical
position and of his cosmology as well. And since Peirce's
views on some of the main aspects of Christian theology are
to be found in his *credo* which is beyond the scope of this
paper, it may prove worthwhile to consider at this juncture
only the most striking of his pronouncements both in theology and about theology. Hence the following points will
be treated: *(a)* the use of reason in vital matters in so far as
it concerns method in theology; *(b)* argument as distinct
from argumentation in relation to *musement; (c)* the doctrine of vagueness in its bearing on theology; *(d)* the somewhat puzzling *Neglected Argument; (e)* the positive content
of the idea of God based on Peirce's pragmaticism. As will
become apparent, *a, b,* and *c* may be considered together,
since what Peirce called argument is related to a necessary
vagueness in concepts, and *d* and *e* may likewise be considered together because of their close relationship.

(a–c) In keeping with his sharp separation of theory and
practice, Peirce refused to classify theology as knowledge
because, as concerned with a matter of vital importance, he
did not believe it was produced under the motive of dis-
interestedness required for genuine theoretical knowledge.[27] There is an additional reason why theology cannot

26. Needless to say Peirce knew that "catholic" is simply a synonym for
"universal."
27. See 1.576.

be regarded as knowledge which is characteristic of Peirce's thought as a whole, namely his emphasis on the importance of method. As one who believed in the supreme importance of logical analysis, Peirce insisted that truth can be attained only if correct methods are employed and employed rigorously. Theology, he contended, precisely because it is designed to serve only as a distinguishing mark of those who belong to the church and are "saved" by accepting it, is not developed under the conditions and by the use of methods necessary for the discovery of truth. Theology serves practical purposes only and consequently it cannot be regarded as genuine knowledge.[28]

Yet theology does represent an effort of reason to say something about such topics as God, prayer, the purposeful character of the three universes, conscience, etc.; because of this Peirce accorded it a place of no small significance. In the article entitled "A Neglected Argument for the Reality of God" (1908),[29] Peirce distinguished between an *argument* and an *argumentation*. Peirce's development of this highly original distinction shows his deep insight into the nature of religious belief in its relation to rational apprehension. He defined an argument as "any process of thought reasonably tending to produce a definite belief" (6.456), and distinguished this from an argumentation which he defined as "an Argument proceeding upon definitely formulated premises" (ibid.). Peirce rejected as a prejudice the idea that all reasoning is of the form of argumentation.[30] There are processes of reasoning which are directed

28. See 6.450, where Peirce referred to theology as the "platform" of the church formulated "under the impulses of ecclesiastical ambition and the *odium* of priests." Truth, on the other hand, Peirce pointed out on many occasions, can never be discovered under such circumstances.

29. This first appeared in the *Hibbert Journal*, 7 (1908), 90–112. It is reproduced in 6.452–491, and since it is easier to identify passages there I shall use the sections of the *Collected Papers*.

30. See 6.457.

solely toward the production of belief in matters of vital
importance and which, because of their generality and ultimate import, must be content to employ vague concepts
and consequently premises not definitely formulated. Belief,[31] he maintained, ought to be confined to what pertains
to *action,* and accordingly pure science results not in belief
but rather in opinion, because in itself it has nothing to do
with action.[32] In situations where the shaping of personal
character is concerned and where decision affecting the
total life and even destiny of persons is in question, situations pertaining to action in a very broad sense, the purely
disinterested attitude of science has been transcended, and
whatever ideas, principles, etc. form the basis of action in
such cases must be said to constitute the *beliefs* held by the
persons involved, no matter how long their conscious classification as such may be postponed.[33] Life, Peirce saw, as
Marcus Aurelius long before him had seen well enough, is
not sufficiently long for us to take up genuine doubts about
everything. Some propositions pertaining to the ultimate
basis of life and conduct must be believed, in order that the
span of conscious life and activity which is ours by nature
may be lived to the full. Consequently, argument tending
to produce belief in matters of vital importance is not only
adequate to perform its task, but it is as much as can be
attained in such matters, because an ineradicable vagueness

31. In this discussion Peirce has used the term "belief" to refer to the
convictions of religion, despite the fact that in another context he rejected
such usage. See above, n. 17.

32. See 1.635 for a beautifully clear statement of the sense in which Peirce
was here using the terms "belief" and "opinion."

33. See 6.467, where Peirce said: "Now to be deliberately and thoroughly
prepared to shape one's conduct into conformity with a proposition is neither more nor less than the state of mind called Believing that proposition,
however long the conscious classification of it under that head be postponed." Cf. 4.64.

always persists, rendering impossible any extended argumentation.

Having decided that what he called an argument was the adequate instrument for the task of theology, Peirce went on to discuss the attitude of the arguer. For an argument to be successful a certain attitude of receptiveness on the part of the inquirer is necessary, and this is the attitude of the "muser," or one who indulges in "musement."[34] Peirce was aware that an attitude of theoretical detachment may often prevent an argument from leading to the belief to which it would otherwise inevitably lead in the consciousness of the person who had already developed the attitude of the muser. The question now is: What is musement and exactly what attitude should accompany it? The answer to this will indicate what it is that Peirce considered requisite for the success of an argument as distinct from an argumentation.

Peirce outlined his idea of musement in only one place, the article on the Neglected Argument, and all that can be said about this remarkable activity must be derived from that discussion.[35] There is an occupation of the mind which "involves no purpose save that of casting aside all serious purpose" (6.458), and which consists in wonder either at some striking characteristic within one of the universes or at some purposeful connection between two of the universes, together with speculation about the cause of these features. The attitude of mind involved is closest to *pure play* because it is not fraught with serious purpose of any kind; on the contrary, it is actually an attempt to cut through the layers of conscious purpose and arrive at that state of mind

34. See 2.266 ff. Musement seems closest to *abduction*.
35. One hesitates to say that Peirce has mentioned something in "only one place" because of the wealth of material he has left behind. So far as I know he touches on musement in no other place than in the article from the *Hibbert Journal*.

which is close to the naïveté and freshness of children in the face of some awe-inspiring wonder. If, however, some ulterior purpose is allowed to enter, the proper attitude is destroyed. "One who sits down," said Peirce, "with the purpose of becoming convinced of the truth of religion is plainly not inquiring in scientific singleness of heart, and must always suspect himself of reasoning unfairly" (6.458).

When, on the other hand, the proper attitude is achieved, speculation concerning the cause of some wonder in the world (particularly what he often referred to as the marvelous adaptation of purposes between the three universes) may begin, and the end result should be the serious entertainment of and belief in the hypothesis of God's reality. This forms the basis of what Peirce called the Neglected Argument (hereafter referred to in this paper as "N.A."—the abbreviation Peirce himself used). It may be pointed out that although the theoretical element has entered in here, albeit in a strange way, Peirce always kept the practical significance of the argument before him, which is shown by the fact that he spoke of it as an argument in "a form directly applicable to the conduct of life and full of nutrition for man's highest growth" (6.457). Nevertheless, there is clearly a rational, if not actually a strictly theoretical, element in the argument, although the concern with the psychological make-up of the inquirer sharply distinguishes this way of approach from the process of argumentation with its necessary theoretical detachment and logical precision. The wonder at and speculation on the whole which Peirce called musement inevitably leads, he contended, to the acceptance of the N.A., if the inquirer really seeks in the proper spirit and with the proper attitude. To the question of the precise nature of the reasoning involved in the speculation born of musement Peirce had an answer which is somewhat surprising: "There is no kind of reasoning that I should wish to discourage in Musement; and I should lament to find anybody confining it to a method of such moderate fertility as logical analysis" (6.461).[36]

Musement is to be free and unfettered in order to develop along whatever lines are suggested to the inquirer when confronted with the wonders exhibited by the universes. The muser looks for a truth which is "beneath the phenomena," and which, when discovered, is of vital importance to the person himself. The muser must not allow any predilection for extreme clarity or logical rigor to destroy the fruits of his musement, since, in the consideration of questions properly metaphysical and religious, ideas of such vagueness and of such ultimate importance are involved that the possession of the truth is of much greater significance than its fine analysis. Peirce even went so far as to suggest that belief in God is often rejected as groundless by men of science simply because they have *precided* (6.496)[37] the vague and instinctive belief in God which they possess, and having thereby altered it in the attempt to express it clearly, they have made it contradictory in some respect. According to him, it is better to depend on the vague deliverances of instinct where first principles are concerned, since in the long run such ideas are more trustworthy than the established results of science which presupposes them, although they cannot and should not be rendered precise. Peirce's own illustration is instructive at this point. That the element of order exists in the universe, everybody admits, and this is a more trustworthy belief when based on instinctive grounds (involving common sense) than any particular laboratory ex-

36. Cf. 6.463, where in speaking about the properly metaphysical questions bound to arise in musement, Peirce said: "But problems of metaphysics will inevitably present themselves that logical analysis will not suffice to solve."

37. Cf. 1.549, where Peirce defined "precision" or "abstraction" as the giving of attention to one element to the neglect of another." See below, n. 51.

periment could render it. But, Peirce continued, if anyone were to undertake "to say *precisely* what that order consists in, he will quickly find he outruns all logical warrant" (6.496). Furthermore, "men who are given to defining too much inevitably run themselves into confusion in dealing with the vague concepts of common sense" (ibid.).

(d, e) Now that the use of reason in theology, the nature of argument, and the idea of vagueness have all been briefly touched upon, there remains the task of discussing the N.A. and Peirce's view of the positive content of the idea of God based on his doctrine of pragmaticism. Actually (although the reader will not discover this until he comes virtually to the end of Peirce's paper), the N.A. consists in three arguments for the reality of God: (1) a "Humble Argument" based directly on musement and involving a direct perception of God's reality;[38] (2) reflection on (1) resulting in the inference, which involves argumentation, that belief in God is instinctive because it is the result of free meditation, and that as a universal feature of human nature it is not a superstition; and (3) a study of the nature of thought and of scientific procedure, particularly retroduction, in relation to the Humble Argument, leading to the view that the purposeful character of the relations between the universes is illustrated par excellence in man's power of framing hypotheses. Or to state the third argument differently, the fact of the success of *il lume naturale* in framing hypotheses is a sign that there is an attunement between man's mind and the universe. In the first part of Peirce's paper these three processes of reasoning are not always kept distinct, and the first two can be distinguished only with difficulty. Despite Peirce's great interest in the metaphysical implications of man's power to frame relevant and most often verifiable

38. Sometimes Peirce said musement "upon the Idea of God" (6.486), sometimes "on the whole" or on the "relations between the universes." See 6.458.

hypotheses, it is the first argument[39] rather than either of
the other two which he properly regarded as the N.A.[40]
This is perfectly consistent with his general outlook, because the Humble Argument is direct, and has, in his view,
a religious vitality not possessed by the other two. Compared to it they rank as secondary, being largely apologetic
in character, while the first is "humble" and is based on
direct perception.

In the Humble Argument the hypothesis which is to be
suggested, first through musement and finally by speculation on the homogeneities and connections between the universes, is that there is a "creator of all three Universes of
Experience"[41] and that the purposeful adaptations discovered therein are to be interpreted in the light of this hypothesis. The hypothesis is initially vague, because God is an
"infinitely incomprehensible object," but in the course of
time, that is, as the purposeful character of the universes
becomes more and more manifest, the hypothesis undergoes
a development toward definiteness which has no assignable
limit. Adopting a position not unlike that of the theologian
Schleiermacher, Peirce held that what the hypothesis of God
as creator suggests concerning the universes is to be fully
maintained, but that its precise implications concerning the
essence of God as such must be partly disavowed or negat-
ed.[42] The reason for such disavowal or negation is that

39. Actually, according to Peirce's own definitions, this is the only one of
the three which is an *argument;* the other two are *argumentations.*

40. See 6.487. Cf. 6.483.

41. See 6.452.

42. Hartshorne, in the article previously mentioned (see above, n. 2), is
undoubtedly correct in noting Peirce's affinity with the tradition of *negative
theology* found in Christian thought, as he also is in noting at least the
prima facie inconsistency of this with Peirce's frequent defenses of anthropomorphism. Hartshorne is not sufficiently just to Peirce, however, in his
failure to recognize Peirce's dialectical attempt to preserve both features,
just as the Trinitarian theology of Augustine attempted to do. See Hartshorne, "A Critique of Peirce's Idea of God," *Philosophical Review, 50*
(1941), 522–23.

since purpose involves growth it should follow, on a strict interpretation, that God undergoes a process of development. That this is the case cannot be asserted unequivocally, he said, although (and Peirce adopted this as a general rule) it is less mistaken to represent God in this way than to represent him as altogether purposeless.

The second facet of the N.A., which like the third is properly an argumentation and not an argument at all, depends on the previous Humble Argument. Actually, it is an attempt by the reflective mind to commend the belief in God resulting from that argument by means of a demonstration exhibiting its simplicity and inevitability. Analysis of the Humble Argument will, according to Peirce, show that if the layers of conscious purpose and intellectual sophistication can only be stripped away, man's instinctive belief in God as the creator of the universes will inevitably present itself with great force. Natural theology, he believed, can make use of such analysis to show the pervasive and instinctive character of belief in God and thereby defend such belief against the charge of being wholly factitious and illusory. However, since Peirce did not believe that argumentation could produce conviction (belief) in religion apart from direct experience, he did not attribute any great force to this second line of reasoning. This second argumentation has a significant place in theology nevertheless, because Peirce regarded it as superior to much of that rationalistic argument in theology which ignores the limitations of reason where matters of vital importance are concerned. Peirce, as is manifest from the above, had little sympathy with an apologetic theology employing argumentation wholly apart from any vital roots in immediate religious experience.

The third part of the N.A. is by far the most intricate of the "nest." It consists in an analysis of the logic of scientific procedure which seeks to develop the idea that the hypothesis of God's reality resulting from the Humble Argument is the first stage of a "scientific inquiry into the origin of the three Universes" (6.485). No full treatment of Peirce's discussion is possible here, but the main points can be indicated. He regarded the Humble Argument as an illustration of the first stage of scientific inquiry, that of proposing a hypothesis to explain or in some way relate certain phenomena. The framing of hypotheses is what Peirce called *abduction* or *retroduction,* and it is to this stage that he attached the greatest significance in the interpretation of scientific method.[43] The testing of hypotheses by means of deduction and induction, while it may appear to be the only part of scientific procedure worthy of attention, is dependent in the first instance on a hypothesis actually having been proposed. In the case of the hypothesis of God's reality, Peirce noted three significant particulars in which it differs from a hypothesis designed, for example, to explain certain electrical phenomena. *First,* the initial[44] plausibility of this hypothesis is much greater than that of any deliberately framed hypothesis. (The point of the Humble Argument, it must be remembered, is that in musement the inquirer frames the hypothesis of God's reality in a mood closely approximating that of pure play, i.e. he arrives at it instinctively and not as a result of deliberate reasoning.) There is the danger that inquiry will never commence at this first stage because it is so difficult to start testing, and consequently doubting, what was in the first instance the deliverance of instinct. The high degree of initial plausibility which this particular hypothesis commands is "an argument

43. See 5.172, where Peirce said, "Every single item of scientific theory which stands established today has been due to abduction."

44. "Initial" means "before deduction and induction have been employed in the testing." See 6.488. Of course, in the case of the hypothesis of God's reality the initial plausibility is dependent on the proper attitude of musement and upon instinct.

of no small weight in favor of the truth of the hypothesis."
Second, when a useful hypothesis is entertained, sufficient
clarity should be attainable to ensure the prediction of consequences and the specification of conditions, and in the
special sciences such clarity can generally be secured. In
the case of the hypothesis of God's reality, however, no such
clarity is possible, and therefore it is not possible to predict
the conduct of an omniscient being, save in exceptional
cases.[45] *Third,* the practical consequences of the hypothesis,
i.e. the all-embracing influence which it has on the conduct
of the sincere believer, tends to counteract the theoretical
difficulties introduced by the vagueness of the hypothesis.
Presumably, in the case of any other hypothesis, Peirce
would not have allowed such considerations to enter in,
since in strictly scientific investigation vagueness is to be
eliminated whenever possible. Nevertheless, he went on to
defend his own pragmaticism in an attempt to support the
view that the real meaning of the hypothesis of God's reality
is to be found in its determination of conduct.[46]

Actually, the "second" and "third" arguments are indirect because they were not meant to prove the reality of
God but only to develop certain features of the Humble
Argument in order to show that it is well founded because
founded on instinct.[47] This means that whatever there is of
a theoretically compelling nature in these arguments is ultimately dependent on the inquirer's already having arrived

45. In 6.502 Peirce seems to run counter to this position. Hartshorne is
correct in saying that Peirce often contradicted himself on theological
questions, mainly, I believe, because he was not convinced of the importance
of theology as a theoretical discipline.

46. Since Peirce's papers on theology and religion are apt to be overlooked
by those whose interest in him is confined to logical and mathematical considerations, it may be that the criticism he makes of certain features of
pragmatism has not been noticed. 6.485 is striking in this respect, and, as it
may prove to some, not a little surprising.

47. See 6.500, where Peirce himself made this point.

at the hypothesis of God's reality in musement. The Humble Argument is, as Peirce repeatedly insisted, the basic one, and with it comes the immediate experience and direct perception without which no religious belief is at all possible.

The central idea behind Peirce's apologetic (argumentation) for the N.A., although the point is obscured by his disjointed manner of presentation, is the idea that man's ability to frame relevant hypotheses suggests "that there is something in nature to which the human mind is analogous" (1.316). This was a favorite theme and one which he developed on many occasions. It is at the back of what he intended by his frequent claim that to engage in science is to believe in God.[48] The fact that man is able to discover, out of the countless hypotheses that have no relevance in a given inquiry, just those which are relevant and verifiable was a crucial one for Peirce, and on it he based his belief that there is an ultimate purpose (the hypothesis of God's reality) behind the three universes. As a final explanation of the attunement of man's mind to the structure of the universe, Peirce rejected absolute chance: "You may say that evolution accounts for the thing. I don't doubt it is evolution. But as for explaining evolution by chance, there has not been time enough" (5.172). Thus at the basis of the N.A. on the theoretical side was Peirce's belief in the significance of just those aspects of reality which have traditionally supported the various theistic arguments from design. The novel aspect of Peirce's version is the analysis of abduction accompanying it which was made possible by

48. See 1.127, 316; 2.24, 769; 5.107, 172 ff.; 6.496, 503. See also Hartshorne's article, before mentioned, where he points out that, on other occasions (e.g. 2.794) Peirce denied that inference needs a ground. This is not noted by Hartshorne, but the paper entitled "Grounds of Validity of the Laws of Logic" (5.318 ff.) is the best illustration of such a denial. In this paper the scientific community is said to supply whatever ground the laws of logic can be said to require.

his intimate acquaintance with the logical foundations of scientific method.

The final point to be considered is the positive content of his idea of God. He constantly emphasized that, as an instinctive belief, belief in God is vague. Yet, despite necessary vagueness, something of a positive nature concerning God may be asserted which even in its limited application is still more accurate than its absolute denial would be. He formally defined God as *Ens necessarium* and as the creator of the three universes; however it is quite clear that Peirce's pragmaticism makes it not only impossible but even unnecessary to continue analysis and speculation along this line toward the development of a fully articulated theology. When the pragmaticist is asked what he means by "God," he can only answer by referring to conduct and practical experience. Peirce illustrated this point by an analogy. Just as long acquaintance with a man of great character will have a marked influence on one's conduct, so may contemplation and musing upon those features of the universe stressed in the Humble Argument lead to a similar influencing of conduct. For the pragmaticist this analogue is what is meant by God or a disembodied spirit. As to the question whether there *really is* such a God, Peirce took this to be the same as the question whether or not any of the great prophets, Socrates, Confucius, etc., men whose conduct was influenced by meditation upon the universe, really discovered *Truth*. God, in this view, is the Truth at the center of the universe, analogous to the mind of man but ultimately known only by those who have experienced the power of this Truth as manifested in the structure and conduct of their own lives.

In at least one place Peirce did try, despite his remark that "the pragmatistic definition of *Ens necessarium* would require many pages" (6.490),[49] to give some hints to the

49. What follows in the text is dependent on this section.

understanding of the term "God." These are brief and undeveloped; hence it seems best to summarize them succinctly, allowing for the fact that they are far from clear. God has his being out of time since all that a pure mind is destined to think is within itself at any time. Order is thought embodied in some regular way or structure. There is as well something that may be called "Superorder" of which order and uniformity can be said to be particular varieties. Pure mind as manifested in time is related to habit and this is analogous to the relation between superorder and uniformity. As such, pure mind must be capable of thinking of a state of nility, i.e. the absence of superorder ("since, after all, no contradiction can be involved in mere nonexistence"), and from one premise formulated in this state the universes must be shown to follow. The nility of this state requires that the one premise employed must be such that it does not suppose the universes to exist at all, and they are, consequently, "absolutely necessary results of a state of utter nothingness" (6.490). Peirce did not enlarge further upon these remarks, partly because he was more interested in the consequences of asserting God's reality than in the further analysis of what is meant by *Ens necessarium*.

In criticizing those features of Peirce's theology just outlined, one can make the obvious remark that so far as the preceding hints about the meaning of *Ens necessarium* are concerned, Peirce may be regarded as the "dark philosopher" indeed. For further consideration it would seem best to concentrate on one main feature, Peirce's pragmaticism. Nothing could be more revealing of his position than his hesitation in dealing with the positive content of the idea of God. Despite his frequent spirited defenses of anthropomorphism in theology, Peirce was convinced that the purely human attributes falling within our own experience cannot be applied to God literally.[50] For this reason he hesitated to

50. See especially 6.502.

develop a positive theology. Perhaps even more fundamental, however, was his view of the practical character of religion, and of the primacy of instinct and sentiment over clear concepts and reasoning. A mind that is not convinced of the significance of theology as a theoretical discipline will never possess the patience to deal with the intricacies and paradoxes facing the Christian theologian. Peirce lacked such patience just because he saw no need for theology beyond the practical one of serving as a "platform" for the church, enabling it to make clear its position and to indicate the conditions for salvation. Since, in his view, belief in God stems from instinct and is directed toward conduct, it is not necessary to spend much time in "preciding"[51] this belief. It is sufficient unto itself and more powerful when left in its vague and instinctive form.

Peirce was certainly correct in pointing to the moral significance of theology, although his restriction of it to a "platform" is too narrow and is not supported by historical facts. Even considered historically, theology has had a more extensive role to play in the history of Christianity than Peirce seemed to think. The most significant limitation of his view, a limitation of pragmatism generally and also of overzealous "existentialism" in theology, is that it fails to take seriously enough the *cognitive* or *interpretative* element in all religious traditions. Religion is practical indeed, but not wholly so, because it offers an *interpretation* of human existence as well as a directive and a goal for human striving. This interpretative element implies a cognitive element and for this reason it is necessary that as much clarity

51. See above, n. 37. According to Peirce "precision" has two meanings closely related to each other; on the one hand it means "a high degree of approximation, only attainable by the thorough application of the most refined methods of science," and on the other hand, "the act of supposing (whether with consciousness of fiction or not) something about one element of a percept, upon which the thought dwells, without paying any regard to other elements" (1.549 n.).

and precision as possible be achieved. If the theologian encounters contradictions, antinomies, and paradoxes, these must be stated and clarified, even if they cannot be satisfactorily overcome or resolved. Peirce's restrictions on theology precluded any further development of its main ideas at his hands, because, save for a few places, he neglected the interpretative aspect of religion, which is what theology really is. It is obvious that any thinker who views religion as a wholly practical affair must either discard theology altogether or accord it a place of decidedly secondary importance.

Finally, in addition to theology's function as a religious interpretation of existence, it may not be vain to hope that the element of wonder and curiosity in man of which Aristotle made so much may still be appealed to as one of the bases of careful theological thought. Religion must ultimately be traced back to a mystery and, as Paul Tillich has indicated, theology is the attempt to understand this mystery (θεός) with such reason (λόγος) as we possess. This persistent attempt reveals man's desire to know, with as much precision as is feasible, even that which may forever surpass his powers. The theology of Augustine reveals this in a striking way. Starting with the faith that a sincere and devoted quest will lead to truth and understanding, he searched out the mysteries in a clear and cogent manner, because no matter how often he prayed that he had not blasphemed or reasoned erroneously about God's nature, his desire to find God out persisted. He could not rest until he knew, even as he was known. This quest for clear knowledge of the mystery at the heart of human existence has not stirred the souls of most pragmatists to direct their ideal of "scientific" knowledge to the domain of theology. Peirce was no exception.

5. John Dewey: Philosopher of Experience

IN REASSESSING Dewey's philosophy as a whole, we should attempt to do him the only honor which philosophers ought to acknowledge, namely, to consider his ideas as sufficiently important to be the subject of continued interpretation and critical judgment. Philosophers, to be sure, always desire to be understood and to communicate with their contemporaries, but, much as they wish to be understood, philosophers would rather have their ideas discussed in a critical yet sympathetic fashion. To attempt this appraisal upon the basis of a clear notion of what a philosopher has wanted to say is the most substantial tribute that can be paid to him. And in carrying on the critical dialogue, we will be working toward a clearer understanding of the present and the factors that have made it what it is.

Let it be clear at the outset that in reappraising Dewey's thought we have to do with no minute philosopher. In breadth of interest and range of thought he belongs with the great comprehensive thinkers of the past. And in contrast to many thinkers both in his own time and since, he had a constructive program. Philosophy for him meant more than analysis, even though analysis is an important part of the philosophic enterprise. Dewey's constructive philosophy has too often been lost in polemic discussion. I subscribe to the confession made some years ago by Ernest Hocking in which he said that he began to understand Dewey when he started reading him for enjoyment and not for the purpose of showing that he was all wrong! As

Dewey's work shapes up in historical perspective, it assumes a great substantiality. One may disagree and one may correct, but in comparison with philosophy of a wholly technical and professional sort, Dewey's large-minded approach to genuinely philosophic questions places him among philosophers of stature.

I will single out the concepts of evolution and experience for special attention because I want to show how the evolutionary idea—what Dewey called the "biological contribution" to philosophy—shaped both his theory of experience and his general outlook on things. In focusing on the meaning of experience, I want to make clear the manner in which Dewey's broader or reconstructed view formed the basis of a metaphysic of nature and a conception of man's place in the universe. It is especially important that we take notice of the criticism leveled by Dewey against the view of experience bequeathed to us by the British tradition in philosophy from Locke to Bertrand Russell. And in so doing we shall have occasion to remark on the positive resources which are contained in Dewey's broader conception. It will be possible, moreover, to show in what comprehensive fashion Dewey elaborated his ideas into a full-blown metaphysical scheme. With this before us we shall be in a position to put several critical questions aimed at assessing the adequacy of Dewey's philosophy for the present situation.

EVOLUTION

Should the theory of evolution ever lose its grip upon the scientific mind, it might be rehabilitated almost at one stroke by citing the fact that in 1859 the evolutionary process brought forth both the *Origin of Species* and the philosopher whose ideas were to prove so remarkably well adapted to its main thesis. John Dewey hailed the publication of Darwin's work as "marking an epoch in the development of the natural sciences"[1] and he was not slow in claiming that the prominence given to change over fixity in the theory of evolution was bound "to transform the logic of knowledge, and hence the treatment of morals, politics and religion."[2]

Dewey was stimulated by the idea that the very title of Darwin's work represents an abrupt change and an about-face; by long association the term "species" denoted fixed forms in the universe, and the theory that these forms themselves have origins meant, for Dewey, a protest against the past and a vote in favor of change over fixity. The emphasis here placed upon change and its omnipresence is at the heart of Dewey's picture of existence as precarious and perilous, characteristics which drive us at once to a concern about the future. Closely connected with the primacy of change is the idea that everything must be understood as *in the making* and not as once and for all *finished* or *made*. If things are in the making, Dewey reasoned, perhaps we ourselves can have a hand in the process.

Change means development and this in turn means a process moving in some direction. A philosophy of change must attend both to the mechanism of individual changes and to the direction which they take. Dewey understood Darwin's theory of organic adaptation through constant variation and the elimination of harmful variations through struggle to mean the directing of attention away from *ultimate* purposes and toward an *intramundane* type of explanation. The general or pervasive character of nature can be understood from within its confines; there is no need to transcend nature. Explanation must become a piecemeal and retail affair focused on specific changes and specific outcomes. Attention and energy should be directed to the

1. "The Influence of Darwinism on Philosophy," in *The Influence of Darwin on Philosophy and Other Essays* (New York, 1910), p. 1.
2. Ibid., p. 2.

specific alone, a prescription as binding upon philosophy as upon the natural sciences. "Philosophy," wrote Dewey, "forswears inquiry after absolute origins and absolute finalities in order to explore specific values and the specific conditions that generate them." This is what I shall call the *dominance of the focal point;* the idea that reflective thought is called forth and fully determined by the occasion of a specific problem so that its whole being consists in the resolution of the focal point or problem that brings it into play.

A constant undercurrent in Dewey's thought is suspicion of speculation directed toward what he called "wholesale" problems. We have, he thought, neither time nor resources for dealing with such questions; the relevance of every idea or inquiry to the focal point is always decisive. Dewey is interested in change only insofar as it has reference to human purposes. He is interested in specific changes because he wants to know how they "serve and defeat concrete purposes." Man, bounded by an evolving environment, seeks to shape it in accord with his own aims of living and of living well. Our concern for changes, he thinks, is directed by the way we view the bearing of these changes upon the issues of life. There is thus an ineradicable teleology in Dewey's conception of things; nature turns out to be a most human affair. For reflective beings the processes of nature are not just there in the form of brute fact; they take on the traits of being harmful or beneficial as they support life or render its survival precarious. Thus concern for special changes is simultaneous with concern for knowing what their outcome will be and how they take place so that we may be able to use such knowledge to anticipate and control the course of events. Concern for anything other than the specific distracts attention from the attack at hand and weakens our effort.

The contribution of Darwinism is the establishing of the

primacy of change and the banishing of ultimate origins and finalities: the focus upon specific problems and changes; the discovery of the outcomes of such change for the purpose of inserting ourselves and our knowledge into the stream of things so as to influence the results in accord with human plans and purposes; the shift of interest in philosophy away from wholesale and ultimate questions.

If we are to succeed in a world of struggle, we must have a weapon both for defense and attack. For Dewey experience *is* that weapon and indeed this is exactly what he meant by saying that experience is a method, a way of going about things.

EXPERIENCE

It is no secret that modern thought, and not only philosophical thought, has been dominated since the eighteenth century by the appeal to experience. When Locke and other figures of the Enlightenment challenged rationalism in thought and hereditary authority in politics, they did so in large part in the name of experience. Experience became the touchstone of all theories and all claims to knowledge. It was, however, not long before the demands of a critical self-consciousness led to thoroughgoing analyses of the nature of experience and to inquiry into the grounds of its claim to be the final criterion. In the face of such criticism the empiricism of Locke and the British school—what Dewey called the classical theory of experience—continued to dominate the philosophical scene. The key to Dewey's metaphysic of nature is to be found in the fact that his own theory of experience represents a thorough criticism and rejection of most of the classical view. This crucial fact and its implications have still not been sufficiently understood.

Dewey's emphasis upon science as *method* and his consequent stress upon the operations required for experimental science have led many to suppose that Dewey's empiricism is the same as that of so-called scientific or logical empiricism. This is an error. Dewey was an empiricist; this was his repeated claim, but he was not an empiricist in the sense of the term that would define and link together in one common tradition the succession of thinkers from William of Occam through Hume and Mill to Bertrand Russell. This being the case, we are led once again to the topic of experience and to Dewey's understanding of its nature.

In a paper written late in his life, Dewey said: "For many years I have consistently—and rather persistently—maintained that the key to a philosophic theory of experience must proceed from initially linking it with the processes and functions of life as the latter are disclosed in biological science."[3] No more explicit statement could be given to show the connection between Dewey's theory of experience and the biological setting of life. Unless we start with the conception of an organism interacting or carrying on transactions with the environment, we shall never understand Dewey's metaphysic of experience.

In an important but not very frequently read essay, "The Need for a Recovery of Philosophy," Dewey asserted: "Experience means primarily not knowledge, but ways of doing and suffering."[4] From this text we can grasp the leading idea of the entire theory. Experience is a dynamic or temporal affair which is reciprocal and constituted by all the modes of intercourse between a conscious being and the environment, both physical and social. The view here expressed is as important for the negations it implies as for

3. *The Philosophy of John Dewey*, ed. Schilpp (Evanston, Chicago, Northwestern University Press, 1939), p. 530.

4. "The Need for a Recovery of Philosophy," in *Creative Intelligence*, Dewey et al. (New York, 1917), p. 37.

what it positively affirms; it is a criticism of older views as
well as a program for the future. It was his aim not only
to show the shortcomings of the older interpretation but
at the same time to establish the closer relation of his own
theory to the actual facts.

When he considered what experience meant for the
classical empiricists, Dewey came up with the following
fivefold description: first, experience means *knowledge*
primarily; secondly, it is a *psychical,* subjective, or mental
content; thirdly, it is largely confined to the *present moment* although it may also be taken as the record of past
or finished fact; fourthly, it is all *particular* and without
connective tissue between its atomic items; finally, experience stands as a *contrast domain* to thought and it is set
over against reason as something other than conceptual
thought. We can see in these characterizations the antithesis of his own view at every point.

On the *first* count, experience for Dewey is not exclusively an affair of knowledge, nor should it be understood as if
it were exclusively material for science. Knowing is an activity that goes on within experience and is controlled by
the conditions of empirical inquiry, but the organism also
sustains other relationships with the environment and these
equally belong to experience. Since Dewey did not identify
knowing with either experience or consciousness, knowing
could not be ubiquitous. On the *second* count, experience
is not taken as exhausted by what is immediately present
to an individual or private mind; the behavioristic drift of
Dewey's philosophy rules out such an interpretation from
the start. By contrast Dewey took experience, except on its
purely qualitative or aesthetic side, as all *public fact.* And
this feature is dictated by the function that experience is
to perform. As an instrument or tool for shaping the environment, experience could not be taken as a private affair;
control demands a means that shall consist of public, im-

personal, and intersubjective content. In *Reconstruction in Philosophy* Dewey even defended the development of a purely mechanical conception of nature as a necessary stage in our becoming aware of the possibilities of controlling nature. As long as natural things were viewed as having their own teleological interiors, man was prevented from treating them as objects of control; taking nature as a mechanical system was a necessary stage in the development of instrumentalism.

On the *third* count, Dewey was uneasy over the passivity attributed to experience in the classical view. Experience as merely the passive reception and record of the present datum seemed to him no more than an opportunity lost. The secret of Dewey's instrumentalism lies in his view that the present (and the past also as retained) is not chiefly for observation but is to be *used* by us in a strategic way; from it we have our only chance to obtain a foothold on the future, which alone counts. Taking experience as merely the record or duplication of present fact would spoil the instrumentalist program; our task is not to conform to the world but to transform it through the renewal of intelligence.

On the *fourth* count, Dewey could not accept what he termed the "particularism" of classical empiricism. In their programs for clarifying our ideas, Locke, Berkeley, and Hume all sought to trace them back to their appropriate sensory data and thus to establish a one-to-one correlation between terms and impressions or ideas. In so doing they came to regard the ultimate or primitive data of experience as distinct, clear-cut, first-person awarenesses that are everlastingly singular in character. Dewey objected to such translation on the grounds that clear-cut sense data are actually the result of reflection and intellectual refinement; his charge is that a "reflected product" is being identified with what is supposed to be experientially primitive. Moreover, Dewey could not accept the atomism implicit in this approach. If experience is composed of atomic data, it is deprived of its own connections and transitions; this made it possible for rationalists to reintroduce relations as the peculiar contribution of the mind. It is difficult to be sure how far Dewey's objection here is based on the conviction that the classical view distorts the actual facts and how far he wanted merely to find a way of preventing rationalists from capitalizing on the omissions of sensory empiricism. But whatever the answer to that question may be, he had a further reason for his view and it takes us back again to the biological orientation. In a striking use of scientific theory to support a philosophical thesis, Dewey claimed that the fact of survival in the human species is incompatible with experience as atomistically interpreted. "No living creature," he wrote, "could survive, save by sheer accident, if its experiences had no more reach, scope or content, than traditional, particularistic empiricism provides for."[5] Here Dewey joins hands with the advocates of "radical empiricism," the contention that experience is never of isolated singular fact, but contains relations or connective tissue within itself. Survival requires some command of things and this is impossible without knowledge of the extended and temporal working of nature and especially of the network of relations existing between its parts. If experience did not embrace this knowledge and disclose such relations but gave only a report, a sort of mental duplicate, of purely present and particular occurrences, it could not serve as the needed instrument for success. The future can neither be anticipated nor controlled by a mere image of the present in the form of discrete, singular data.

On the *fifth* count in Dewey's critique we have a point that refers to all the others. He rejected the idea that ex-

5. *The Philosophy of John Dewey,* p. 544.

perience is a single subject matter—the domain of sense—which is to stand as different in kind from and in contrast with thought. For him all statements of the form "experience is X" where "X" means a single quality, object, or kind of datum are incorrect. Experience cannot be identified with any of its proper parts and it is no longer the given in contrast with concepts. Dewey's main concern was that experience taken in this way must inevitably exclude inference, the activity of reason. For Dewey's program this exclusion would be disastrous; experience in its main significance is *connected meaning* enabling us to handle processes and their outcomes; if it excludes the connections of inference, it must again be reduced to the reception of disjointed singulars. An intelligent being does not merely *react* to the environment, but he is capable of *responding* to it; mind is the response to the doubtful as such. But response involves both an apprehension of the connections between presently discriminated items and the relations to the past from which they come no less than to the future in which they issue. All of this involves inference and other activities of thought. In thus making essential to experience the activity of the thinking mind, Dewey proved himself a good Kantian. Unlike Kant, however, Dewey claimed to learn all these things from the biologist; Kant, it might be recalled, though he had himself made actual contributions to natural science, had a higher regard for philosophical reflection.

The answer to the question, "What is experience?" is given in the form of a complex description of what goes on when an intelligent organism stands in thoroughgoing interaction with the environment. The result is a vast complex of objects, qualities, events, meanings, or habits which determine some future response. And when experience is controlled by the method of the sciences, it yields that knowledge of the workings of things which furnishes us with the power to shape the course of events. Experience has many facets; in the nature of the case it cannot be identified with any *one* sort of thing. It embraces not only science and art but morality, politics, and religion at the same time. If at times Dewey appears to give to experience a singular or differential meaning by identifying it with a method for control, that is because he shared with William James the belief that method is neutral and does not of itself commit us to special theses about the nature of things. It is difficult to understand what leads anyone to suppose that methods remain free of assumptions and that they invariably enjoy protective neutrality. When someone tells us *how* to obtain something, he is assuming that he knows the general sort of thing he is after and has some idea of where it is to be found. To suppose that one-sidedness and special pleading attach only to results and conclusions and not to methods has been one of the most cherished fancies of the entire pragmatic tradition.

Before leaving the topic of experience, a word is in order concerning the seeming disappearance of the individual experienc*er* in Dewey's view. I shall return to this point later on; here we need but note the impression shared by many that Dewey's dominantly social interpretation of experience as public fact makes it difficult to locate the individual for whom experience is an actual fact. It is true that Dewey sought to deal with this problem by means of the doctrine of pervasive quality and what he called having *an* experience; the aesthetic dimension, it would appear, makes room for the individual and the private. But even in this context Dewey retained his suspicion of the private; emotions, he wrote, "are not, save in pathological instances, private,"[6] but are occurrences in the development of experience to some issue or conclusion. This seems to place the

6. John Dewey, *Art as Experience* (Capricorn Books, New York, G. P. Putnam's Sons), p. 42.

most individualized of all experiences once again in the public context where it falls under the dominant motive to control events.

Dewey used with considerable success his doctrine of method for the purpose of establishing continuity between knowing and evaluating in the ethical sense. And this he could achieve because he viewed each as a process aiming at some sort of control. Connecting the scientific and the aesthetic, however, is more difficult because the aesthetic is not supposed to be a matter of instrumentalities at all, but of intrinsic finality. The aesthetic for him must either lose the consummatory value claimed for it, or we must admit a genuine, individualized, final center of experience. Thus our difficulty in locating the individual who has first-person experience stems from the fact that even in the aesthetic dimension Dewey is not always able to avoid slipping back into his thoroughgoing instrumentalism.

We may now come to our third theme, Dewey's metaphysics. It is clearly impossible to set forth even a skeleton outline of the substantive position contained in Dewey's most comprehensive metaphysical book, *Experience and Nature*. But we shall, nevertheless, use it as a guide in the development of our third theme. The persistent neglect of that important book has been largely responsible for the truncated view of Dewey's philosophy that has been entertained no less by his followers than by his avowed critics.

METAPHYSICS

Dewey developed his position into a full-blown metaphysical system which he described as naturalistic empiricism. There can be no question that in the final construction of his naturalistic philosophy, Dewey was guided largely by the evolutionary idea and the reconstructed conception of experience. Each determines an aspect of his theory of nature and of his view of man as a creature firmly planted in the natural process.

At the outset of *Experience and Nature* Dewey distinguishes between philosophy and metaphysics: "If we follow classical terminology," he writes, "philosophy is love of wisdom, while metaphysics is cognizance of the generic traits of existence."[7] The upshot of this distinction is that metaphysics should mean the delineation of the most general and pervasive traits exhibited by anything that exists, whereas philosophy is bound up with the basic aims and strategy of life. Existence and individuality, event and relation, function and structure, and many other categories become the appropriate concern of metaphysical analysis. Dewey objected vigorously, however, to the idea that the pervasive structure disclosed by analysis is to be set off as a timeless realm more real than the world of contingency and change. He objected, moreover, to metaphysics taken in any sense other than the one he had set out. The aim of metaphysics is to arrive at a structural catalogue; there is to be no synthetic interpretation of things by selecting any one aspect or feature as the clue to the unity of the whole.

He repeatedly maintained that the generic traits of existence are themselves involved in time and change and that man is related to these features of nature in a practical way. This fact shows us that metaphysics is not enough; if man is to succeed and improve his lot in a precarious world, he needs what Dewey called the wisdom that is philosophy as well. This latter note is sounded with special force in his final chapter where he returns again to the connections between philosophy and metaphysics. There we see emerging the idea that philosophy is essentially *criticism*, that is, appraisal and judgment directed toward goods or values. The aim of philosophy as criticism is the relating of differ-

7. John Dewey, *Experience and Nature* (New York, Norton, 1929), p. 51.

ent aspects of experience to each other and the reflective discovery of genuine or lasting values as distinct from what is trivial or evanescent. It is in this way and at one stroke that Dewey settled accounts with the classical conception of philosophy as love of wisdom and introduced into his system a wisdom which is not knowledge but which cannot be separated from knowledge.[8]

But howsoever we interpret the wisdom that is philosophy, we still need further clarification as to the relation it bears to metaphysics, the relation, that is, between the wisdom that is to guide life and the pervasive or generic nature of the universe in which it is to be lived. We come here to the heart of Dewey's philosophical vision, and it makes no difference by what name we choose to call it. The principal point is that for him there is a vital and practical relation existing between the generic traits of the universe, on the one hand, and the issues of life and death faced by those who live in it, on the other. Dewey described this relationship as raising the "most far reaching question of all criticism" and as the problem of problems for reflective thought—the relation between existence and value. If, for example, we discover precariousness as a trait of all things, that fact by itself has no more significance than that of a trait noted and recorded. When, however, precariousness is seen as connected with the concrete situations in which men choose, live, and die, it takes on, says Dewey, "that fear of the Lord which is at least the beginning of wisdom."[9] All, then, finally turns on man, the emphasis in Dewey's philosophy which led Santayana to accuse him of natural impiety. To the extent to which natural process affects us or we intervene in natural process, the situation becomes decisively related to values. As if to secure the point more firmly, Dewey writes: "The more sure one is that the world

8. *Experience and Nature*, p. 409.
9. Ibid., p. 413.

which encompasses human life is of such and such a character (no matter what his definition), the more one is committed to try to direct the conduct of life, that of others as
well as of himself, upon the basis of the character assigned
to the world."[10]

If we stand off and try to view Dewey's vast and complex
philosophy without regard to the technical apparatus of
philosophers, we see an enormous spread of nature, of
things and processes, of powers and their effects; these constitute the environment in its nonhuman aspect. And we
see man, the being with intelligence in whom the human
predicament, as Dewey says, "becomes aware of itself." That
is the whole picture, nature and man. There is no third
party, and indeed man is so completely a part of nature
that it often seems as though there were no second party.
Nature is an evolving affair, filled with change and marked
by precariousness and instability; man has experience, that
product of his mind and his transactions with the environment containing within itself both the knowledge born of
science and the wisdom of philosophy that is supposed to
guide him in its use. Living, then, becomes the grand strategy of seeking to *control* the passage of things so as to make
life not only sufficiently stable for survival but to enhance
its quality and enjoyment through the cultivation of those
lasting goods discovered in experience and approved on reflection. The futurism of Dewey's thought is dictated by
this grand strategy; every present has its being as an opportunity for discovering the secrets of things, how they work
and where they lead, so that we may gain power over the
future. In this reading life is not so much lived as it is
taken by storm. There is an experimental spirit and a rest-
lessness hanging over it all, for in the final reach there is no
fulfillment in Dewey's universe; one never possesses but

10. Ibid., pp. 413–14.

is always on the way to possess. The past is gone, the present is unstable and pregnant with care; besides, the present is but an instrument for the future and the future never comes. For every present is analyzed not in terms of what it *is* but rather by reference to what it *will do* and we are once again put off to the future. The point is most clearly illustrated in the case of the knowledge process. Dewey always distinguished between *having* and *knowing*, the former meaning direct, present experience. But if we ask whether *knowledge* is ever *had* as distinct from the having of "an experience of knowing," Dewey would have to answer in the negative. Knowledge is never had but is always infinitely postponed; what we can have in the present is an hypothesis or theory, the meaning and justification of which always lies in the future.

It is impossible to expound or interpret philosophical ideas without giving at least implicit critical judgment, but implicit criticism is not enough; appraisal of a more positive sort is called for. I shall, therefore, focus upon three issues raised by the themes I have set forth. And in considering these criticisms we do well to bear in mind that insofar as Dewey stands as *the* American philosopher for the first half of our century at least, we pass critical judgment upon ourselves.

The first issue concerns whether Dewey was right in his insistent and persistent claim that man must forswear what he called "wholesale" questions in favor of specific or retail problems. How far, in other words, is it valid to admit what I have called the dominance of the focal point? Are the so-called practical and urgently focused predicaments the only human concerns? In considering this question we must begin by admitting that Dewey's aim in emphasizing the specific and piecemeal problem is clear and not without its measure of truth. We have limited resources and limited opportunities for strengthening our hand; much of our energy

must be directed toward meeting the immediate challenge
of the environment. No effort is to be wasted on inquiries
into large "useless" questions such as why there is evil in
the world, whether there is God, how one and the same individual can retain identity while still changing from day
to day. As far as this goes we may accept his doctrine of the
need for intelligent attack upon the evils and threats of the
environment. But a major difficulty at once confronts us:
How shall we determine what is *relevant* to resolving the
piecemeal problem and indeed how shall we know when it
is resolved? To what extent are ultimate and apparently
useless questions at the heart of a difficulty which seems
overwhelmingly specific and practical? No natural science
will answer these questions all by itself.

It is not, however, merely a matter of showing the *practical* relevance of wholesale or ultimate questions; this can
always be done, and Dewey at times acknowledges the point
himself when he thinks of reflective thought as criticism.
But more important, ultimate questions point to our human concern for some understanding about aspects of our
life and world beyond the reach of what is taken into account by a philosophy directed only to the instrumental control of things. The only point in Dewey's thought where
an attempt is made to transcend the instrumental attitude
is in the aesthetic; this is the one aspect of experience that
is offered *for itself* and not as a means to something else.
But we may well ask whether the aesthetic is enough; there
are in addition large questions of a *distinctively moral* nature that are not the same as choice between technical alternatives, and there are problems perennial in metaphysical analysis and speculation, to say nothing of the concerns
of religion. What are we to do in the face of the persistent
human demand—I almost said *natural* demand—for answers to such questions as whether an individual is responsible for a world and a self he never made; whether human

purpose and choice are but the inner appearance of a supposedly real world composed only of physical events; what we are to make of the fact that the universe contains a self-reflexive or self-representative being in the form of self-consciousness; whether there is self-dependent being. These are questions which the philosopher cannot avoid because, if I may borrow a phrase from Dewey, they belong to the "problems of men." But they will be ignored, as indeed they were by Dewey, from the standpoint of a philosophy acknowledging only specific problems and the instrumental response.

The second issue is closely related to the foregoing; it concerns the theory of experience and especially whether Dewey's interpretation of it as an instrument and public fact does not mean the disappearance of the individual self or experiencer. In making the criticism I must confess to a certain ambivalence; on the one hand I hold that his account of experience conforms more closely to the facts than does the classical theory. His account, it must be admitted, brings within experience much that is actually encountered but which had to be denied experiential status on the classical view. On the other hand, however, Dewey went so far in the direction of behaviorism or the translation of experience into external, public fact and function that the individual experiencer becomes insignificant. The individual and the private always made Dewey uneasy; it is not that he denied either, he was too good an empiricist for that, but he wanted to keep them confined to a place where they would do no public damage. He intended to provide for the privacy of experience by his theory of art and through what he called the enhancing and enriching of experienced goods. But when it comes to experience as the instrument or weapon of attack on the environment, privacy and individuality are of no account. The fact that an individual self is always the locus of experience, that experience, as

William James put it, is always somebody's experience, somewhere and somewhen, is not taken seriously; as either overt behavior or impersonal public fact, experience virtually closes with nature, and the individual is forced to abscond into the realm of art.

It is no accident that Dewey was forced to acknowledge this deficiency in the face of psychological criticism. In reply to Allport's questions concerning his psychology, Dewey candidly replied: "I am obliged to admit what he says about the absence of an adequate theory of personality."[11] And the reason offered by Dewey in his own defense was his desire to avoid "spiritualistic" theories of the self as individual substance. But even if we admit the inadequacy of the concept of substance, surely the problem of locating the unity and identity of the individual self remains. This problem cannot be resolved, as William James' entire philosophical development testifies, by a purely functional theory. Every functional theory of the self ends by translating it into activities of a sort which only a center of consciousness can perform. "I would point out," Dewey wrote in 1939, "that I hold that the word 'subject' if it is to be used at all, has the organism for its proper *designatum*. Hence it refers to an *agency of doing*, not to a knower, mind, consciousness or whatever."[12] I confess that I fail to follow when I am told that a person is not a consciousness or a knower, but even more I fail to understand how an "agency of doing" can become aware of itself, how it can remember, and how it can become divided within itself.

How, for example, are we to understand the divided self as an unhealthy or undesirable state of affairs unless we presuppose an underlying unity and center of the self? Dewey could not really introduce such questions into his theoreti-

11. *The Philosophy of John Dewey,* p. 555.
12. Ibid., p. 542.

cal treatment because for him all theory is instrumental to further control; if the answer to a given question does not contribute directly to the manipulation of a portion of nature, it is of no account. The more a problem relates either to the ultimate constitution of things or to the interior life of an individual self, the further removed it is from the surface of public fact and the less powerful would be its theoretical solution for the control of the environment. But not all human problems are directly a matter of overt and external control of things; some of them have to do with the interpretation of individual life and its purpose. When these "useless" questions are neglected, they do not simply evaporate; on the contrary, they take on an explosive urgency just to the extent to which they are ignored. And if all the available intellectual discipline for treating them is at work elsewhere, we should not be surprised when others seek to resolve the problems confronting the individual, his freedom, his purpose, and his life in the world in what appears as an irrational way. We earn the right to criticize these attempts at solution only when we are seeking to answer the same questions. To refuse to raise a question is to forfeit the right to assess the answers offered by others.

The third and final issue concerns the nature and function of metaphysics itself. Dewey repeatedly rejected what he took to be the main distinction behind classical metaphysics, the distinction between appearance and reality. He was fond of saying that the proper contrast to appearance is not reality but disappearance. The point of his rejection is that no one aspect of things and no one portion of experience can be taken as the clue to or as definitive of the exclusively real, so that everything else is reduced to the domain of appearance. Selective preference must be overcome; nothing special or limited can be elevated to an absolute position. Everything must be taken into account

and given its due, and the singling out of any one thing o
trait as a clue for interpreting all the rest appears as hope
less partiality and special pleading. Now when such a thesi
is advanced in the contemporary world, it has an undeniabl
democratic tone which commends it to many; it especiall
satisfies our interest in remaining neutral in the face o
those hard problems which cannot be solved in what appear
to be a final or definitive way. But our concern is neithe
with the overtones of such a view nor with the fact that i
satisfies a current interest, but with the question as t
whether it is true and most adequately expresses the natur
of metaphysics. I believe that it does not and for two mai
reasons.

First, there is no point whatever in bothering our head
over the general nature of things if the only conclusion a
which we shall arrive is one we know well enough in th
beginning, namely, that reality is a quite miscellaneou
collection of things related in some fairly constant ways
We scarcely need metaphysical inquiry to achieve that re
sult any more than we would need it to conclude that what
ever is, is. Without a differential standpoint or interpreta
tive principle such as organism, matter, selfhood from whicl
we attempt to understand reality in its wholeness, we hav
no insight and ultimately no philosophy. I do not say tha
the interpreting principle need imply any static monism
I wish only to point out that a radical pluralism will not dc
as an adequate metaphysical principle because it can neve
get beyond repeating in the form of what purports to be
critical conclusion the fact known to all at the outset
namely, that reality contains as many things as it does i
fact contain.

Secondly, it is not merely a matter of making a plea fo
the employment of a differential principle of interpretatio
in philosophy but rather of pointing to the unavoidabilit
of such a principle. Hegel, for example, surpassed all phi

losophers in his attempt to avoid a limited or special vantage point from which to estimate the whole, but if we attend to what actually happens in his system, we find that he was in fact asking for a special principle rich enough to interpret the whole of reality. This principle in his system is self-consciousness or spirit; on any interpretation what we are given is certainly a differential principle. It is not in fact different with Dewey's own philosophy. For all of his criticism of absolutes and of an ultimate context, Dewey's naturalistic empiricism does not avoid a vantage point from which it interprets reality as a whole. A great deal of the power of Dewey's thought in American life has in fact been due to the circumstance that he did not follow his own prescriptions. Dewey's thought is deeply involved in a differential principle governing the interpretation of the whole of nature and of man's place in it; the biological situation—the interaction of organism and environment plus the mutual adjustment required for survival—furnishes the key to understanding the human predicament; experience in the form of science provides us with the exclusive instrument for coping with it.

Dewey's view of what he called the human predicament is thoroughly dependent upon taking biological theory as the clue to man's place in the universe. Existence changes and is precarious: the environment is not all favorable to the sustained life of man; as a peculiar type of biological organism, man is capable of experience or the attainment of public knowledge. When shot through with intelligent method, experience can intervene to control the environment and thus make possible the turning of nature's processes to human ends. This basic vision controlling the whole of Dewey's philosophy is itself totally dependent upon taking one aspect of the full situation of man in the universe and using it as a clue to the nature of the whole. The biological and the social, as Dewey repeatedly stressed, determine his outlook; if they had not, he would have produced no philosophy but only a social theory.

I cannot pass over the problem of selective emphasis without a final word about the most glaring form in which it is raised by Dewey's thought. For Dewey the name for the real is Nature, and we are often told by him that no differential meaning should be attached to the term. Nature is all there is and we must not suppose that the concept of nature derives its meaning from the contrast situation in which it stood in the traditional "great chain of being" where it was bounded by man at one end and by God at the other. But if the term Nature is to have no differential meaning and simply denotes "whatever is," then it is gratuitous. For we encounter persons and poems, tables and chairs, hopes and fears. All are real and stand in need of analysis and interpretation, but exactly what is contributed by using the term Nature to denote all these different kinds of things? The term Nature is far from innocent. By it Dewey means to denote the environment, including man and perhaps all his potentialities but nothing more. That Nature, however, taken in some differential sense exhausts reality, Dewey has nowhere shown.

Negative notes need cause no embarrassment, for what better tribute to a distinguished philosopher can one offer than the attempt to think his thoughts after him and thus become engaged in a critical way with the problems he has faced? We respect most those philosophers we take seriously enough to criticize.

II. The Present

6. Is Existence a Valid Philosophical Concept?

THERE can be little doubt that, in one form or another, existence has been at the center of philosophical discussion since the founding of medieval thought in the philosophy and theology of Augustine. No further evidence than, for example, the history of the ontological argument would be needed to show the truth of this statement. Prior to the time of Hume and Kant, philosophers spoke more directly and without hesitation about existence itself; since the penetrating analysis of the transcendental dialectic in Kant's first *Critique,* the tendency has been to discuss the idea of existence or, even more recently, the nature and status of existence propositions. Whatever the form in which they are raised, however, questions concerning existence are no novelty in philosophy.

The question posed in the title is, like all good rhetorical questions, somewhat vague initially and in need of interpretation and clarification. This is particularly true of our proposed question, since it clearly makes reference to the validity of a concept, and, insofar as we generally do not use the term "valid" in relation to concepts, the import of the question will have to be conveyed by another question or questions that will obviate this special difficulty as well as the initial vagueness.

I propose to deal with the situation in the following way: I shall consider briefly four questions which may be taken, either singly or in conjunction, as expressive of the meaning of the original question. This does not mean that anyone dealing with that question would have, of necessity, to be dealing with the questions I shall propose, but only that these questions may be taken as more precise formulations of some of the considerations that might legitimately be discussed under the general question, "Is existence a valid philosophical concept?" It is important, I believe, to be as clear as possible at the outset concerning the question which is actually being asked. Moore, wherever else he may have been mistaken, was surely correct in his insistence on this point, and I can only leave it to you to decide whether I have avoided another pitfall also pointed out by him, namely, whether I have consistently tried to answer the questions I have actually proposed and not some other questions.

The four questions to be considered briefly are the following:

1. Is there a *concept* of existence?
2. Is existence a predicate?
3. Is the question, "Why does anything exist?" meaningful?
4. Is it the "proper business" of philosophy to study existence, and, if so, in what sense?

1. *Is there a* concept *of existence?* Both a part of the meaning and much of the relevance of this question become obvious when it is recalled that in the past many philosophers have believed existence to be supradefinitional or something which in the strict sense cannot be thought. Thus Kierkegaard said, "The only thing-in-itself which cannot be thought, is existence, and this does not come within the province of thought to think."[1] Or again, Hume, in his discussion of the idea of existence,[2] maintained that this

1. *Concluding Unscientific Postscript,* trans. David Swenson (Princeton, Princeton University Press, 1941), p. 292.
2. *Treatise,* I.2.6; italics mine.

idea must either "be derived from a distinct impression," or be "conjoined with every perception or object of our thought," or "be the very same with the idea of the perception or object." In conformity with his general position Hume accepted only the third possibility, holding that "the idea of existence . . . is the very same with the idea of *what* we conceive to be existent." And this is virtually the same as saying that there is no *idea of existence* as distinct from *what is existent* at all.

In choosing the above illustrations I should not want to be interpreted as having said that these two views are by any means identical, but, although I cannot discuss them further here, they are noteworthy insofar as they express the view that existence, as such, cannot be thought, which I take to mean that there is no concept of existence, as such. Many philosophers have asserted, in one form or another, the view that there is an irreducible or surd aspect of existing things to be found simply in the fact *that* they actually *do* exist, and are not nonexistent or only possible. This fact has been taken as the limit of thought, precisely because thought is, according to its own nature, concerned with the generic and its degrees, while existence is always particular and unique, thus defying thought. The truth in such a view might be more readily acknowledged, so it seems, if it were not so frequently stated in a paradoxical way. On the one hand it is said that existence as such cannot be thought, and then the reason often given in support of this shows clearly that there must be at least one sense in which existence can be thought, namely, it must be known that the proposition "all existence is particular and unique" is true. For unless this were known to be true (together with some such proposition as "all thought is of the general and is expressed in conceptual signs"), the conclusion that existence cannot be thought would not follow. It is obvious, nevertheless, that a proposition like "all existence is particular and unique" expresses a view of the nature of existence as such and thereby constitutes a thinking of existence, in some sense.

Even if the view that existence as such cannot be thought is paradoxical, there is a truth in it nevertheless, and that truth can best be indicated by the fact that any conceptual grasp of existence will always be a cognition of "thisness," and not of "this" at all. But "thisness," as Bradley has well shown, does not designate what is existent, since it is universal and not particular, and existents are always particular. "Thisness" is rather an alleged aspect of all that exists, while that alone is an existent which can be the referent of a statement of the form, "This is . . . ." It is of great interest in this connection to note that Russell, in his analysis of the term "this" in the *Inquiry,* recognizes that, taken as a name, "this" "applies to only one object at a time,"[3] and consequently always designates some particular existent under consideration, and nothing else. However, when Russell pushes the analysis further, it becomes clear that all attempts to conceptualize "this" necessarily involve, at some point, the introduction of what he calls "undesired generality," and this can only mean that there is some feature of any situation in which something is designated by "this" which defies further analysis and conceptual formulation. Hartshorne is, I believe, calling attention to the same point when he says, "Why should not 'existence' be a demonstrative pronoun? Pointing is prior to naming and describing."[4]

Let us now return to the original question: Is there a *concept* of existence? Despite the undeniable element of truth in the view that existence as such defies thought, it still seems obvious that if a logical formulation of what is meant when something is said to exist can be given, then

3. Bertrand Russell, *An Inquiry into Meaning and Truth* (New York, Norton, 1940), p. 136.
4. Charles Hartshorne, *Man's Vision of God* (New York, Harper and Bros., 1941), p. 272.

there is a *concept* of existence, taking "concept" in the logical sense specified by Carnap in his *Introduction to Semantics*. Since what is required here, however, is simply to show that there *is* a concept of existence, it will not be necessary to offer and defend any particular concept as *the* concept of existence.

If we say that roses exist, but that unicorns do not, what we mean to say has been well formulated by W. P. Montague in *The Ways of Knowing*.[5] To assert the existence of any particular thing like a rose means to assert that a web of relations of "interaction or spatio-temporal connection" obtains between the rose and "the totality of other things." And, on the contrary, to assert that unicorns do not exist is to assert that no such interaction and system of relations holds, or, what is the same thing, to assert that "unicorns exist nowhere," where "exist" here means exactly what it did in the previous case. Should it be objected, however, that the proposition "unicorns exist in storybooks and in tapestries" is true, and that their "existence" in these places does involve a web of relations similar to that specified above, this objection need only be met by pointing out that everybody would know at once that "exist" in this proposition is not being used in the same sense as in the previous case. And, it should be pointed out, in order for anyone to grasp the basic ambiguity of meaning involved, it would not be necessary for him to be able to offer an exhaustive concept of existence at all, since it is possible to know when a term is being used in two senses without being able to define it exhaustively.

From the foregoing we may conclude that although it may not be possible to exhaust the meaning of "existence" as such in a purely discursive or conceptual way, nevertheless the fact that it is possible to give a logical formulation

---

5. New York (Macmillan, 1925), pp. 110, 111.

of what is meant by the term is evidence that there *is* a *concept* of existence.

2. *Is existence a predicate?* This time-honored question has been discussed by philosophers since the days of Kant, and I believe that the conclusion arrived at both by him and many others to the effect that existence is not a predicate is essentially correct. Consequently, I have virtually nothing which is new to add on this subject. If the term "predicate" is taken in its logical sense as designating some property or attribute of an actual existent, then the analysis of a comparatively few sentences will suffice to show, as Moore and others have done, that "exist" or "exists" is not a predicate or "does not stand for an attribute" in the same sense in which "blue" or "sweet" are predicates.

Russell, it will be recalled, set forth the view in 1919 that existence is not a predicate of individual existents but rather "a property of a propositional function," and Moore in 1936 criticized Russell's view on the ground that it still retains existence as a predicate, though not of individuals but of propositional functions. In addition, Moore correctly pointed out that even if the proposition "some tame tigers exist" means, as Russell once claimed, "some values of 'x is a tame tiger' are true," it does not follow that "exist" *means* "is sometimes true." Here the main difficulty of this approach becomes clear: In the attempt to state in a rigorous way the view that existence is not a predicate, concrete existence gets wholly reduced to the language of logic. Whereas there is, I believe, a simpler but no less cogent way of showing that existence is not a predicate, which does not involve this difficulty.

When we say "the so-and-so is red," "red" is a predicate designating a characteristic of "the so-and-so," and if the proposition is true, we can be said to know something about *what* it is to be "the so-and-so" which would aid us in identifying it should we encounter it in experience. When, however, we say "the so-and-so exists" or "there is a so-and-so," "exists" or "is" is not a predicate designating a characteristic of "the so-and-so" in the above sense at all, since if the proposition is true we could, of course, be said to know something, but we could not be said to know anything whatsoever about *what* it is to be "the so-and-so," and certainly nothing that would aid us in identifying it. From this consideration it seems clear that in the above sense existence is no predicate.

Yet it would be false to conclude that we know nothing whatever *about* a thing when we know that it exists, since it is obvious that at least one considerable difference between lions and unicorns is that the former do exist while the latter do not (in the same sense of "exist"), and again it would be false to say that we could not know this difference without some definite concept of existence, since it is quite certain that many people who are not at all prepared to offer such a concept do know that of lions we can truthfully say "there are lions," while of unicorns we can truthfully say no such thing at all.

3. *Is the question, "Why does anything exist?" meaningful?* In considering this question it is important at the outset to be clear about the meaning of the terms "why" and "anything." Let us begin with the latter. For the purpose of this discussion it is not necessary to offer an exhaustive analysis of the difficult term "any." Strictly speaking, the term cannot be defined because all attempts to do so involve the use of "any" or some synonym in the *definiens;* nevertheless its usage can be indicated. Russell has maintained that "any" always occurs in a "denoting phrase" which consists of a class-concept preceded by such terms as a, the, any, some, etc.[6] It is so used in the above question and

---

6. Bertrand Russell, *The Principles of Mathematics* (2d ed. London, Allen and Unwin, 1937), pp. 56 ff.

"anything," where "thing" is being used to mean a "this," is meant to call attention not to this or that particular member of the class of existing things ("thises"), but rather to "any" member of that class, and the member taken into consideration makes no difference. Thus "anything" means "any 'this.'" The generality introduced by this formulation enables us to consider the fact of existence itself which is precisely what is involved in asking a question about the existence of "anything." And, as will be clear presently, in asking the question, Why does anything exist? we are really asking the question, Why does something exist?, where "something" denotes at least one existent and is the negation of "nothing."

Ordinarily when the question "why" is asked, what is sought is either some reason or some cause, or more precisely some set of necessary conditions, the statement of which can be said to constitute the "explanation" of the phenomenon in question. Thus, for example, if the question, Why is a rainbow often visible after a storm? is put, the answer could be given in the form of a set of physical statements from which the occurrence loosely called "the appearance of a rainbow" can be deduced. Sometimes, however, in asking the question "why" we are asking not simply for an explanation of the type provided in the special sciences but for a cosmic *purpose* or *ground,* as, for example, when we ask the question, Why do men die? In asking such a question we may, of course, be seeking a zoological or physiological explanation, and we may even hold that the question is meaningful only when it can be answered in this way, but quite often, particularly as philosophers and as religious beings, we are asking a superempirical and perhaps not strictly cognitive question, born both from philosophic curiosity and from religious concern, about why what we discover to be the case about ourselves and our world is the case, particularly since there is no contradiction in supposing that "the case" might have been otherwise. And in asking the question, Why does anything exist?, taking "why" in this second sense, we are really asking, Why is something the case at all?

I am well aware that at the present time there is a widely held theory of meaning on the basis of which the question, Why does anything exist? would be judged at once to be a meaningless question, and for at least two reasons: First, because, according to this view, questions beginning with "why" are meaningful only to the extent to which they can be answered (either actually or in principle) by the assertion of propositions occurring in the natural sciences, and this, of course, eliminates any asking of "why" in the above noted second sense, which is the genuine purport of the original question. And, second, since none of the natural sciences deals with the fact of existence itself, an answer which would save this particular question from being a pseudo-question cannot be given and the question becomes meaningless. However much prestige this theory of meaning may enjoy at the present time, it does not seem to me to be a theory with which philosophers can finally be satisfied. For it is doubtful whether science itself is wholly consistent with such a view and also whether a theory containing as many assumptions about what reality must be like in order to be "meaningfully" interpreted can legitimately lay exclusive claim to the title "empirical." And besides these considerations, there is the far weightier one (for philosophers at least) that the consistent application of this criterion of meaning results in the elimination of all philosophy, at least in the sense of metaphysics. The paradox that philosophers should devise and defend a theory of meaning which eliminates philosophy except for logic certainly calls for interpretation which is beyond the scope of this volume.

Hence, although I have not yet tried to say precisely in what sense the original question is meaningful, I cannot accept at the outset the view that it is meaningless because it is a frankly metaphysical question. For it might be the case that it is meaningful for the philosopher, even if not for the natural scientist, or, more precisely, if not for the philosopher claiming to speak either *for* or *like* the natural scientist. Those who are overzealous in regarding all metaphysical questions as meaningless ought not to overlook the possible errors involved in condemning a whole class of questions, since there might be special considerations relevant only to one member of the class which would seriously alter the situation. In other words, if metaphysics is to be condemned, it must be condemned at retail and not at wholesale.

Such special considerations must, it seems to me, be taken into account in dealing with the question, Why does anything exist? It is not always noticed that if the existence of anything is not a logical determination of its nature—not a part of its "what"—and also, if actual existence is contingent and never determined by logic alone,[7] then there is no logical contradiction whatsoever in the supposition that "anything" might not have existed, which is equivalent to saying that it might have been the case that nothing whatsoever should have existed. And that if as a matter of actual fact "something" does exist instead of nothing, the reason why might be asked by the frankly speculative philosopher. Moore seems to have had something of direct relevance to this in mind, though of course in a different context, when he said, referring to an individual existent, "it seems to me that you can clearly say *with truth* of any such object 'This *might* not have existed. It is *logically possible* that this should not have existed.' . . . The statement 'It is logically possible that this should not have existed' seems to

7. Cf. J. M. E. McTaggart, *The Nature of Existence* (Cambridge, England, the University Press, 1921–27), *1*, 59: " 'Something exists' is not a proposition of which we can be certain simply by pure logic."

mean 'The sentence "This does not exist" is significant.' "[8]

We encounter in experience no finite "this" about which it is false to say "This might not have existed," which means that, despite the actual fact of the existence of many "this-es," no one of them exists of necessity or, to put it another way, for *any* "this," " 'this' might not have existed" is always true. If this is the case, it is legitimate to ask the question, Why does anything exist? when this means "Why does at least one 'this' exist when any 'this' might not have existed?" even if we cannot supply a cognitive answer, for so far as anyone has proved to the contrary, there might be meaning-ful questions which cannot be answered by us, which is to say that there might be mystery in the world which in prin-ciple cannot be dispelled by thought.

Nothing in the preceding argument, however, should lead us to overlook the fundamental contingency of finite existence. Stated ontologically this means that "existence" denotes dependent existence, and stated logically it means "if *x* is a 'this,' for any *x*, '*x* does not exist' is not self-con-tradictory." Whether something exists or not cannot be discovered by a logical analysis of its structure,[9] and hence there is no possibility of ever proving that something *must* exist. Actually, we never argue toward existence but always away from it, in the sense that, for example, we do not prove that a traitor exists, but that someone who exists is a traitor. This point is often overlooked and has led to no end of confusion in the past to the extent to which philos-ophers have sought to prove that such and such *must* exist, or that the world *must* contain certain existents.

4. *Is it the "proper business" of philosophy to study exist-ence and, if so, in what sense?* In asking this question we at the same time raise one of the most embarrassing issues

8. *Aristotelian Society*, Suppl. Vol. *15* (1936), 186.

9. Montague, "We can never learn whether a perceived object really exists by studying its internal nature."

which philosophy has to face: what is the nature of philosophy? This question, however difficult, is unavoidable in any period for at least two reasons: first, unlike the situation in the special sciences, philosophers at different times have held different views of the nature and scope of philosophy, and, second, part of the content of philosophy itself is a statement of the nature and scope of philosophy, a fact that puts philosophy in the unique position of containing *within* itself statements *about* itself.

In seeking the proper business of philosophy, the expression is being used in the sense of the subject matter of philosophy, or the questions to be answered by philosophy. In this sense most philosophers would agree that the question of the meaning of such concepts as individual, possibility, substance, event, etc., together with the resolution of problems arising in connection with them, is the proper business of philosophy, whereas answering questions like, "Is any number the sum of 4 squares?" or "Are the sulfides of silver, mercury, and lead soluble in cold water?" is not the proper business of philosophy (even though logicians may be concerned with the logical form and related aspects of such questions). The most obvious answer to the original question is that the study of existence is the proper business of philosophy, but while this much may be obvious, what is not is the precise sense in which philosophy is to perform this task. Before dealing with this, it may be well to explain briefly the reasons for using the term "existence" rather than the traditional term "being." The distinction between being and existence in modern philosophy has, for reasons too complex to be introduced here, caused no end of confusion. If being means the unity of essence (the "what") and existence (the "that") in all things, it has a clear meaning and an important function. There are, however, at least two reasons for using the term "existence" in this situation: One is the fact that many modern philosophers do use it, as, for example, Dewey when he speaks of the "generic traits of existence" or Whitehead when he refers to the "categories of existence"; the other is that in our experience we only encounter the "that" and the "what" together in actual existents, or simply in existence. Furthermore, if philosophy is to begin with what is, and it can hardly begin anywhere else, then it must begin with existence, in the sense of "all that there is."

Assuming that philosophy does begin with existence, what is it to do? Philosophy has, I believe, the task of the *analysis* and *interpretation* of existence. More specifically, the philosopher must direct his attention first to the discovery, by analysis and precise formulation, of the basic structure in which all existents participate and which they exhibit, and, second, to the interpretation of existence either by employing some category like "importance" or by the use of what has been called a cosmic "root metaphor." The former, or *analytic* aspect of philosophy, has been well characterized by Whitehead when he defined metaphysics as "the science which seeks to discover the general ideas which are indispensably relevant to the analysis of everything that happens."[10] If the basic importance of events in his thought is borne in mind, it will be obvious that the expression "everything that happens" designates "existence" in the above sense. The latter aspect of philosophy, that of *interpretation,* involves the perennial human concern for some intelligible account of the whole of existence, and it was forcibly put by Royce some years ago in the following words: "Philosophers have actually devoted themselves, in the main, neither to perceiving the world, nor to spinning webs of conceptual theory, but to interpreting the meaning of the civilizations which they have represented, and to attempting

10. A. N. Whitehead, *Religion in the Making* (New York, Macmillan, 1926), p. 48.

the interpretation of whatever minds in the universe, human or divine, they believed to be real."[11]

However these two aspects of philosophy may have been related to each other in the past, the fact remains that philosophers have always studied existence in this way. And even though there have been philosophers like Plato and Hegel, for example, in whom the emphasis on *essence* or idea has tended to swallow up existence in its given or contingent character, it would still be difficult to show that these philosophers were not making an analysis and offering an interpretation of existence.

If the study of existence is the proper business of philosophy, then one aspect at least of the present situation in philosophy calls for interpretation: What does it mean that there appears on the philosophical scene a special *philosophy of existence?* If the study of existence is the proper business of philosophy, it would seem, then, that any philosophy, be it idealist, materialist, etc., would ipso facto be a philosophy of existence, and that it is paradoxical, if not downright redundant, that a philosophical movement should characterize itself specifically as *the* philosophy of existence.

There are, I believe, two considerations in the thought of the past century which, if they do not fully explain the situation, at least tend to clarify it to a great extent. They are: *(a)* the submerging of existence in essence in Hegel's great system, leading to what may be called a "revolt of existence" in the thought of subsequent philosophers, theologians, political theorists, and social reformers, and *(b)* the tendency of recent philosophy to confine itself to logic and the analysis of scientific language, leading to the neglect of the existing self and its problems, particularly the interest of the self in the *interpretation* of existence. The philosophy

11. *The Problem of Christianity* (New York, Macmillan, 1914), 2, 255.

of existence was born with Kierkegaard because of the first consideration, and it continues to thrive at present in large measure because of the second. Before continuing this line of interpretation, however, it will be helpful to be clear about the sense in which "existence" is being used in the contemporary philosophy of existence.

From the beginning this movement has taken *human existence,* in one or another of its aspects, as its point of departure, and this peculiar sense of "existence" is central whether in Kierkegaard, Jaspers, Heidegger, or in the more sensational current "existentialism." Thus the "existence" of which these philosophers speak is "human existence" as distinct from the more general sense of existence as "all that there is." The distinction can be made more clear and precise by citing a few passages from Jaspers and Heidegger. In German, *Dasein,* in its ordinary usage, means "existence" in the sense of all spatio-temporal actuality, and, for example, Leibniz and Hegel, not to mention many others, used it in this sense. The term *Existenz,* however, denotes "human existence" as in Jaspers' *Vernunft und Existenz,*[12] where he characterizes it as "the dark ground of self-existence, the hiddenness out of which I encounter myself, and for which transcendence first becomes a reality." Heidegger, it is true, complicates the situation by using the ordinary word *"Dasein"* for his own peculiar idea of self-existence, which however is similar to (but not identical with) *Existenz* in Jaspers. Heidegger characterizes *Dasein* as "human actuality"[13] and for him it clearly means the existence of the conscious self faced with the contingency of active life, and especially with the problem of human significance and destiny. In thus making individual human existence their starting point, the philosophers of existence are led to deal with only one level of existence, i.e. the existence of the

12. Bremen (Storm Verlag, 1947), pp. 42 ff.
13. *Sein und Zeit* (Tübingen, M. Niemeyer, 1953), pp. 7, 25.

concrete self, and consequently the questions which they raise border on the *religious,* the *psychological,* and the *anthropological* much more than on the properly philosophic. While philosophy is not, and must not be, unconcerned with human existence, it on the other hand seeks to study all existence and to view human existence in its proper setting. This means that philosophy has to do with existence in some more inclusive sense than these philosophers would allow.

With the above in mind, it is possible to understand more clearly the reason for the appearance of a special philosophy of existence. Not only have the existential philosophers been primarily grasped both by the radical givenness of all existence together with the contingency and fragmentariness of concrete existence, which resists form and essence, but they have believed that there is one and only one point at which existence as such can be apprehended directly, and that is in human existence. Existential philosophy has been driven to its characteristic sense of existence both by the rationalism of Hegel and his emphasis on an all-embracing logic to the neglect of the full dimensions of the *individual* self, and by the tendency in the philosophic thought of the past century to move closer and closer to the tasks of logical analysis, and further and further away from the peculiar philosophic problems of great interest to the concrete existing self. In attempting to prevent concrete existence from being swallowed up, either by Hegel's rationalism or by the technical problems of logic, existentialism has not only tended to destroy reason and form, but it has reduced "existence" to "human existence," a concept having a much narrower extension than that of existence in the sense of "all that there is," since what "exists" in the peculiar sense of *Existenz* also exists in the former sense, but the converse of this does not hold.

The question which poses itself, then, is this: Is the sense of existence current in the philosophy of existence ultimately adequate for philosophy? The direct answer to this question must, I think, be *no*. Philosophy deals with all existence and on this account it must not restrict itself to the narrower range of *Existenz*. Insofar as it deals with all existence, philosophy must attempt to include within itself all levels of existence. It must, however, attempt not only the analysis of existence but also the interpretation of existence, and this means that it must attempt to deal seriously with the concretely existing self. For it is only at the level of human existence that the problem of interpreting the whole of existence arises. If, however, philosophy confines itself only to logic and to the analysis of the language of science, however important such analysis undoubtedly is, then it can and will give no consideration to that type of meaning and interpretation which the self, as a total living personality facing all the risks of human existence, requires. To the extent to which philosophy, under the banner of a narrow empiricism which is basically rationalistic, continues to neglect the level of human existence, a separate philosophy of existence with irrationalist tendencies seems inevitable.

7. Christianity and Philosophy

EVERY DISCUSSION in which Christianity is brought into relation to some special branch of knowledge or sphere of secular life is bound at the very same time to raise the more fundamental and perennial question of the relation between Christianity and culture. Our chief concern in the present instance, however, is with the aims and tasks of the Christian who is at present engaged in teaching and writing about the meaning of philosophical ideas and systems and in thinking with some originality about significant philosophical problems.

The first question that arises is whether there are any special problems involved in the relation between Christianity and philosophy which might not also arise for the relation between Christianity and, let us say, physics, mathematics, or psychology. Where these subjects are concerned, the principal task of the Christian is to be a good physicist or mathematician, remaining faithful to the aims and methods of these disciplines, being careful not to attempt to dictate conclusions on the basis of religious considerations. It should be obvious that the relations between Christianity and most of the special sciences will be largely *external* and that they do not cease to be so until reflection enters and philosophical extrapolation begins. In this regard the Christian in physics or mathematics will be concerned, as a Christian, in these subjects only insofar as there are philosophical implications to be drawn from them, that is, only insofar as their conclusions are related to a general theory of the cosmos and of man's place in it. Tillich is right when he points to the pivotal position of philosophy between theology and the special sciences. "The point of contact," he writes, "between scientific research and theology lies in the philosophical element of both, the sciences and theology. Therefore, the question of the relation of theology to the special sciences merges into the question of the relation between theology and philosophy."[1]

The fact is that Christianity and philosophy, quite apart from the details of their long historical association, are what we may call "near relations." Their exchanges with each other, if we may continue the figure, take place within the family and, as everyone is aware, near relations are capable of both more intimate cooperation and mutual antagonism than is possible either for casual friends or total strangers. Philosophy, unlike most of the special sciences, overlaps the borders of religion and theology, a fact which is most apparent at times when philosophers are devoting the majority of their attention to their classical *metaphysical* tasks. It is the overlap which in the past has so often led to both mutual cooperation and mutual suspicion.

Time and again Christianity has rejected philosophy, because it sees that philosophy, in virtue of its comprehensiveness and scope, has the capacity to function as a substitute for religion, thus rendering it superfluous and irrelevant for large numbers of thoughtful people. Philosophy, on the other hand, has often sought to cut itself off from Christianity because of the fear that Christianity seeks to supply answers to some of the fundamental questions simply by appeal to the pronouncements of an authoritative church or to the contents of a set of sacred writings. When this set of circumstances prevails, philosophy feels that its own rational quest, marked as it is by patience and dialectical persistence, is made useless.

1. *Systematic Theology* (Chicago, University of Chicago Press, 1951), *1*, 18.

History has shown, however, that antagonism and suspicion between the two is not the whole story. The two can and have dwelt together in a relationship which has been fruitful; philosophy has contributed critical clarification as well as supplying categories and concepts out of which constructive theology was first achieved, while Christianity has contributed its distinctive concerns and convictions, keeping philosophical thought focused upon the speculative questions, those questions which ask about the foundation of existence itself. My own belief is that what is most necessary at the present time is a reconsideration of the positive or constructive relationship between the two, for, among other reasons, it is only upon such a basis that a Christian can be both a Christian and legitimately engaged in philosophy at the same time. If no such basis can be agreed upon, Christians in philosophy may indeed still exist, but the two allegiances will have to remain radically distinct, and the sides will either be irrelevant to each other or one will have to be sacrificed to the other, for it is still true that two cannot walk together if they have no common understanding between them.

Moreover, the tasks of the Christian in philosophy become impossible to fulfill unless there stands, as a basic presupposition acknowledged by each side, respect for the relative autonomy of the other. The nature of autonomy and the crucial problems it poses in a situation where ultimacy itself is part of what is at issue cannot, of course, be dealt with here, but it is essential that both Christianity and philosophy retain a certain autonomy in relation to each other. In this regard, before entering upon a detailed account of the tasks of the Christian in philosophy, the situation will be greatly clarified if we note three approaches to the problem which, although they have had and still do have strong support, nevertheless make a positive and fruitful exchange between the two impossible.

First, there is the position of complete or radical separation in which the autonomy of each side is expressed in its having nothing whatever to do with the other. Here we are supposed to have two wholly distinct sets of problems and bodies of doctrine, such that one may work legitimately within one or the other, or even in both, as long as it is explicitly understood that there is to be no logical dialectic between them, *dialectic* being taken to imply mutual analysis and criticism. From the vantage point of Christianity, this solution means that theology, either as a whole or in some special part, is beyond all criticism from the "wisdom of this world," and from the standpoint of philosophy it means either that religion has nothing whatever to contribute to philosophy or that philosophy is being taken as so completely a rational pursuit that it cannot be asked to take seriously any claim to the discovery of truth through the medium of revelatory events or persons. This solution, it is sometimes claimed, is superior to any other because it logically delimits the spheres, thus protecting the integrity and autonomy of each. What those who defend this view (or some variation upon it) do not always point out is that, if it does preserve the distinctness of the spheres, the division is achieved at the cost of making each irrelevant to the other, regardless of the extent to which they may appear to be influencing each other on the surface. Christianity and philosophy have nothing to do but go their separate ways, each supposedly respecting the other while at the same time seeing to it that the other has nothing to do with the conduct of its internal affairs. In this view, it is obvious, there really is and can be no Christian in philosophy.

The other two untenable views are the reverse of each other, and they are untenable because both violate the basic principle of mutual autonomy and respect. First, there is the view in which Christianity sets itself up in uncompromising fashion as having primacy over philosophy and indeed over all secular thought. According to this view, Christian theology forms a system of certain propositions in no way dependent upon philosophy, either in form or content, and philosophy is regarded merely as an enterprise based upon the presumption of human reason to be competent enough to attain truth concerning God, man, and nature. Philosophy in this view is not necessarily set aside, for it may be used as an apologetic tool for theology and the justification for such a procedure is the primary status of theology among all disciplines. Philosophy is thus reduced to the level of a means for communicating a truth already possessed at the same time that it is deprived of the power to make any contribution, critical or constructive, to the content thus communicated. This proposed solution cannot stand because philosophy is denied as philosophy and, furthermore, it leads to a form of bad apologetic which is little more than special pleading. Quite apart from the fact that this sort of apologetic never convinces those to whom it is principally addressed, it soon exposes itself for what it is, a pretense at being philosophical which is neither serious nor altogether honest. Thoughtful people see that the attempt to communicate religious beliefs through the medium of a philosophy which has been, as it were, previously disinfected or shorn of its critical powers, is a sign of fear and of religious bankruptcy. In such a situation philosophy resists, and rightly so, being assigned the status of a means for achieving a goal it has no part in framing. In this view, the Christian in philosophy is driven into the unenviable and impossible position of action as a "fifth columnist" in the ranks of worldly wisdom.

The reverse view, we may say at once, is equally indefensible. Here we find philosophy attempting to set itself up as the final arbiter of all questions of experience and existence, with the result that Christianity, both as experience and as doctrine, is accorded no independent place of standing. The refusal on the part of philosophy to admit the claim of Christianity may result from either of two developments within itself. It may come from the narrowing of philosophy to the proportions of a discipline interested only in questions of logic, epistemology, and semantics, in short from a philosophy which has taken a decidely antimetaphysical turn, or it may come from a too rationalistic view of constructive metaphysics, as tends to be the case in Hegel, for example, but in both cases the result is the same. To be sure, the situation is far worse when the rejection of the claim of theology comes as a result of philosophy's having become positivistic, than in the case of an unchecked metaphysical rationalism. For in the latter case there are at least possibilities of discussion and creative tension, both of which are in principle precluded when philosophy stands upon wholly positivistic ground. Whichever reason is uppermost at a given time, however, makes no difference to the basic principle that there cannot be a positive, creative relation between Christianity and philosophy when the latter refuses to acknowledge the legitimate autonomy of the religious standpoint. In this view the Christian in philosophy is driven to the position where he can introduce the religious pole into his thought only at the cost of being denied by his colleagues the status of a genuine philosopher. In addition, the consequence for philosophy is further impoverishment, because the supposedly universal character of the experience upon which all philosophy must depend is deprived of its religious dimension.

Whatever the truth about the relation between Christianity and philosophy, it should be fairly clear that the three alternatives just sketched must be rejected. The two cannot remain in complete isolation, nor can we rest with a solution in which either one dominates, thereby reducing the other to the status of a means or a tool. If the relations of separation and subordination are excluded, there remain

only the possibilities either that Christianity and philosophy
are to be fused in a so-called "Christian philosophy" or that
the two are to remain distinct and autonomous in relation
to each other, at the same time that they engage in mutual
criticism and mutual aid to each other. I believe that only
the last alternative contains the truth of the relationship
and that it alone makes possible legitimate tasks for the
Christian in philosophy. As for the idea of a "Christian philosophy," I shall indicate later in the chapter why I think
this solution is not tenable.

My aim now is to develop the meaning of the alternative
I accept, first by calling attention to two principles, and
then by describing and illustrating six tasks which the Christian in philosophy can and must perform.

The Christian in philosophy can perform his tasks in the
knowledge that Christian theology and philosophy have
been related to each other *historically* and that they can be
seen to be related to each other *essentially* as well. Throughout its history, Christian theology has developed in continuous relation with philosophy. In fact it is difficult to
overestimate the importance of this connection. Of all the
great historical religions, Christianity alone has developed
theology with systematic rigor and with a logical conscience
surpassing that of religions content to rely upon *mythos*
alone. Its willingness to incorporate, along with the concept
of *Logos* in the special Christian sense, what Tillich has
called the logos principle in the universal sense, has made
possible within Christianity more comprehensive and abiding formulations of religious faith than have been possible
for traditions relying more exclusively upon ordinary language and mythological speech. Not only has the initial contact with philosophy been decisive for the form of Christian
theology, but in every historical period significant Christian thinkers, alive to the demands of their particular situation, have used in their own work leading ideas and cate-

gories supplied by the creative philosophy of their own time. At present even Karl Barth, who has been so uncompromising in his rejection of philosophy, seems to recognize the validity of this point in his book on Protestant theology in the nineteenth century. And it is clear that his own thought, despite anything he may say, has been very far from developing in a vacuum; as time passes the involvement of his own theology in the basic thought of the philosophy of existence will become increasingly apparent. And this is the way it has always been.

Christianity is involved with philosophy not only historically but essentially as well, the relationship being based upon the intrinsic natures of the two enterprises. Christianity, as a faith deeply concerned with the world as it is, participates in and makes statements about a world which it shares in common with all men, Christian and non-Christian. There are no basic parts of Christian doctrine which do not make some reference to or imply some relation to this common world and to the human experience taking place within it. In setting forth its faith, Christianity becomes involved at the same time in the general or pervasive structures of that world and that experience. These structures are pervasive in the sense that they determine to a specifiable extent certain aspects of the nature of whatever participates in them. It is, for example, impossible to construct theology without making use of such concepts as space, number, causality, freedom, nature, etc., but, while these concepts, when used for theology, will have to take on a meaning appropriate to the formulation of Christian faith, they are not themselves "Christian" concepts. They have been derived from general experience and from careful analysis of the world and human life open to men in all times and places. In order to think at all, the Christian theologian must use these concepts, and their discovery and systematic connection is the proper business of the philosopher. It is this fact which makes the activity of the Christian in philosophy both possible and unavoidable.

Let us turn now to the brief description and illustration of the six tasks which can and must be performed by the Christian in philosophy.

1. The foremost obligation of the Christian in philosophy is to be a good philosopher, to carry on the philosophical enterprise with the same standards of rigor and detachment which have characterized philosophical thought at its best throughout Western history. For the Christian in philosophy can make his contribution only if he respects philosophy for its own sake and seeks to pursue its problems with candor. Without setting himself up as final arbiter, the philosopher can supply an "outside" criticism and appraisal of the Christian world view which may be used for purposes of clarification and comparison. If Hartshorne is correct we may begin by defining metaphysics as a "rational and secular study of the universal traits of experience and existence,"[2] and follow him further in defining a "secular" study as one which "assumes no evidence other than such as is accessible to any intelligent man who *sufficiently* reflects upon our common human experience."[3] The Christian in philosophy must pursue philosophy in this secular sense and then seek to relate its conclusions in various ways to the classical content of Christianity. For he is attempting to see what plausibility and relevance Christian ideas have in relation to secular experience when they are subjected to critical comparison with a view of the world based not upon the "special occasions" (to use the language of Whitehead) of Christian experience but upon the "general occasions" of secular experience. The Christian in philosophy must dare to consider the possibility that the truths of Christian-

2. Charles Hartshorne, *Reality as Social Process* (Glencoe, Illinois, Free Press, 1953), p. 130.
3. Ibid.

ity, when exposed to such critical comparison with an "outside" view, can be shown to be both plausible and relevant from a perspective which is not, *in the first instance,* a Christian perspective. Perhaps two illustrations drawn from two different areas of philosophy will help to make the point more clear.

If the well-known dictum of St. Paul, "The good I would, I do not . . ." is literally true and relevant to moral philosophy, then it is not true just for Christians, but should manifest itself in the general structure of human life, that is, it should become clear in the experience of *anyone* paying sufficient attention to his experience. If, to use a parallel case, we are not phenomenalists and do not believe that the world consists exclusively of what some philosophers call "sense data" but believe instead that there is an objective physical world, we shall not allow those who are phenomenalists to maintain that the world really is constructed of sense data in their case but not in ours. Instead, we shall maintain that if the thesis of an objective physical world is true, it is not true simply for those who believe it but holds true for others as well, regardless of the view which they may take. So it is with the Christian in philosophy: He must see how the case stands from the secular perspective and then dare to consider the possibility that the Christian affirmations can be given a plausibility and relevance from this outside perspective.

To take a second illustration, if the Christian thesis that every created, finite being is contingent, in the sense of having the source of its being outside itself, is true, then again it is not true just for Christians but should be manifest to anyone paying sufficient attention to his experience. The question which the Christian may ask as a philosopher is, is his truth manifested in general or secular experience, and can it be grasped from his outside standpoint as a secular philosopher? To the extent to which the general structure of the world and human life shows itself to possess just the character which Christianity either asserts or implies that it has, we may be said to have a sort of confirmation of Christianity which is not derived in the first instance from the adopting of the Christian faith.

I do not say that the Christian in philosophy either can or should attempt to "prove" either deductively or inductively the truth of Christianity from general experience alone, but that from his secular perspective he has the possibility of critical comparison which may lead to an intelligible confirmation of the plausibility and relevance of Christian beliefs. If we as Christians refuse to admit the validity of this sort of critical comparison with a secular metaphysic, we are implying that the truth of Christianity does not in any way depend upon its exhibiting that truth in the structures of the world and of human life, but rather that its truth rests upon some wholly authoritarian or purely dogmatic basis.

2. The second task of the Christian is to attack all forms of narrow empiricism in philosophy and especially to fight against reductive types of philosophy which exclude metaphysics. The Christian in philosophy has a double allegiance: on the one hand to Christianity and on the other to philosophy. Narrow empiricism and reductionism seek not only to discredit religion but to eliminate the constructive metaphysical aspect of philosophy as well. Sometimes Christian thinkers, either in the name of Biblicism or as a result of their suspicion of philosophy, are tempted to side with the opponents of metaphysics within philosophy, because they see an opportunity to destroy the pretensions of a form of thought they regard as a dangerous rival. I believe this is a disastrous point of view, for Christianity has a double stake in the survival of metaphysical thought. Christian thinkers are naïve if they fail to see that attacks upon metaphysics are also attacks upon theology. It is not possible

to acquiesce in the arguments which tend toward the elimination of metaphysics while at the same time supposing that theology can be preserved safe from these attacks or that theology is untouched by these attacks.

Christianity has a second stake in the survival of metaphysical thought, for the most fruitful interplay between Christianity and philosophy can occur only when philosophy is concerned with the perennial metaphysical questions. This is not to say that critical philosophy—theory of knowledge, logic, and analysis—has no creative relation to Christianity, but the fact remains that if we look to the past we can see that great theology has always developed in periods of immense metaphysical activity in philosophy. And we can see the implications of this in our own time; one of the embarrassments for the philosopher who wants Christianity to take philosophy seriously is that current philosophy has so little to offer in the way of constructive metaphysics. St. Augustine, Anselm, Bonaventura, and Thomas Aquinas could carry on their creative dialectic with Plato and with Aristotle because they were the masters of the metaphysical tradition, but how is any such dialectic possible in our own day between Barth and Bertrand Russell!

3. The third task of the Christian in philosophy is to attempt to discover those particular philosophical views on specific problems which are *relevant* to the Christian faith in the sense that the truth or falsity of these views implies the truth or falsity of certain contentions made by Christianity. To hold, as some current Christian thinkers do, that all philosophical assertions are equally distant from Christianity is to say that all philosophy is equally irrelevant. But, as has been pointed out before, this position is untenable. Christianity has always to relate itself creatively to the scientific and philosophical thought of a given time, and it is of the utmost importance for theology that it keep aware of the stake it has in different interpretations made

by philosophers of new discoveries in the investigation of man and the physical world. What, for example, are the implications for theology of the modern interpretation of the physical universe? Is the Christian world view in no way affected by the philosophical thesis that universal causality must be given up? What stake has Christianity in various philosophical interpretations of this situation? Or again, could Christian faith be held to be true in a world as externally related or as loose-jointed as the world of Hume and his followers is believed to be? And if we answer in the negative, as I believe we must, what view should Christianity take of the counterthesis, so forcefully and carefully defended by thinkers like Bosanquet and Blanshard, that reality is one all-embracing system in which all the parts are internally related to all the others? If Hume's view makes the world ultimately unintelligible, does not the counterproposal make reality so completely transparent to reason that finitude, tragedy, and sin must lose their meaning?

4. The fourth task of the Christian in philosophy is to pay attention to the critical side of philosophy—logic, epistemology, semantics—in order to be able to deal with problems concerning the truth value of religious affirmations and particularly with the linguistic forms in which theology is cast and worship is carried on. One of the most significant developments in recent theology, for example, has been the re-emphasis upon the historical foundation of Christianity and upon its continuing concern for the historical process. I know of no philosophical study of greater importance at the present time than the philosophy of history, not so much in the grand sense of a speculative construction of the world historical process, but in the humbler sense of a critical examination of possible differences between history as a form of knowledge and some of the natural sciences. There are a whole host of intricate problems surrounding the nature of historical knowledge, the meaning of an historical

event, the connotation of such concepts as "unique" and "decisive" or "crucial." We need to know, for example, in what sense a given event or condition can be singled out as being "more decisive than" some other, or what is meant by the oft-repeated phrase "the presuppositions of the secular historian." Consideration of such critical questions marks the proper business of the Christian in philosophy, because responsible Christian thought cannot be content simply to take over common sense assumptions about these issues.

Another sphere of contemporary critical discussion in philosophy concerns the philosophy of language. Christianity can as little afford to neglect the human word as it can the divine word and, however difficult it may be to engage in modern linguistic philosophy without being swallowed up by the shallow metaphysics that frequently accompany it, the Christian in philosophy can make an important contribution in this domain. Such questions as the nature of symbols, their relation to signs and to other devices used in expression, the function of imagination in religious thought, the status of myth and its relation to conceptual thought—these questions and countless others are the important ones. Consider, for example, the extent to which Protestant theology has been hampered by not having at its disposal any such neat and authoritative doctrine of religious expression as the Thomist doctrine of analogy. I am not overlooking the fact that the structure of Protestant Christianity precludes this sort of authoritative approach, but the fact remains that to have arrived at some clear ideas about the precise form and structure of religious assertions would greatly facilitate the work of the Protestant theologian.

There are other problems for the Christian in philosophy centering on the analysis and interpretation of language. Time and again, misunderstandings arise as a result of failure to attend to the different functions of language and to the different purposes for which they are introduced. More often than not, attacks upon theology come from the uncritical use on the part of theologians themselves of *devotional* language in a context where *theological* language is called for. There is, to be sure, an intimate connection between these two types of language, but this fact should not be permitted to obscure the equally important consideration that their aims are not the same. The Christian in philosophy has the obligation of making such distinctions clearly, of calling them to the attention of theologians themselves, and of incorporating them into such disciplines as the philosophy of religion.

5. The fifth task of the Christian in philosophy is that of acting as interpreter in the situation of misunderstanding between Christianity and the special branches of knowledge. Sometimes, especially in periods of deep alienation between different points of view and different approaches to the same subject matter, there is so complete a failure of communication that neither side has any clear understanding of what the other is talking about. It will be recalled that earlier in this discussion I referred to Tillich's idea that philosophy stands as a buffer between theology and the special disciplines. There is no more important office it can fulfill in this regard than to act as interpreter, to bring about clear understanding and dispel misunderstanding.

So many disputes, especially among those seeking to interpret the same material from differing points of view, stem from mutual failure to comprehend. It is not a matter of agreement or disagreement, in the first instance at least; it is more elemental than that. Agreement and disagreement are possible only when there is mutual understanding, but so often in the discussion of issues revolving around religion, there is no genuine basis for discussion because there is no initial understanding of what each side wants to assert.

The philosopher, as Royce used to point out, can assume the role of interpreter and become something of a roving ambassador, using his powers on analysis and interpretation to help settle some of the border disputes so common in the intellectual and cultural world.

Out of the attempt at mutual understanding may come some surprising results of considerable importance for Christianity. Is will be of importance, for example, if we can show that when the social scientists talk about the "cultural lag," they are discovering and expressing in their own language a truth which Christianity has always known, namely, that you do not transform the moral and spiritual natures of men simply by putting more knowledge and technical skill at their disposal, or merely by making it possible for all of them to vote. The discovery that two different minds or groups of minds really mean to say very much the same thing, although they express it in different language, is a matter of no small importance in a period when most minds seem readiest to misunderstand and misjudge. The interpreting of one perspective to another perspective requires a third point of view, one not explicitly identified with the divided parties. The Christian in philosophy can well function as this third party in the protracted attempt to interpret Christianity to the modern mind. It must be acknowledged, of course, that understanding does not of itself lead either to agreement or to conviction, but it is equally certain that without such understanding there can be no civilized adjudication of disputes, and the only alternative is that of naked force.

6. The sixth task of the Christian in philosophy is his obligation to show the contribution of the theological tradition to the history of Western philosophy. There are in this domain a great many points of interpretation which need to be stressed. Mr. Casserley in his book, *The Christian in Philosophy,* has covered what needs to be done and he

has offered excellent illustrations. Those chiefly concerned will be philosophers whose main work is in the history of philosophy. We are all familiar with the way in which the history of philosophy is most frequently taught, especially the period from c. 400 to 1500. Or perhaps we should say that we are all familiar with the way in which this period is not taught! More often than not, it is passed over altogether or accorded nothing more than a superficial description summed up in some such catch slogan as "philosophy in this period was the handmaiden of theology." The latter treatment is bad enough, but almost as if to add insult to injury, those teaching the material in this way who are not trained in the development of theology are invariably in no position to interpret the cliché (which is true if properly interpreted).

This task of the Christian in philosophy seems to me so important that I should like to offer several other illustrations of the sort of thing that needs to be done. Study of Enlightenment philosophy cannot be carried on without taking into account the pronouncements of many thinkers about Christianity, its history and doctrines. Whereas these Enlightenment thinkers thought they spoke in behalf of classical Christianity, it is clear to anyone acquainted with theology that what they regarded as the Christian view on this or that topic was often very far indeed from what actually was maintained in the classical creeds or by the great theologians. The difficulty is that the modern man is almost invariably ignorant of the discrepancy, which is why so many people at present are under the impression that the eighteenth century is one place to go if you want to discover what Christianity is all about. The situation is all the more tragic in view of the fact that it is largely unconscious; the modern mind still remains unaware of how far the Enlightenment really was from any living contact with classical Christianity. Try, for example, to tell the modern man, even the modern Christian, that Christianity is more concerned with the concept of eternal life than with that of immortality, and he will most likely regard you with suspicion as an innovator. Failure to distinguish between Enlightenment views of Christianity and the classical tradition has played a large part in such shallowness and confusion. The Christian in philosophy engaged in historical work can do a great deal to remedy the situation.

Another example has to do with the tendency of some historical interpreters to lose patience and overlook what they regard as small differences and details where matters of religion and theology are concerned. Thus students are taught to speak of *the* ontological argument for the existence of God, and in this connection it is usually the formulation of Descartes to which they have been introduced. The origin of the approach with Anselm and especially the absolutely decisive differences between his formulation and that of Descartes are not even mentioned. Nor is it made clear that there were other formulations of the ontological approach: Bonaventura, the Victors, and the later Franciscans. Since this part of the historical account is generally passed over lightly anyway, most teachers feel no obligation to do better and the result is a permanent distortion. Here again, the Christian in philosophy can provide the necessary clarification and discrimination.

It has no doubt been noticed that I have been speaking of "the Christian in philosophy," but I have not argued for a "Christian philosophy." The main reason is that I do not believe there can be such a discipline. I shall not attempt to consider what Christian philosophy means in the Roman Catholic tradition nor shall I discuss the views of some recent attempts at Christian philosophy within the ranks of Protestant ultraconservatism. There is, however, the suggestion that Christian philosophy represents the system of propositions expressing the views which Christianity would maintain on all matters pertaining to the world and its nature. Such a system would, presumably, be based solely on the Bible. What is not clear to me about this proposal is the relation between Christian theology and this projected Christian philosophy. I fail to see what topics would be contained within the latter which are not treated in the former. Theology is not simply discourse about "God" and nothing else; it contains an elaboration of the full Christian world view, including its relations to the cultural situation out of which it springs and to which it speaks. If this is so, what is left to be done by a so-called Christian philosophy?

There is a deeper objection to the idea of a Christian philosophy and it is this: If this enterprise is not a disguised form of theology, it can only be the claim to be the presentation of *the* Christian answer to classical philosophical problems, and I find it very hard to see that there is any such thing as *the* Christian answer to a host of philosophical problems I can name. What, for example, is *the* Christian answer to the problem of internal and external relations, or to the mind-body problem, or to the problem of the validity of a genetic analysis of the nature of a thing, or to the issue between nominalism and realism—what, we may ask the Christian philosopher, is *the* Christian answer to any or all of these problems? I submit that no such answers are to be found, because Christianity does not contain within itself as a religion of salvation the resources for providing a unique answer to these questions. I referred previously to the Christian *in* philosophy rather than to Christian philosophy just in order to deal with this problem. The Christian who is also a secular philosopher can ask for the *relevance* of certain philosophical solutions to the Christian faith, and he can try to discover the extent to which Christianity is involved in various alternative interpretations proposed by secular philosophy. But there is no such thing as *the* Christian answer to the perennial problems of secular philosophy. Moreover, if the would-be Christian philosopher replies by maintaining that Christian philosophy is directed toward the answering not of questions posed by secular philosophy but of questions posed by Christianity, then I should want to know in what sense Christian philosophy differs from Christian theology, since Christianity is primarily a religion in itself and not a philosophical inquiry. If, as Whitehead has suggested, Christianity is a religion seeking a metaphysic, that metaphysic, if found, will not be a Christian philosophy supposedly uniquely derived from the Bible, but a secular metaphysic based upon the analysis of general occasions, which is compatible with Christianity. I would urge again that while there can be a Christian in philosophy, I do not believe there is or that there can be a Christian philosophy.

The problem raised here is at once so important and elusive that it will be helpful to offer an illustration which may make clear the particular view I hold of the relation between what has previously been called "secular" metaphysics and Christian thought. Let us take as our example the doctrine of Incarnation. No one, I believe, will deny that this doctrine is a legitimate and absolutely essential part of Christian theology. That is, no one, not even the most violent objector to secular or speculative metaphysics, will want to maintain that this doctrine is not a part of a biblically based theology but represents instead a metaphysical construction. As soon, however, as we seek to formulate the doctrine in a way which is more clear and critical than traditional devotional language permits, we are led to make some assertion such as the following: There is an event or series of events within recorded human history which we describe as the appearance of the Christ, and this event is both a legitimate part of the historical process and a unique revelation of the meaning (in the sense of divine purpose) of that process as a whole. In this sample formulation (or in any similar one which purports to express the meaning of the Incarnation) there are at least three concepts —event, unique, history—whose meaning cannot be determined apart from a metaphysical or reflective analysis of human experience. We do not and cannot learn, for example, the meaning of a concept like "unique" from the Bible alone without recourse to an analysis of our general human experience. It is false to claim that the Bible alone[4] gives the Christian theologian an adequate account of the meaning of these concepts (including others in the previous formulation not mentioned, such as the troublesome "is" and all the connectives), and yet he cannot formulate clearly this most central Christian doctrine without making use of them. It follows that he must derive their meaning, *in part* at least, from *another* source. It is necessary to stress "in part" here since I am *not* claiming that the Bible itself and the general biblical perspective contributes nothing to the meaning of these concepts.

The "other source" in question will always be either common sense ("everyone knows what an 'event' is") or some more critical and explicitly formulated metaphysical theory. It is important to notice that those who simply assume the so-called ordinary meanings current at a given time are inclined to believe that they are free of all metaphysics and "speculation." This is not so. The distinction between the ordinary view and a critical metaphysics is not one of type or kind, since the ordinary view is itself (or contains) a theory of reality, but rather it is a distinction between the more and less explicit in thought. The fact is that common sense meaning always represents implicit metaphysics.

4. If it is claimed that it is illegitimate to confine the theologian to the Bible alone since he has the whole "Christian tradition" at his disposal, the reply is that the creedal formulations and theological constructions denoted by the expression "Christian thought" already involve the very dependence on philosophical analysis which is in question.

The problem which remains, and it is a problem which has determined the theological situation, whether consciously or not, in every period of thought, is this: *From what "other source" will the Christian theologian derive the meaning of concepts which are exhibited in all experience and are thus unavoidable, but whose meaning is not completely and uniquely furnished by the classical religious content which is given to him?* My own contention is that the theologian must look to the analyses of general experience furnished by philosophy for the meaning of those concepts which he always uses without at the same time being able to maintain that he is in possession of a single "Christian" meaning for them. And the principal reason why there is no such meaning is that Christianity is primarily a religion and not a metaphysic. On the other hand, as a religion it appears in a world and claims to be true of a world which is itself the appropriate object of metaphysical thought, except that the general metaphysics which would be wholly true about that same world is not contained within the confines of Christianity alone.

In looking to philosophy to supply what is not given to him from his own tradition exclusively, the theologian is not, however, forced to adopt uncritically the results which the philosopher offers. The theologian must attempt the difficult but inescapable task of deciding among the various alternatives which of the available views is compatible with the general Christian perspective. This is what was meant above when it was said that, since the view that *all* philosophical positions are equally irrelevant for theology is false, it becomes necessary for the theologian to decide which of the available views is relevant to and compatible with Christian faith. For example, a metaphysical theory of time and history which precluded the possibility of the temporal process being viewed as one whole or which made it nonsense for us to speak about *the* meaning of history would be inadequate for the Christian theologian and could not ultimately be used by him. But it does not follow from this assertion that all philosophy is equally useless. On the contrary, the twin fact that philosophy is unavoidable and at the same time inclusive of positions which are hostile to Christianity (or incompatible with it in some crucial respects) makes it imperative for the theologian to enter into a critical discussion or dialectic with philosophy aimed at the discovery of those philosophical analyses which are able to be used by him in the clear and critical formulation of his own basic doctrines.

There are, of course, many unsolved problems confronting the position I have just outlined, but I hope the preceding paragraphs have served to make more clear what was meant above by the doctrine that philosophy and theology are to remain autonomous in relation to each other at the same time that they engage in mutual aid and criticism.

The current tendency within Protestant Christianity to recover the classical content of the faith and to reassess the views of the great Reformers is a tendency with which I am in sympathy. Such a process of recovery is of the first importance. On the other hand, if Protestantism is willing to trade its cultural relevance and particularly its creative relation to philosophy simply for the recovery of its past, it will have made the worst bargain in its history.

8. The Present Status of Natural Theology

IF WE CONSIDER the status of natural or philosophical theology within the present philosophical or theological situation, three distinguishable problems confront us. There is *first* the rejection of all theological and metaphysical thought from the standpoint of logical empiricism and certain related types of analytic philosophy. From this extreme position natural theology has no legitimate status whatever since it falls beyond the boundary of cognitive significance. Whether all so-called analytic philosophers would accept this extreme conclusion is difficult to say, especially in view of the fact that the substantive position as regards the truth of religion and theology held by those who approach them through a study of language is often very far from clear. *Secondly,* there is the rejection of a philosophical approach to theological questions from the standpoint of the purely biblical or dogmatic theologian. Here the use of philosophical concepts and methods is looked upon as a violation of the rights of theology, and the claim is made that the content of the Judeo–Christian religious tradition is unique and discontinuous either with ordinary experience and knowledge or with the conceptual framework of any philosophical system. Natural or philosophical theology is thus set at such a distance from the classical religious tradition and its theological expression that there is no point of contact between the two. As those following the lead of Barth would say, there is no identity of meaning whatever between the use of the term "God" by the biblical theologian and its use by the natural theologian or metaphysical interpreter. Moreover, there is no way from the world and human experience to God. *Thirdly*, there is a more subtle problem presented which concerns not the rejection of a philosophical or natural theology from some outside dogmatic point of view but rather a most significant difference in approach among those who accept the legitimacy of philosophical analysis and argument in the treatment of theological questions. The difference is that between the ontological–religious approach represented by Tillich on the one hand and the cosmological–scientific approach represented by Tennant on the other. Each way allows for some form of critical or philosophical treatment in confronting theological questions, but they rather sharply diverge on the exact nature of this treatment. The difference is not precisely the same as that traditionally existing between the ontological and cosmological arguments, since one of the issues dividing the two is the status of inference or argument in the theological domain, and whether the proper import of the ontological approach is understood if it is taken as an argument in the sense that is characteristic of the cosmological arguments. In order to keep the discussion within manageable proportions and, even more important, to raise substantive questions of philosophical theology rather than the question of its possibility, it is advisable to concentrate upon the third problem and to devote but brief comment to the other two.

As the historical development of logical empiricism plainly shows, the basic meaning principle upon which it rests cannot be justified without the employment of an argument that is circular in the vicious sense or a persuasive appeal to the need for clarity if we are to have successful communication. On the other hand, the alternative of claiming that the positivist principle is in effect a recommendation for the use of language is generally thought to be too weak. Positivists want to do more than define the term "meaning";

they want to make a *normative* claim for their principle so that it represents more than one proposal besides others for the use of language. But this normative claim is just what cannot be directly supported. Insofar, then, as the rejection of theological discourse as meaningless is based upon the positivist meaning criterion, this rejection must itself be rejected as dogmatic. In doing so, however, we still leave undetermined the status of those approaches to theological questions through the analysis of religious language which are *not* admittedly based upon any explicit positivist meaning criterion.

The discontinuity thesis of much current Protestant theology involves the denial of any rational way to God from either the cosmos or man's experience and the consequent irrelevance of philosophy for theological inquiry. This position is mistaken in at least two important points. First, it can give no valid argument for holding that a God who in the religious tradition is conceived as having created man and nature cannot in any way be known through those creatures. Secondly, this position cannot consistently maintain that it avoids all appeal to philosophy and to natural knowledge in the elaboration of its religious doctrines. We have but to scrutinize any doctrine asserted within the framework of the allegedly pure biblical theology in order to discover its dependence upon concepts derived from both general experience (often presupposed as the "common sense" meaning of a term) and philosophical refinement.

For example, one of the most significant contentions of current neo-Protestant theology concerns the claim that the Christ represents the unique, final, and only genuine revelation of God. In order to state this doctrine it becomes necessary to employ the concept of the *unique*. This concept at once involves intricate philosophical issues, and the theologian, no matter how rigorously he tries to confine himself to Biblical material alone, requires a philosophical theory at this point, and such a theory is not available to him wholly from the religious tradition of revelation within which he works. The theologian who hopes to avoid involvement in general metaphysical problems by remaining within the confines of revealed fact is in no better position than the logical positivist. Neither can avoid either implying or asserting some thesis of a metaphysical sort which has alternatives of the same logical type. In confronting the purely dogmatic theologian, it is sufficient to show that in the very execution of his own project he is already involved in philosophical thought and is dependent upon that same appeal to general experience which it is his expressed aim to avoid.

To the third or central problem of this discussion we may now turn. The issue more precisely stated concerns the distinction and relative merits of the ontological–religious way of approach and the cosmological–scientific line of argument. In order to focus the discussion most clearly, we shall take Tillich as representative of the former way and Tennant as representative of the latter. It will be most instructive to compare their views in the following respects: (1) their points of departure; (2) their conceptions of the source of the idea of God and their views concerning the relation between religious and philosophical elements; (3) their views of the nature of reason and its function in the theological context.

The point of departure for the ontological–religious type is the *self*, its consciousness both of its own being and of truth as presupposed in every inquiry, especially in critical doubt and questioning. In describing this way of approach as Augustinian, Tillich says of the scholastic developers of the position:

> The Franciscan school of the 13th century . . . developed the Augustinian solution into a doctrine of the

principles of theology and maintained . . . the ontological type of the philosophy of religion. Their whole
emphasis was on the immediacy of the knowledge of
God. According to Bonaventura "God is most truly
present to the very soul and immediately knowable; he
is knowable in himself and without media."[1]

It is important to notice that for this way the religious consciousness is presupposed; there is no going outside the self
and its awareness of itself in order to find a proper beginning for reflection. "Enter the inner chamber of thy mind"
is the first and chief text, and the aim is to discover or,
better, recover the *presence* of God in the form of some
ultimate such as truth immediately grasped. In referring to
the eternal light as it appears in the logical and mathematical axioms and in the ultimate categorial notions, Tillich
says, "These principles are not created functions *of* our
mind, but the presence of truth itself and therefore of God,
in our mind."[2] Hence through a process of reflection initiated by the individual self there is attained a recovery of
what is always there and something not confined wholly
to any individual self. "These ultimate principles," Tillich
continues, "and knowledge of them are independent of the
changes and relativities of the individual mind; they are
the unchangeable, eternal light."[3] There is a mystical element in this conception in virtue of the fact that the first
principles are said to carry immediate evidence with them
whenever they are noticed; Tillich sometimes describes this

1. Paul Tillich, "The Two Types of the Philosophy of Religion," *Union
Seminary Quarterly Review, I* (May 1946), 4. What Tillich here calls "philosophy of religion," some would call "natural theology," although there
are those who would reserve the latter term for the cosmological approach
upon the assumption that it alone confines itself to the "natural" world
and avoids "revelation."

2. Ibid., p. 5.
3. Ibid., p. 4.

element as an apprehension of a point beyond the split of knower and known. To say that the religious consciousness is here presupposed is to say that the identity of this immediately grasped ultimate with God is already assumed. Thus God is said to be present in the apprehension of the first rational principles, in the apprehension of the Holy, in the apprehension and acknowledgment of unconditional obligation. Since Tillich and Augustinian tradition generally understand the apprehension required as part of a reflective process which can be carried through only by each individual for himself, the necessity of starting with the self is easily seen.

The point of departure for the cosmological–scientific type is, on the other hand, the *world* of limited things and processes as they are known both through ordinary experience and the precisely formulated knowledge of the natural sciences. This way of approach, often called the "way from Nature to God," begins the quest with a world of fact beyond the self, although this world is often said to include man as well. One of the problems to be considered is the precise extent to which man and the *whole range* of his experience are excluded or included in the "nature" with which we are to begin. However this question may be decided, it is essential to distinguish within this general approach between starting with the *fact of existence* as given with finite things and starting with some *particular character* of what exists. In the former case we have the approach through the contingency of existence as such, while in the latter case we are concerned not with the general fact of existence but with the particular character of the natural world—that it forms an order of nature and presents an adaptation of structure and function which suggests that it is the work of a designer. F. R. Tennant, in his most comprehensive work, *Philosophical Theology,* has given systematic form to the cosmological–scientific approach in the second sense. His program is to defend a refined form of the argument from design under the title of a cosmic teleology. If the first way of approach begins with the self and presupposes the religious consciousness, this second starts with physical fact and presupposes the validity of science as a method and its picture of the world. "Natural Theology," says Tennant, describing his own approach, "sets out from facts and inductions; its premises are as firmly established and as universally acknowledged as any of the stable generalizations of science."[4] And in so characterizing his starting point Tennant means to claim that his approach is empirical and not to be confused in any particular with that rational theology which, in his view, begins not with actuality but with a priori conceptions. "The empirically-minded theologian," says Tennant, ". . . would let the Actual world tell its own story and offer its own suggestions; not silence it while abstractive speculation . . . weaves a system of thought which may prove to conflict with facts."[5] In claiming to start with experience, it seems clear that Tennant understands the term in the sense of the classical British empiricism as the domain of sensible appearance. What is not so clear about his starting point is the status of man within the actual world and the experience with which we are to begin; he often claims that this world includes man, but if this is true we may still entertain doubts as to the terms upon which man is taken into account. The central question is whether Tennant's conception of experience is broad enough to permit consideration of the whole range of distinctively human experience made possible by the fact that man is a *subject*, or whether man will be included only as one *object* beside others in virtue of the fact that the scientific knowledge with which we are bound to begin is incapable of regarding man in any other way.

4. *Philosophical Theology*, 2, 79.
5. Ibid., 2, 78.

Tillich's ontological approach aims at relating the "two Absolutes"—the God of the Judeo–Christian tradition and the philosophical conception of Being—in some determinate way. The most important consequence of this attempt for the present topic is that the idea of God is taken over from the religious tradition and is not the result of any induction from the facts of the known world. This does not mean that God is understood in any simple-minded or anthropomorphic way or even that the religious understanding of God undergoes no modification when it is expressed in ontological terms. It does mean, nevertheless, that the idea of God's nature is not derivative from the nature of the cosmos and is not subsequent upon an examination of what would be required for explaining the existence of the world of finite things. Instead, the idea of God is presupposed as being given through the religious consciousness, and it becomes identified with Being itself by means of the concept of truth. In referring to what he has called the "two Absolutes" Tillich tells us: "They coincide in the nature of truth. *Veritas* is presupposed in every philosophical argument; and *veritas* is God."[6] Absolutely essential to and even more basic than any of these concepts stands the concept of the Ultimate or the Unconditioned; it is the presence of this common concept that enables Tillich to find a point of contact between the two sides. Both the philosophical quest and the religious affirmation find their essence in an ultimate that is unconditioned; this is, as in Kant's description, the condition or ground upon which everything depends while it is not itself conditioned by anything outside itself. Although the Ultimate forms the common ground for the synthesis of God and Being, we must not overlook the fact that each of these concepts possesses its own content from its own side. Thus God is understood

6. Tillich, p. 4.

in accordance with the classical Judeo–Christian conception, and Being is understood as that power in all things which makes them what they are and enables them to maintain themselves against the threat of dissolution and distortion. The two Ultimates are made to coincide in a point which is described by Tillich sometimes as the point of identity beyond the split between being and knowing and sometimes as the *prius* which cannot be directly expressed without introducing a point of nonidentity into the formulation. Metaphorically, the *prius* represents the light itself in which everything is seen, although it is itself not always noticed as such and cannot itself be described in the same manner as finite things seen in and through it.

For this approach the religious tradition and the philosophical enterprise are seen both as distinguishable and as related in an essential way. Neither is derived from the other but they are made to coincide in a point. The serious question which presents itself is this: Since the idea of God is already presupposed from the religious tradition and the contribution from the side of philosophy is rigorously confined to the ontological principles, what place if any can be given to nature and to cosmological description; in short, how shall we avoid the conclusion that the ontological approach, starting as it does with the self and attempting to reach God, is but one more doctrine of God and the soul with nature left out of account? Moreover, what possibility is there in this approach for our knowledge of the natural world to enter into the description of the divine nature, and for our continuing experience both of the world and ourselves to exercise any critical influence upon traditional conceptions, both religious and ontological? These are questions to which we must return.

Tennant's cosmological approach is distinguished by the fact that he refuses to begin with any idea of God derived from an historic or "revealed" religious tradition or indeed with any conception of God which he takes to be a priori. In this regard he states:

> The classical proofs of the being of God sought to demonstrate that there is a real counterpart to a pre-conceived idea of God, such as was molded in the course of the development of religion. . . . The empir-ically-minded theologian adopts a different procedure. . . . The *explicanda* which he investigates, and the re-sults of his investigation, alone will determine the con-tent or essence of the explicative idea of God to which he is led, as well as the grounds for belief that such an essence exists.[7]

According to this view the substantive meaning of the con-cept of God[8] is wholly derived from the facts which serve as a basis for the inquiry, and there is said to be no ini-tial dependence upon religious considerations. Thus such concepts as creation, eternity, infinitude, perfection, and others can have no meaning for this type of theism which they do not receive from the cosmological facts requiring explanation. And although it is claimed that man no less than the world forms part of the starting point for this type of theology, there exists within it no tendency to allow man's religious dimension and experience to dictate the meaning of the theistic concepts. This is not to say that man is excluded altogether from the facts which determine the content of the divine idea, but Tennant is inclined rather to confine himself to the moral or aesthetic aspects of hu-man experience and to admit the religious only *after* his

7. Tennant, 2, 78.

8. It is interesting to notice that Tennant claims to borrow from religion no more than the *name* when he identifies as God the Being required for explaining his cosmic teleology (2, 121). This is legitimate only if we can de-fend the thesis that proper names are purely denotative and without con-notation; I believe that this cannot be done.

empirical theism has been established. In this regard religion may be said to be postponed or left out of account until the constitutive idea of God has been elaborated; it is then introduced only as a means of enriching and enhancing a theistic idea which it had no hand in shaping. God appears primarily as the explanation of the world conceived as a certain type of teleological system, and theology stands not as a discipline coordinate with philosophy or the theory of being but rather as an extension of or extrapolation from science. "Teleology," says Tennant, "is therefore a development from science along its own lines."[9] The difference between Tillich's view and that of Tennant becomes particularly sharp and profound at this point; whereas Tillich tries to synthesize the ontological and religious ultimates, Tennant works not at all with ontological conceptions but begins instead with science and attempts to establish God as the explanation of the cosmic teleology; he then brings in the beliefs of the historic religious tradition as "the final phase of natural religion." Thus he does not confront the issue as to the identity of the two ultimates, although it is clear that he assumes and accepts this identity.

The ontological way is the way of *immediacy* where apprehension, understanding, and acceptance are all one, and certainty comes, as Tillich says, "out of the things themselves without a medium." This is intuitive rationalism operating, as in the Platonic dialectic, to bring the mind to a recognition of what was there all along but is only noticed upon reflection. For this approach God as the Unconditional or *veritas* is the basic certainty and, as such, not a matter of faith; the "risk of faith" of which Tillich speaks refers not to any uncertainty or probability in the awareness of the Unconditional but rather to the *relation between* it and the

9. Ibid., 2, 120.

world of contingent things including human life. Faith and its risk enter when the Unconditional is identified with some concrete embodiment such as Jesus or the "God of Abraham, Isaac, and Jacob." Throughout, however, there is a careful avoidance of any explicitly inferential process; the function of reason is that of grasping and understanding, not that of mediated proof. In keeping with this doctrine Tillich speaks not of the ontological argument but of the ontological way or approach.

The cosmological way is that of *inference* from certain characteristics of the cosmic order to the being of a divine intelligence. Reason here appears in a discursive function, and whatever special thought processes may be involved in the performance of this function, the basic consideration is that a mediated conclusion results and that this conclusion carries with it some coercive force. Unlike older proponents of the cosmological way, Tennant does *not* maintain that the argument of empirical theism is demonstrative in nature. Demonstrative proofs are in fact criticized and rejected with the result that the final rational basis of this form of empirical theism is in "a cumulative argument for a reasonable, if indemonstrable, teleological interpretation."[10] Thus, though mediated argument continues to be relied upon as the only possible rational ground, this is frequently taken to mean "common reasonableness"; and, in one place at least, we are told by Tennant that in using what he calls the aesthetic argument for theism it "becomes more persuasive when it renounces all claim to proof and appeals to alogical probability."[11] Thus, reason in the theological domain does not issue in deductive proof but rather in reasonable explanation, and as such it is said to provide a sufficient ground for reasonable belief. *If the ontological way starts with an initial certainty and encounters uncer-*

10. Ibid., 2, 83.
11. Ibid., 2, 91.

tainty when it attempts to relate its basic apprehension to the conditioned and contingent world, the cosmological way starts with initial probabilities and tries to attain certainty through the cumulative force of mediate argument.

First, as regards the respective starting points, the ontological way has a certain advantage. Since the idea of God cannot fail to contain some conception of the identity of thought and being or at least of their internal relatedness, we are driven at once to ask where there might be found some apprehension of, or analogue for, this identity. Whether or not such an identity is to be found in the world beyond the self remains open, but it is clear that an *apprehension* of it will be found if anywhere at all, only in ourselves. The only point at which we find the togetherness of thought and being directly is in man; we are led to the self as a starting point. In man as an existing being, however, the identity is not fully exhibited, since the being of man is not identical with his thought. But if the identity is not in man himself, might it perhaps be present in a thought which is capable of being grasped by every individual? Such an identity is given to us, as the Platonic–Augustinian tradition has always held, in the logical and mathematical principles which are constitutive. We have at this point an apprehension within the mind of the required identity, but, *and this is the crucial difficulty with the ontological approach,* that this identity is God or the presence of God is not itself a matter of further insight. When it was said previously that the idea of God *must contain* some conception of the identity of thought and being, the necessity involved can be but an *intensional* one taking us back to the initial meaning of the idea. The justification of this meaning represents the contingent element in the ontological approach and explains why it becomes necessary for that approach to appeal to the religious tradition at this point.

Why, then, may we not appeal to the cosmological starting point? The answer is that although the cosmological approach must be allowed to make a much greater contribution to the determination of the divine idea than has been acknowledged in the past, it is not correct to suppose that in this approach the idea of God is wholly a posteriori and derivative from external fact alone. *Some* idea of God is present at the outset in order for any inquiry to be possible. When Tennant says that this or that is the case for the world "as theistically interpreted," he cannot mean that the interpretation is made on the basis of an idea of God wholly subsequent to his argument. To investigate the cosmos for God requires that *some* antecedent conception of God be presupposed. Thus, in both approaches the idea of God is present at the outset; the superiority of the ontological way resides in the possibility it offers of some *apprehension* of a meaning in which God is exhibited. This apprehension can be direct, but it is not absolutely immediate as Tillich claims.

Secondly, the main issue concerning the source of the idea of God is whether or not the idea of God can be determined apart from considering the nature of the world. And at this point the importance of the cosmological way becomes very great. While it is not true that the theistic conception maintained by Tennant, for example, is wholly derived from and subsequent to his analysis of the world, it is true that no complete idea of God is possible apart from considering the structure of the world and even of cultural-historical existence. The way to the world cannot be simply, as Tillich maintains, a tracing out in nature of an Unconditional already fully apprehended. The nature of God is given throughout the full range of finite being, and such being must be consulted at every level if we are to be clear about the meaning of the divine attributes. Moreover, the ontological way, based as it must be upon a fixed point *(sapientia),* is unable to anticipate the actual developments in knowledge *(scientia)* that come and cannot be denied to have bearing upon the nature of God. In this regard the cosmological way has the superiority of being open to the novel in experience. If the cosmological way runs the risk of losing the contribution of man's religious dimension, the ontological way runs an even greater risk of losing nature and its processes.

Thirdly, the issue posed by the contrast between the way of immediacy and that of argument is too complex to be argued here. It is, however, worth noting that there is a curious instability in each position which continually drives toward the other side. The proponents of the ontological way eschew mediated argument, and yet, unless a complete mysticism is maintained—a religion and philosophy of pure experience—the position falls back perpetually into an ontological *argument* involving one logical transition. The development from Augustine to Anselm forms the classic example. The way of immediacy can never be wholly self-consistent, for besides the ever-present tendency to state the position as an argument, there is dialectical interpretation involved in the process of *recovering* the uncreated light; this can hardly be styled immediacy. On the other hand, the proponents of the cosmological way defend the argumentative approach, but in the face of repeated criticism they have been forced to give up maintaining that the approach provides a demonstration or "knockdown" proof. Tennant retreats to providing "reasonable belief," and he more than once refers to his empirical theism as "teleological explanation" or "interpretation" of the cosmos from a "theistic point of view." When the way of explicit argument turns away from proof and moves in the direction of interpreting the world from a certain perspective, an appeal is being made to direct apprehension and the gap between it and the way of immediacy begins to narrow.

The points of mutual involvement lead me to suggest that not nearly enough attention has been paid in recent thinking to the possibility of synthesizing the two ways of approach—through the self and through the cosmos—by means of a more comprehensive theory of being directed to the problem of the relation between man and the cosmos. If God appears in each pole and the two poles are themselves essentially involved in each other, then it seems likely that neither approach can be prior to the other and that both will be needed.

9. The Experiential Foundations of Religion

ONE of the difficulties to be faced by any inquiry into the empirical foundations of religion is the formidable one of first having to answer the equally perplexing question, What is experience? It is, of course, always possible to avoid this question, particularly if it is supposed to call for a theory of the general nature of experience, by confining attention to specific experiences and their analysis. And indeed this view is not without merit because it is true that specific problems involving actual experience cannot be adequately treated upon the basis of general considerations alone; a theory of the nature of experience is no substitute for those actual experiences which must be taken into account whenever questions about empirical foundations are raised. And yet the direct approach betrays its insufficiency as soon as it is seen that every appeal to individual experience to settle a question always carries with it a further appeal, whether implicit or explicit, to some criteria that determine what is to count as an experience or as the content of experience. Moreover, this preliminary critical question cannot be side-stepped, because all attempts to proceed in a wholly direct way are subject to the same objection: Without criteria experience becomes so broad that nothing is excluded. It loses its differential meaning and its effectiveness as a means of bringing general concepts and theories to the test is greatly reduced. A critical approach is unavoidable even if it is subject to becoming a new rationalism unless great care is exercised; a too zealous concern for the application of rational criteria may result in the elimination from experience of a great deal that is really encountered. Despite this difficulty, the fact remains that the critical approach is unavoidable; the best solution is to follow it through, making every effort to preserve for actual experience the right to speak for itself.

Modern thought has included two principal types of empiricism: the classical or British type which found its most incisive expression in the thought of David Hume and for which experience is ultimately an affair of sense impressions, and the broader, vaguer type sometimes called "radical" which characterizes, in different degrees, the thought of an entire group of critics of the classical type—Hegel, Bradley, Peirce, James, Dewey, Whitehead, and perhaps even Heidegger. According to this radical type, experience is not a single affair, an identifiable subject matter such as sense, or particulars, or impressions of the mind, but it is something initially far more complex and vague; it is a great mass of contents[1] resulting from the interplay between the self and the world in which it lives. Experience becomes the great matrix out of which all distinctions arise, but it is itself not wholly identical in nature with any of its contents. There are, to be sure, more recent forms of empiricism than either of these, but insofar as they have been concerned with experience and not merely with the means of expressing it, they do not constitute a special case since they are interpretable as refinements of the classical type.

1. It is necessary to choose some neutral term here such as "contents" even if it is vague, because a more precise term would be too narrow. If, for example, one were to say "awarenesses" or "motor activities" or "qualities," one would speak truly, since these are all included within experience according to the radical type viewpoint; but the narrowing of experience down to any one of these, to one specific type of thing, is exactly what this viewpoint wants to avoid.

The main concern of this chapter is to consider briefly the bearing of these two conceptions of experience upon the experience of God and the content of religion, in order to discover in what sense religion may be said to be based upon or rooted in experience.

For the classical viewpoint, experience was a concept specifically aimed at eliminating rationalism in thought and at bringing what were regarded as "abstract" ideas to some sort of decisive test. The result was the identification of experience by such characteristics as the following:

> (a) Immediate data of sense isolable from each other because of their sharp outlines and devoid of directionality or purpose.
>
> (b) A set of contents, particular in nature, placed in opposition to thought or reason.
>
> (c) The domain of sensible objects.
>
> (d) A "mental" or private content set in contrast to the public or external world known to science.

The attempt, however, to interpret the whole of human experience by these characteristics soon made it evident that there could be no room for God *within experience,* i.e. as matter of experience, if the empirical viewpoint were strictly interpreted and rigidly followed. The main point was, of course, the problem created by characteristic (c), for in no way could the supreme object of religion be found within the domain of sensible objects and thus as a genuine deliverance of experience in the sense required by the theory. This was not, however, the only difficulty, since a careful examination of classical type empiricism will reveal that a feature implied in all the characteristics of that view is that whatever can be experienced must be an *object* of some sort. The first and most serious consequence of such a theory is that selves cannot be matters of experience; only Berkeley seems to have taken that problem seriously. Since

God can never be understood as an object but only as a center of purposes, the classical empiricism furnishes still another reason why God was forced beyond the confines of experience.

Recognition of these troublesome facts led to the proposal of four alternatives:

1. Deny the reality of God altogether on the grounds that we are dealing with either a human fantasy or a merely abstract idea.

2. Introduce one exception into the system so that the idea of God is admitted as a valid idea upon some basis other than that of "experience" as defined by the theory.

3. Introduce a special sense—a "religious sense"— by means of which God is apprehended without radically modifying the basic thesis that experience is co-extensive with the domain of sensed particulars.

4. Contend that God, while never a matter of direct experience, may yet be known through rational inference alone.

It will be noticed that the first alternative is the only one which is thoroughly consistent with classical empiricism, since all the others make it quite clear that if God is to be admitted as *matter of experience* from this perspective, it must be at the cost of an essential change in the theory itself. It is at this point that the approach of Kant to the problem is most instructive for our purpose, for among other reasons Kant is a pivotal figure who attacks the classical conception of experience and broadens the idea but does so from a standpoint which still retains as a proper part of itself several of the very assumptions essential to the theory he was trying to show up as inadequate. Kant, nevertheless, saw the problem clearly and his entire theory of the Ideas was an acknowledgment of the reality of certain regions of experience which must be forced beyond or outside of "experience" if it is still understood in the classical sense. God was, of course, the chief among the realities expressed in the Ideas; and, in making God into the Ideal of Pure Reason (in one of the senses in which God figures in the system), Kant was underlining the truth that, from the standpoint of the classical conception of experience, God is no longer a matter of experience but, if known at all, must be known in some other way. Without pursuing Kant in his solution, the point of importance here is that, although he did not leave the older view of experience standing, he *did leave too much of it uncriticized* and, instead of modifying it radically, he was content simply to add new dimensions to it.

Following the lead of Kant, it was for Hegel to launch a more radical attack upon the classical conception of experience. He did not negate it as has so often been thought, nor did he leave it standing where it was; instead he attempted a radical reconstruction of experience in which it would become clear that the classical conception was too narrow, that it left out of account a great deal which no responsible philosophy can ignore. Without implying that the other representatives of what I am calling the radical conception of experience are "Hegelians" in any sense whatever, the fact is that later proponents of the broader view have followed the line of thought which he charted. Several sentences from Hegel's *Shorter Logic* are most instructive in this regard. In discussing the Enlightenment conception of experience, the empirical philosophy based upon it, and the natural science standing behind it, he wrote:

> In its own field this empirical knowledge may at first give satisfaction; but in two ways it is seen to come short. In the first place there is another circle of objects

which it does not embrace. These are Freedom, Spirit, and God. They belong to a different sphere *not because it can be said that they have nothing to do with experience;* for though they are certainly not experiences of the senses, it is quite an identical proposition to say that whatever is in consciousness is experienced. The real ground for assigning them to another field of cognition is that in their scope and content these objects evidently show themselves as infinite.[2]

The most important item in this passage is Hegel's apprehension that while religion generally and its basic reality God, cannot be based upon experience if experience is understood in the classical sense, it is nevertheless not true to say that these realities have nothing to do with experience. And this is precisely where the issue needs to be drawn: If we have before us so pervasive an aspect of human experience as religion and so many claims to the experience of God, what are we to say of a theory of experience which compels us to deny to religion all experiential status? One alternative is to hold to the classical view, deny that God is a matter of experience, but contend that he can be reached and known in another way, namely, inferentially and in such wise that direct experience is not required. The other possibility, when the issue is so drawn, is to ask whether a conception of experience which eliminates so much can be adequate. It would seem that another line of thought is called for, a reconstruction of what is meant by experience. And this, of course, is exactly what was attempted by those who formulated the radical or second type of empiricism. According to the broader view, the classical conception must be reassessed for the purpose of discovering whether it is adequate for the full range of human life.

It may, of course, be objected at this point that the

2. Hegel, *Logic,* in *Encyclopedia,* sec. 8 trans. Wallace; italics mine.

discussion has consistently assumed that God *must* be a matter of experience and that religion cannot be based upon pure thought alone. A brief word on this must suffice. If we take seriously, as we must in framing any empirical theory at all, the nature of the subject matter itself, there is one fact which the history of religion makes clear and that is the indispensability of direct experience as a ground for belief in God. The long and involved history of the various rational arguments for the existence of God shows that, although they may be put forward as if they provided a substitute for direct experience, this is not in fact the case. The arguments have no compelling rational force at all unless the self tracing out the rational pattern implicit in them understands what is meant by "God," and this is impossible without certain experiences of the sort generally described as religious. This, however, is not the point to be argued here; the central question is, assuming that religion cannot be severed from experience, Is there a conception of experience which is itself intelligible and by means of which God and religion may once again be understood as matter of experience? This, among other questions, was one which occupied those thinkers previously cited as proponents of a new, broader, and more subtle theory of experience.

The main contention of the present discussion is that the broad or reconstructed conception of experience is required if religion is to be made intelligible as experience; the classical conception, important as it was for certain purposes, is too circumscribed to perform this task. A full-scale treatment of the more adequate conception, as well as consideration of the new problems to which it in turn gives rise, cannot be attempted here. It must suffice to point out four of its features. *First,* according to this view, experience is a reciprocal affair in the sense that it involves an organic togetherness of the experiencing self and the experienced world; *second,* and as a direct consequence, experience is impossible without interpretation from the side of the self and cannot be taken as the passive reception of "bare" data ready and waiting to impress themselves upon us; *third,* experience cannot be limited to "sense" and the supposed simple and clear-cut deliverances of the standard five senses, because these data do not represent what is ultimate and primitive in experience but are rather, in the language of Dewey, "reflected products," the result of prior analysis. As a means of correcting the deficiency, this conception maintains the fluidity and continuity of experience and especially the presence of *relation* and *directionality* or purpose within it. In its eagerness to eliminate all but what presented itself directly to sense, the classical conception had virtually done away with the connecting tissue of experience and consequently could not do justice to the fact of tendency, of direction and movement toward a goal. This feature, as will become clear, is of the utmost importance to religion. *Fourth,* in addition to bringing relation back into experience, the broader conception focused attention as well upon what might be called the "intensive quality" of experience for the concrete self. Such quality has two principal forms. On the one hand, it means the whole range of comprehensive qualities describing what the aesthetic and moral aspect of experience is for a self—that, for example, experiences are poignant or dull, decisive or trivial, etc.; and, on the other hand, it means the manner in which the self "takes" experience, the quality which describes its total reaction both to the world encountered and to the vicissitudes of its own self as an adventurer in that world. Such responses as the *anxiety* so much stressed by the philosophy of existence, the *optimistic* and hopeful outlook of the liberal rationalist, the *ultimate concern* for being and the *courage* which Tillich has singled out as the defining characteristic of religion itself, the *satis-*

faction or joy with which one may respond to the world as a place of self-realization—all these are excellent examples of intensive quality describing the total or final response of the self to the world and to the situation within which it exists. In accordance with the broader view of experience this intensive quality must be taken as a genuine part of experience, because it shows itself to be a pervasive feature in human life, identifiable across cultural boundaries. It remains now to show how the features of purpose or directionality and intensive quality, omitted or slighted in classical empiricism or reduced to the level of the "merely psychological" in more recent forms, are needed to clarify exactly how God may once again be understood as matter of experience.

Without being able to enter into discussion of the perplexing question of whether there is any purely immediate experience, either of God or of any feature of the cosmos, I shall have to state my own view shortly and, unfortunately, dogmatically, and I shall do so with the mitigating comment that the view is in accord with the form of empiricism I am calling the broad or reconstructive view. It is that experience, and the experience of God particularly, is always *direct* but not *immediate*. The distinction may be explained briefly. I take a purely immediate experience to be one which excludes and is effectively beyond the interpretative pole in experience, the source which provides it with meaning and import or bearing for the life of the one who has it. Consequently, a purely immediate experience would have to be empty of all discrimination, a condition which renders it indistinguishable from nothing. All experience contains meaning of some sort and all meaning implies determination and discrimination. This means that were there totally immediate experience, it would have to remain fully inarticulate even for the self who has it. The denial of absolute immediacy does not mean, however, that all experience of God is inferential or at secondhand; there is no inconsistency in holding that a given item of experience can be *present* to a concrete individual and thus *directly experienced* by that self without that experience being immediate or exclusive of a reflective medium through which its meaning comes to the self. And although the distinction needs to be maintained throughout the whole of experience, it is especially important for the experience of God since, in any view, God cannot be understood as an object in the ordinary sense but must be taken as a ground of all things which does not appear as one more thing. It is the chief characteristic of such a ground, especially when understood as a center of purpose, to be present and to lend itself to direct experience but not to be immediately known. To be encountered by another, a center of purpose must be present, but to penetrate beyond the encounter to the interior of that center is a process which takes not only time but endless attempts at interpretation or mediation. This fact proved to be a stumbling block not only for the classical conception of experience when it directed its attention toward the problem of God, but even for the broader or radical conception of experience, as more recent theories aimed at pointing up the peculiarities of the experience of selves have shown.

If we maintain, as we must, that experience of God is experience of a center of purpose of the nature of a self, then we must go on to ask not only how selves are experienced but how this would be possible in the case of a divine self. The answer can only be stated; there is no opportunity for development and defense. Wherever there is *self-conscious purpose* running through experience and wherever there is what was previously called *intensive quality* in life, there must also be found selfhood, for these are not possible without it. But these two features, it will be recalled, are among those which the broadened conception of experience has sought to rehabilitate as genuine aspects or constituents of experience. The point to be developed is that the divine self can be present in experience at two points—at the point where the self believes it has experienced the *ultimate purpose* of its life, that ultimate good without which life would not be, as we say, worth living, and secondly, where the self experiences its total reaction to life describable both by the self and others as *intensive quality*. The thesis, then, is that the divine self is present in these direct experiences.

It must, of course, be objected that the very fact, and the most important one, which we do not know to be the case is being assumed without argument, namely, that these experiences are in fact the ones in which the divine center of purpose is present. The objection is correct and it re-enforces the need for mediation and interpretation, for in order to know that the divine self is present in experience, we need signs or marks, since neither that self nor those signs are sufficiently transparent for us to recognize their meaning immediately. That certain experiences are indeed the presence of God needs to be established. Nevertheless, however important it may be, this is not the main point to be raised here. The present discussion has been confined instead to the task of showing that the broadened or reconstructed type of empiricism makes the experience of God a real possibility since it has provided for the experiences selected—purposiveness and intensive quality—a genuine status in experience. This is exactly what classical empiricism could not do.

10. Religion and Morality

THE relation of religion to morality is a theme well known to every student of the history of religion. Not only has it been the subject of much discussion within the various religious traditions themselves, but it has been at the center of the philosophical discussion of ethics in Western culture since the age of the Enlightenment. When in ancient times the Old Testament prophets first apprehended the ideal of justice and preached the necessity of righteousness before God, they were at the same time criticizing both directly and indirectly certain popular religious beliefs about God on the basis of their newly acquired standard. From such criticism it was inevitable that there should arise the question concerning the relation between the standard regulating the conduct of life, on the one hand, and traditional belief about God's nature, on the other. This posed one aspect of the problem of the relation between religion and morality. The same aspect is illustrated again, at another time and in a vastly different culture, by the Greek philosopher Xenophanes. In a well-known fragment, he considers the alarming discrepancy between a certain ideal of the good life and current beliefs about the nature of the gods:

> Homer and Hesiod say that the gods
> Do all manner of things which men would consider disgraceful:
> Adultery, stealing, deceiving each other.[1]

Many other illustrations from the history of religion might be given to illustrate essentially the same problem, but it is not necessary here.

1. B 11, 12 (Diels), quoted by W. Jaeger, *The Theology of the Early Greek Philosophers* (Oxford, 1947), p. 47.

Since the period of the Enlightenment the relation between morality and religion has been the subject of more
general philosophical analysis, as distinct from its treatment
at the hands of theologians working within the Christian
framework. Of all Western thinkers, Kant is perhaps the
one who has set forth most clearly the way in which his
period (and contemporary culture is the heir of the Enlightenment in this respect) conceived the relations between
specifically religious belief and the ideal of the good life.
Stated briefly, that part of Kant's thesis which is relevant
is that morality must be *autonomous* and not be held in
the leading strings of either religion, theology, or dogmatic
metaphysics. Kant was interested, and with good reason,
in rescuing the unconditional character of the moral demand from the relativism, psychologism, and disguised
self-interest which threatened either to destroy it or to transform it into a means to something else. For this reason he
adopted a rigid and uncompromising attitude, the only
one that seemed to him consistent with the holiness and
awe-inspiring character of the categorical command. Consequently, all notions of reward and punishment as the
proper motive for leading the good life, such as were associated with the Deism and the Protestantism of his time and
indeed as they had also been with medieval Catholicism,
were repugnant to him, and he came to reject the doctrine
of moral *heteronomy* in which morality would be dependent on extramoral sanctions or motives.[2]

2. Of course, the fact should not be overlooked that when Kant came
(1793) to consider the relations between morality and religion, he regarded
religion as the outcome of morality in the sense that morality inevitably
leads to religion. The point important to this discussion, however, is that
Kant's view of morality as *autonomous*, together with his rejection of all
supramoral foundations for morality, has been (whether explicitly or not)
the basis of many nineteenth- and twentieth-century attempts to "free"
morality from the tradition and authority of religious belief and theological
doctrine.

Furthermore, Kant's period, because of its suspicion regarding positive or historical religion as distinct from "rational" or "natural" religion, thought of the ideal of the good life as an end in itself and tended either to set positive historical religion aside as outmoded superstition or to take it simply as a means of providing the emotion necessary for leading the life of reason and obeying reason's commands.[3] Many thinkers since Kant have followed him in this main point (although they have rejected the categorical imperative and substituted the values of liberalism or of middle-class culture), and at present a majority of philosophers seem agreed that morality stands on its own feet, so to speak, and is in need of no guidance or support either from religion or from metaphysics. Modern secular culture, based as it is in large measure on the values and ideals of the Enlightenment, accepts this view; and many spokesmen for the contemporary ideal of a "scientific" morality based solely on biological, psychological, and sociological considerations are vehement in their insistence that religion and morality be kept distinct because a true morality can be attained as a result of scientific analysis and hence does not need to be supplemented by what are regarded as the superstitions of religion.[4]

Since a problem cannot be dealt with unless it is carefully formulated, it is necessary at this point to attempt to sharpen the issue in order to consider in somewhat greater detail the matter at hand. When we seek the relation be-

---

3. The seeds of this Enlightenment view are already to be found in Spinoza's *Theologico-political Treatise*. The position is more fully developed by such thinkers as Locke, Rousseau, Voltaire, and Kant. Schleiermacher's *Reden*, it will be recalled, represents a protesting voice against this predominant view, insofar as it is a defense of the autonomy of religion against those who would make religion only a *means* to conduct.

4. See, e.g., the polemics of Sidney Hook against those who believe that religious beliefs have any relevance either for morality or for politics. *Partisan Review* (June, 1948).

tween the nature of God and standards of what is good, we are raising a problem which has two distinct features. On the one hand we may be concerned about a *theological* question, or we may be raising a question falling more specifically within the context of *moral philosophy,* on the other. In the first case the problem centers about the moral character of God, together with the relation between certain ideal moral standards of righteousness and mercy and the nature of the divine. In the second case the problem concerns the extent to which morality—the principles governing the relations between man and man—are based on, or in some way dependent on, concepts and norms derived both from man's continuing religious concern and from historical religious tradition. When the subject of this discussion was loosely referred to at the outset as the "relation of religion to morality," the first aspect of the problem, the theological one, was underscored. Now that it is necessary to deal more specifically with the issues involved, it must be made clear that it is the *second* aspect of the general subject that will be the main concern of this analysis, chiefly because it has a more direct bearing upon the structure and the problems of modern culture than does the more definitely theological question, although the two are by no means unconnected.

Since our problem has, like the problem of evil, been raised not merely by the critics of religion but within the very confines of the Judeo–Christian tradition itself, it seems best to try to develop a certain contrast within that tradition for the purpose of making clear from the beginning the distinguishing marks both of the specifically religious concern and of morality. Such clarification is absolutely essential, since, contrary to both popular belief and the opinions of some philosophers, religion and morality are not synonymous terms signifying some vague concern for "values" or ideals as distinct from "facts." Not only

are the religious concern and the concern for the correct
regulation of conduct not identical, but it is precisely the
fact that they are distinct, although related in some essential
way, that generates the problem with which this analysis
will deal.

Since the development of a complete philosophy of religion is not possible here, it is necessary to proceed simply
by indicating the essential features of both religion and
morality. There is no better way of accomplishing this than
by setting forth a familiar contrast within Western Christianity between what we may call the "pietistic"[5] and the
"activistic" poles within the religious community. The
former pole, as will be shown, while not unmindful of the
moral problem, tends to stress the exclusively religious aspect of experience, while the latter tends to put the greatest
emphasis on morality and the ideal relations between man
and man, often to the exclusion of what is more definitely
the concern of religion. The pietistic pole raises the question of man's ultimate destiny and looks to God as the
supreme object of trust and devotion, at the same time rec-
ognizing the gulf between man and God (sin) and the consequent need for reconciliation (salvation). The activistic
pole, on the other hand, is impatient with this concern for
ultimate questions and foundations, and, being tremen-
dously impressed by the concrete historical situation with
its multitudinous evils, it wants to be engaged in some
concrete task in this world. Its watchword may be summed
up in the questions: What are we to do? What is our duty?
Here the concern is for action that will have, in this world,
a noticeable effect upon the existing state of affairs. Here
the concern is for economic and social justice, for the care

5. This term may have for some a derogatory connotation. Nothing of
the kind is meant here. What the term refers to is made clear enough in
the body of the discussion. The term "mystical" might be better here, but
it has a great variety of connotations.

of the weak and the poor, and for the establishment of
that society on earth which shall be, if not actually the
Kingdom of God, the closest approximation to that ideal
that is possible for man. Both these tendencies are present
in the Judeo–Christian tradition, and they represent not
so much two mutually exclusive concerns (for there are
pietistic elements in the activistic pole and vice versa) as
a difference of emphasis upon either one of two strains that
were always present in both Old and New Testament religion. From these two poles develops the problem of the
relation of religion and morality.

Both these poles may be clarified further by analyzing
certain portions of the biblical and early Christian literature. The following passages may be cited as illustrations
of what has been referred to above as the "pietistic[6] pole":

> (a) God is our refuge and strength,
>   A very present help in trouble.
>   Therefore will we not fear though the earth do
>   change,
>   And though the mountains be shaken unto the
>   heart of the seas. . . .
>   Jehovah of hosts is with us;
>   The God of Jacob is our refuge.
>   [Ps. 46:1, 2, 7]
>
> (b) Out of the depths have I cried unto thee, O Je-
>   hovah.
>   Lord, hear my voice:
>   Let thine ears be attentive
>   To the voice of my supplications.
>   If thou, Jehovah, shouldest mark iniquities,
>   O Lord, who could stand?

6. Since this pole expresses the properly religious concern and the activistic pole the properly moral concern, the more customary expressions "religion" and "morality" will be used to designate these in what follows.

But there is forgiveness with thee,
That thou mayest be feared.
I wait for Jehovah, my soul doth wait,
And in his word do I hope.

[Ps. 130:1–5]

(c)   And it shall come to pass in the latter days that
the mountain of Jehovah's house shall be established on the top of the mountains, and shall be
exalted above the hills; and all nations shall flow
unto it. And many peoples shall go and say, Come
ye, and let us go up to the mountain of Jehovah,
to the house of the God of Jacob; and he will teach
us of his ways, and we will walk in his paths: for
out of Zion shall go forth the law and the word of
Jehovah from Jerusalem. And he will judge between the nations, and will decide concerning
many peoples; and they shall beat their swords
into plowshares, and their spears into pruning-
hooks; nation shall not lift up sword against nation, neither shall they learn war any more.

[Isa. 2:2–4]

(d) Why died I not from the womb?
Why did I not give up the ghost when my mother
   bare me?
Wherefore is light given to him that is in misery,
And life unto the bitter in soul;
Who long for death, but it cometh not,
And dig for it more than for hid treasures;
Who rejoice exceedingly,
And are glad when they can find the grave?
Why is light given to a man whose way is hid,
And whom God hath hedged in?

[Job 3:11, 20–23]

(e)   Great art thou, O Lord, and greatly to be praised; great is Thy power, and of Thy wisdom there is no number. And man desires to praise Thee. He is but a tiny part of all Thou has created. . . . Thou dost so excite him that to praise Thee is his joy. For Thou has made us for Thyself and our hearts are restless till they rest in Thee.

[AUGUSTINE *Confessions* i. 1]

Each of the above passages illustrates clearly a specific characteristic of the religious concern as distinct from the further implications of morality,[7] and these characteristics may be described in some detail as follows:

(a) An expression of supreme trust in God as the reality which does not change amid a world of ceaseless change and ruthless power that threatens man's very existence.

(b) An expression of despair from one who, having experienced the gulf between God and man (iniquity and sin), cries out for forgiveness and trusts that it will be forthcoming because of the merciful nature of God.

(c) The prophet provides an excellent illustration of the religious vision of the goal of all life and a longing for the attainment of that peace which is universal.

(d) Job, in these well-known lines, raises the basically religious question having to do with man's ultimate concern for his destiny: What is the significance of human life, especially in a world which continually crushes us with its misery and bitterness? This riddle of human existence, with all its depths of despair and frustration, is the subject of Job's anguished cry, and it reveals, better than any other expression could, the religious question at the foundation of all life.

---

7. It is true, however, that the moral implications are stated in *(c)*.

(e) Augustine gives classic expression to the religious feeling of joy in the presence of God throughout his *Confessions*. This often quoted prayer reveals joy and is, at the same time, a heartfelt manifestation of that recognition of God as man's true end and of that ultimate completion of the personality which is of the essence of the specifically religious hope.

The characteristics cited above have one striking feature in common: they do not have as their primary feature any reference to the actual conduct of life in human society, nor do they offer any answer to the pressing question: *What are we to do?* Rather they concern certain ultimate (in the sense of *unconditional*) questions and have to do with certain ultimate aspects of human experience which finally touch upon man's destiny as a creature who, while a finite "natural" being like other created things, is yet distinguished as man both by his search for the source of all being and by his attempt to penetrate the mystery of his own existence in order to uncover the meaning of the limited being which he has. All these features point to that aspect of life which is genuinely religious.

On the other hand, morality has as its primary concern the principles ordering the lives of men in society and the consistent means for remaking society in accordance with such ideals. Morality, strictly speaking, knows only of human society in this world together with all its imperfections, and, as such, it neither knows of nor cares for the ultimate destinies of the peoples and societies that recognize its commands.[8] Following the pattern above, these passages may be cited as representative examples of the specifically moral aspect of experience:

8. The analysis of this point in the consideration of religion and morality is made with wisdom and profundity by F. H. Bradley in his much neglected *Ethical Studies* (1st ed. 1876; 2d ed. Oxford, 1927).

(a)   And now, Israel, what doth Jehovah thy God
      require of thee, but to fear Jehovah thy God, to
      walk in all his ways, and to love him, and to serve
      Jehovah thy God with all thy heart and with all
      thy soul.
                                          [Deut. 10:12]

(b)   Woe unto them that decree unrighteous decrees,
      and to the writers that write perverseness; to turn
      aside the needy from justice, and to rob the poor
      of my people of their right, that widows may be
      their spoil, and that they may make the fatherless
      their prey!
                                          [Isa. 10:1, 2]

(c)   Woe to them that devise iniquity and work evil
      upon their beds! When the morning is light, they
      practise it, because it is in the power of their hand.
      And they covet fields, and seize them; and they
      oppress a man and his house, even a man and his
      heritage.
                                          [Mic. 2:1, 2]

(d)   But I say unto you that hear, love your enemies,
      do good to them that hate you, bless them that
      curse you, pray for them that despitefully use you.

                                          [Luke 6:27, 28]

(e)   And why call ye me, Lord, Lord, and do not
      the things which I say? Everyone that cometh unto
      me, and heareth my words, and doeth them, I will
      show you to whom he is like: he is like a man
      building a house, who digged and went deep, and
      laid a foundation upon the rock: and when a flood
      arose, the stream brake against that house and
      could not shake it: because it had been well build-
      ed.
                                          [Luke 6:46–48]

Just as surely as the previously cited illustrations of the religious concern revealed a supreme interest in ultimate questions and a profound dependence on God, so the above statements, drawn from the literature of prophetic religion, are concerned with the standards of individual conduct in human society, and they are directed toward some answering of the question: *What are we to do?* The following analysis of these passages should make the essential features of morality quite clear:

(a) The passage from Deuteronomy, often set forth as containing the essence of Old Testament morality, gives a statement of the supreme law which is to govern life. Men are required to walk in the ways of God and to serve him with a complete devotion that enlists the whole of their being.

(b) and (c) The passages from the Old Testament prophets, Isaiah and Micah, are akin, and they express the most important aspect[9] of the prophetic criticism. In the name of a supreme standard (righteousness) existing evils are denounced: perversions of justice in the law courts, oppression of the poor by the rich and the unscrupulous, covetousness in the acquisition of land so that the less fortunate are left without any portion of what is intended by God to be a dwelling place for all men. All these abuses of the social order are denounced by these prophets, and this is made possible by their possession of a supreme and ultimate standard believed to be normative for regulating the relations between man and man.

(d) In this much discussed injunction of Jesus we find a clear and definite prescription of what relations be

9. See *e* below.

tween persons should obtain if Christian morality is to prevail.

(e) This passage, perhaps more than any of the others, illustrates the basic concern of morality: the passion for the embodiment in the individual life itself of those values which inform the whole duty of the one who sincerely professes the moral principles in question. Here there is no compromise with hypocrisy, no patience with those who pretend to be righteous but who do not *do* the commands and who do not show in their relations with all mankind the ideals in which they have faith and to which they are committed. Actually, Jesus is making the prophetic criticism in its most subtle form: the protest against those who hear the truth and seem to believe but who do not manifest their obedience in some concrete and visible way.

It is obvious from these passages that the moral concern is a concern for right conduct and the proper ordering of human society. In contrast with religion, it is not itself primarily interested in ultimate questions bordering on the nature and final destiny of man, or with the doubts, fears, and despairs of man in search of a faith which answers his questions and quiets his soul. Religion looks ultimately to a homeland of the spirit which passes beyond this world and transcends all time. At bottom the religious attitude is one of trust and of contemplation. Morality, in contradistinction to religion, is interested in the principles of order governing the relations between persons in actual society, and its main business is with the affairs of this world. As morality it neither knows of what is beyond mundane existence, nor does it care; it is interested mainly in the performance and in the accomplishing of such concrete tasks as will make the existing order into a more adequate likeness of the ideals it holds dear.

After the natures of religion and morality have to a certain degree been distinguished, the central problem remains: What is the relation of religion, so conceived, to the content and form of morality? Or the question may be made more concrete by asking: What is the relation between moral standards and moral passion and that faith in God as the ground and goal of life which is the answer to the basically religious question of man's ultimate destiny? As was suggested at the outset, this is a particularly pertinent question at the present time, precisely because it is so widely believed that religion should have nothing to do with morality. In an age of advanced and advancing science, so it is maintained, the method of intelligence either has decided, or in the near future will decide, the answers to all the perplexing questions facing those who seek to order their lives in the light of a rational consciousness of ends and means, of motives and consequences. This means that the idea that religion is at the foundation of morality is abhorrent mainly because what is loosely referred to as "religious morality" is thought to be authoritarian in spirit and hostile to the freedom of inquiry, which is presumably the primary value of those committed to the doctrine that a purely "scientific" morality is both possible and necessary. It is the opposition to authority in the matter both of motives and of norms which most frequently alienates those who reject a morality based on religion. Unfortunately, the possibility that morality might be in need of religious foundations not authoritarian in character is not even considered.

In attempting to meet the issue here, it must be said categorically that Kant and all defenders of the *autonomy* of morality are correct. The good life, as Spinoza has well said, is not a means to something else but is itself a supreme end. Hence morality must be autonomous in this sense, and no alien considerations, such as craven fear[10] of a tyrannical deity or dread of persecution from an absolutistic church, should be admitted as validly determining the conduct of human persons. Nor, again, should any considerations of earthly gain or worldly reward and success be primary conditions determining truly moral conduct. The good is to be chosen for its own sake, just as the good life is to be lived for its own sake; in both these respects morality is truly autonomous and must ever be regarded as such.[11] However, the question still remains as to the relation between morality and religion. We must ask the extent to which morality is dependent for its content on the norms and concepts derived from historical religion, and also from what source comes the inspiration to shun pleasure, wealth, and worldly success in order to live that type of life which is in accord with the most exalted moral principles. In biblical religion the answer to these questions is clear; the ideals (content) which are to govern human existence in society are derived from the nature of the divine, and it is the love of God (form) that furnishes the power to live the good life in a world which often thwarts our most de-

10. It might be of interest to some in this connection to note that Calvin, who, largely because of the one sermon of Jonathan Edwards which everyone knows, is generally thought to have made fear the dominant motive in the Christian life, carefully distinguished between a craven fear and that awe and reverence which comes from *respect* and *love* for a father. Speaking of the man of true faith, Calvin says: "He restrains himself from sin, not merely from a dread of vengeance, but because he loves and reveres God as his Father, honors and worships him as his Lord, and, even though there were no hell, would shudder at the thought of offending him" (*Institutes*, I.2.2).

11. This point has been stated very cleverly by F. H. Bradley in *Ethical Studies* (Oxford, 1927), Essay 2, where it is held that only an immoral man gives an answer to the question: Why should I be moral? It can be shown, however, that the religious man can give an answer to this question and one which does not destroy the autonomy of morality.

termined attempts to embody Christian perfection. In biblical religion man is required to be just and merciful because God is both just and merciful in all relations with his people. Man is required to manifest love in his earthly life because, according to the essence of Christian faith, God is of the nature of love. And in all cases the love of God dwelling within the person of the individual believer is what provides the motive and inspiration for all our human efforts. The relation between religion and morality here stressed is well stated in a blunt and poignant remark in the First Epistle of John: "If a man say, I love God, and hateth his brother, he is a liar."[12] In this passage morality, the principle of order among men, is determined by the object of religion, the nature of God; and the writer regards it as an express contradiction if a man professes love of God and yet fails to manifest this love toward his fellow men. The nature of God provides the norm for conduct (the context of the passage quoted makes this more clear than does the passage itself), and the love of God provides the motive and passion necessary to perform.

Yet those who do not share this view of the relation between the religious and the moral fail to do so generally because they believe that religion at the basis of morality inevitably means that authoritarian sanctions are employed and that human conduct in such a situation is ultimately determined not by a pure love of God but by a craven fear of either divine or ecclesiastical retribution, or both. Historically, this charge cannot be denied; certainly, history offers many illustrations of the perversion of a religious morality in which the pure motive of love has been obscured and replaced by an external (i.e. nonpersonal) authority. We should not, however, too hastily reject the religious foundations of morality simply because of the possi-

12. I John 4:20.

bility of perversion. Love of God, as the foundation for the good life, meant both for Old Testament prophetism and for classical Christianity a basic orientation of the person as a whole toward the divine perfection and from such an orientation (the same as the Platonic turning toward [*converto*] the light or good) the good life was believed to follow as a consistent expression of the personality whose life is turned toward and centered in God. Hence love of God as the basis of morality involves us in no subjugation to an external authority necessitating conduct through fear, but it is rather the underlying attitude and motive of the person who seeks to live the good life and whose life as a member of society then becomes a consistent expression of an individual will and personality rooted in God.

A true morality, as was said above, should be autonomous, i.e. it should be free from any external authority that coerces the personality or that subjects the good life to some further end by reducing it to the status of a means. The protest against religious morality is justified when the religious basis is perverted into an authority. An autonomous morality, however, is not necessarily one that is divorced from religious foundations, and the question remains as to what it is that constitutes the religious basis of morality. Prophetic Judaism and classical Christianity are at one in maintaining that morality without religion is ultimately impossible. Only the main points in this regard can be stated here, but the following relations between the two are defensible:

1. No criticism of the existing state of affairs in any society is possible without the assumption (whether implicit or explicit) of the unconditional validity of standards by reference to which such criticism is made. All critical assertions about human activity of the nature of evaluations (excluding rigorously *descriptive* assertions) either contain or imply a proposition like "such and such *ought* to be done,"

and the term "ought" or some logical equivalent never fails to occur. This holds whether, for example, we are criticized for not loving our neighbors, for not seeking clarity in philosophical thought, or for not employing the method of intelligence in conducting all our affairs. Furthermore, standards intended to tell us what ought to be done (some idea of what is a good life) cannot and, in fact, do not remain neutral with respect to the question which is the properly religious one: the question of and concern for man's final destiny as a creature in his world. Just as surely as moral criticism implies moral standards, so moral standards themselves imply some view concerning the final destiny of man. An analysis of every critical discussion of human conduct containing assertions that are evaluations will reveal that a proposition like "The truth about man's final destiny is such and such" is implied. This fact has been overlooked to an extent that is a scandal for moral philosophy. There is no better way of showing this than by pointing to the ethical writing of Dewey. He calls himself a naturalist, and he is certainly an opponent of the view of religious morality outlined here; yet it is clear to anyone who takes the trouble to raise questions about his thought, that some such proposition as "The final destiny of man is to control his own destiny through technology or the method of intelligence" is assumed throughout. This assumption is an assumption about the basically religious question, and that it functions as an ultimate premise in Dewey's thought is clear from the fact that not only is there nowhere any proof of it, but it is not ever brought up for discussion.[13]

Ultimately, no view of the good life, no serious doctrine of what man ought to do, is ever possible apart from some view of his final destiny; and such a view introduces the re-

13. Why this is the case is beyond the scope of this discussion, but the answer is probably to be sought in an examination of the basic assumptions of modern culture.

ligious element. This is the most important consideration in showing that morality is necessarily related to religion.

2. One of the prevalent dangers confronting all morality is that it may degenerate and become ideology or a cloak for the hypocrisy of self-righteousness. A morality that has no foundation in a reality transcending itself is inevitably subject to corruption precisely because it recognizes no judge beyond its own commands. A morality, however, truly based on a love of God that is religious in character and one that recognizes the power of God as judge is protected, in principle, from such corruption and consequent transformation into ideology. A morality so grounded in religion recognizes that it is subject to the same ultimate principle of criticism (divine judgment) by which it judges existing persons and societies, and a morality rooted in that which transcends all times because it belongs exclusively to no one time possesses within itself its own principle of criticism. Such criticism is brought to bear subjectively by self-conscious judgment on the part of the holders of that morality, and objectively through the medium of historical events at the same time. No morality not based on religion possesses a principle of self-criticism, precisely because it possesses no transcendent reference to which it is itself subject and which judges it. This is not to say that, in fact, religiously grounded morality has not been corrupted in the past. Such an assertion could be made only in ignorance of the facts; but, nevertheless, it remains true that, in addition to determining the content of morality, religion is the final judge of morality. It stands as an ever present guardian, warning morality of its possible pretensions and enabling it to be free from transformation into ideology.

3. Finally, religion supplies the inspiration for the moral life and provides, at the same time, something even more important: the meaning and purpose of moral striving. The man who has morality and nothing more, as Royce

once put it, is like a man who serves an ideal master who is forever in a far country. The servant not only toils on without ever seeing the master, but he may well come to doubt whether there is any master at all. The man, however, whose morality is founded on religion knows the master intimately and believes fully in the ultimately purposeful character of his striving. Furthermore, his vision of the ideal society, the kingdom of God, gives form and substance to his attempts both to regulate his personal life on the basis of certain standards and to labor for the remaking of present society into a likeness of the ideal. Without the vision, the hope, and, finally, the faith of religion, such labor is forever incomplete.

In the above ways[14] religion is a genuine foundation for morality without at the same time being an authoritarian force behind it compelling the good life through fear. Since it is the threat of authority that the opponents of religious morality usually deplore (and rightly so), a religious foundation that eliminates this threat and that at the same time provides the basis without which all morality must be destroyed is able to overcome the objection. Morality is both unsure and incomplete without a living connection with religious faith. The sure recognition of this truth can be hastened if it is made clear, first, that a true religious morality should be free from authoritarianism and, second, that, for the reasons cited above, morality implies religion and when it is not founded on religion it is continually threatened with destruction.

---

14. All the possible relations between religion and morality have not been discussed here. The question of sin and morality, for example, needs extended treatment, for this raises the question of man's ability to live the good life without grace.

11. Poetry, Religion, and Theology

POETRY and religion, theology and philosophy are four facets of cultural life which are almost invariably bound together in some important relationship with each other. It is not simply that they are related in the initially vague sense in which every aspect of life is said to be related to every other, but in the more precise sense that to engage in any one inevitably leads on to one or more of the others. Thus the poets of the world have always drawn heavily upon the religious heritage of their lands, and religion, in turn, has always expressed its deepest convictions in dramatic form and in language which can only be called poetic. Moreover, not only have philosophy and theology either opposed or supplemented each other in every cultural period, but the two have also been in the most intimate relationship with both poetry and religion. Religion cannot avoid the self-scrutiny and reflection from which theology takes its rise, nor can great poetry be written which does not immediately plunge us into philosophical and theological problems, even if the fact is often allowed to pass without recognition.

Two recent works[1] merit our consideration because they help us to focus on the problems that arise from the mutual involvement of the cultural forms we have singled out. Louis Martz in *The Poetry of Meditation* has given a masterful study of the chief poets of the Counter Reformation;

1. Louis L. Martz, *The Poetry of Meditation* (New Haven, Yale University Press, 1954). Malcolm Mackenzie Ross, *Poetry and Dogma* (New Brunswick, Rutgers University Press, 1954).

the work is especially valuable because it argues for the meditative style as characteristic of Roman Catholic sensibility. In *Poetry and Dogma* Malcolm Ross discusses similar issues in his contrast between the poetic tradition in the Anglican Church and transformations made necessary by the impact of Puritan piety. Behind both books stands a concern for that phenomenon in English poetry which T. S. Eliot has called the "dissociation of sensibility"; both writers are agreed in their conception of the basic problem, and both—Martz in his careful, circumspect fashion, and Ross in his doctrinaire, almost blatant style—believe that this dissociation was a result of the decline of *sacramental* religion in the seventeenth century. The researches of the two, in addition to their contribution to literary history and criticism, bring us face to face with the underlying problems of understanding how poetry is related to theology and especially of deciding the status to be accorded the materials of poetry, metaphor and symbol, in a comprehensive view of reality. These more basic problems are less explicit in Martz's work because his main aim is to offer an historical, critical interpretation of English metaphysical poetry, and the underlying questions are permitted to appear only indirectly and intermittently. Ross, on the other hand, is less concerned with poetry itself and more anxious to set forth explicitly his thesis concerning Christian symbolism in relation to Roman, Anglican, and Protestant points of view. In this regard Martz's book is far more informative in its analysis and its contribution to the understanding of the poets selected—Southwell, Donne, Herbert, Crashaw—and much less assertive than that of Ross, who cares little for clarifying the thought of the poets he treats. Instead, he uses them as means of illustrating and re-enforcing his thesis that the rejection by Protestants of certain Roman (and Anglican?) theological doctrines led to the dissolution of the poetic symbols connected with these doc-

trines. Actually Ross's thesis extends beyond simply corre-
lating poetic symbols with specific doctrines, but it includes
the further and more basic contention that the Incarnation,
and its interpretation as the consecration of the sensory
world, forms the ultimate ground upon which any symbol
can be validly used by a religious poet. Rejection of the
Incarnation in this sense, the thesis runs, means the destruction of the "firmament," to use the favorite term of Ross,
within which Christian poetry must exist. Martz seems to
accept a similar view, though it is nowhere clearly asserted.

Perhaps comparisons of this and a similar sort will be
more profitably made by the reader himself after the central
theses of the two books have been stated and some main
points examined.

The description of certain English poets as "metaphysical" goes back to Dr. Johnson and his biographical-type
criticism of such men as Donne, Cleveland, and Cowley.
The term, as T. S. Eliot said in his review of Grierson's
Metaphysical Lyrics and Poems of the Seventeenth Century,
has long "done duty as a term of abuse or as the label of a
quaint and pleasant taste." And students of these poets
well know how many since Johnson's time have had a hand
in explaining the "essence" of metaphysical poetry to us.
At the end of the same review, after briefly reconsidering
some of the characteristics suggested by Johnson as definitive of metaphysical poetry, Eliot says, "It would be a fruitful work, and one requiring a substantial book, to break
up the classification of Johnson . . . and exhibit these poets
in all their difference of kind and of degree."[2] While we
should not suppose that Martz was consciously following
Eliot's suggestion, it is legitimate, I believe, to regard *The
Poetry of Meditation* as just the sort of "substantial book"
about the metaphysical poets which Eliot had in mind.

2. T. S. Eliot, "The Metaphysical Poets," in *Selected Essays 1917–1932*
(New York, Harcourt-Brace, 1932), p. 250.

As Martz points out on many occasions, his study is a protracted attempt to place metaphysical poetry, or in his suggested new phrase, the "poetry of meditation" (p. 4), in a tradition of religious meditation stemming from the type of spirituality characteristic of Counter Reformation Christianity, Martz goes deeper than Johnson who was impressed by one striking feature of this type of poetry, its paradox ("The most heterogeneous ideas are yoked by violence together"); he was in fact inclined to single out this formal or stylistic feature as definitive. Martz seeks a more substantial basis in human life itself and thus looks behind and beyond the poetry for the human concerns which the metaphysical poets were attempting to express. The conclusion of his search is that the poetry of meditation must be understood as the attempt to bring out of the conflict and chaos of ordinary life *a unified self*, a self at one with itself, with nature and with God. Such unification must be achieved, insofar as it is achieved at all, through the discipline of religious meditation upon the nature of God, the things of religion and man's duty to his fellow man. The book's brief conclusion (pp. 321 ff.) brings out this latter point very clearly, although I suspect that the reader will be somewhat surprised if not puzzled by the sudden leap from Herbert to Yeats and Gerard Hopkins which the conclusion makes.

By setting the poetry of Donne, Southwell, and Herbert against a detailed background of meditation such as is to be found in the writings of Ignatius Loyola and François de Sales, Martz aims to show that poetic works like Donne's "Anniversaries" and Herbert's "The Temple" become intelligible as meditation symbolically and metaphorically expressed. Meditation, in the sense of the term characteristic of the *Spiritual Exercises*, thus forms the link between religion and poetry; in each the ultimate purpose is the same—to focus the attention of the self upon itself and to enable the self in so doing to discover God as that Self in which it can find fulfillment. Meditative poetry using the materials of the religious imagination and the doctrines of theology becomes what De Rougemont has called "a calculated trap for meditation." And the extent of the aesthetic quality depends upon the type and subtlety of the "calculation" employed.

The chief merit of Martz's way of establishing his thesis is its directness. He does not confine himself to showing that certain meditative works were available to be read by the poets (and this is fortunate, because such argument is always hazardous), but seeks to make out his case by showing how the poems themselves can actually be interpreted, obscurities cleared up, seemingly disparate lines connected, etc., if they are read as poetry of meditation.

Despite Martz's primary interest in the poetic problem, his discussion takes him into the general religious history of the seventeenth century. In addition to interpreting the metaphysical poets he wants to show that "the Counter Reformation penetrated to English literature through methods of religious meditation that lay at the heart of the century's spiritual life . . . " (p. 13). Consequently a large part of his treatment consists of the marshaling of evidence, mostly data about the circulation of Catholic books in England, to show the widespread influence of Counter Reformation spirituality on English religious life. It is, as we shall note, in his defense of the general contribution made by Roman theology to the poetic sensibility, that Martz is led to discuss theological questions which can and must be considered in their own right quite apart from their connection with literary interpretation.

Critical discussion of the soundness of the principal literary thesis of the book, especially as it concerns detailed comparison with other interpretations of metaphysical poetry, is beyond my competence. This task must be left to those literary critics and historians who are well versed in the poetic material. And they will, I am sure, devote to this impressive book the attention and sharp scrutiny which it merits. A work as comprehensive as this, however, must touch upon themes theological and philosophical which are by no means confined to their precise relationship to seventeenth-century English poetry. These themes must be considered in their own right and it is more than likely that they will not be given the attention they deserve by those whose interest is more strictly literary.

In his presentation of the development of earlier medieval theology, Martz leaves out of account one very important influence, and oversimplifies a certain contrast in Christian thought which is of central importance for the sensibility possessed by his meditating poets. In his very helpful account of the structure of the type of meditation he is considering (pp. 33 ff.), Martz introduces the all-important idea of the threefold division of the soul and the correlation of these powers with the Trinity. In this connection he rightly cites Bernard as the most striking example of this way of approaching the divine nature. But the entire account would have been improved had Martz gone back to the source of the meditative or reflective approach to God in the *De Trinitate* of Augustine. It was Augustine above all others to whom later medieval thinkers were indebted for the theory of the image of God in man. No other thinker can be credited with such brilliance in theological speculation as Augustine displayed in his attempt to find within the trinity of the soul's powers an analogue of the triune God. Augustine was the first to stamp the reflective approach upon Christian thought and it was he who first seriously and systematically attempted to understand and attain to God through the reflective progress of recovering the divine image in his own self. In this regard all later followers of the reflective or ontological approach—the Victorines, Bernard, Bonaventura—find their ultimate source in the *De Trinitate*. Martz, to be sure, could not have been expected to include everything, but omission of a source as important as Augustine is unfortunate.

Moreover, if Augustine's thought had been given a more prominent place, Martz would have been in a better position to clarify a contrast upon which he depends in his poetic theory. He rightly notes a cleavage which developed in later medieval thought between those who, like Bernard, stressed the primary importance of piety and of the direct relation between the individual soul and God, and those who, like Abelard and Thomas Aquinas, placed more stress upon the discursive and dialectical elaboration of Christian faith in a vast system embracing the whole of known reality. Largely because he is uncritical in his use of oversimplified pairs of opposites (for example, "theology—emotion," "abstract—concrete," "divine—human," together with the implication that all the left-hand members correlate with each other), Martz is led to formulate the difference between Bonaventura and Bernard on the one side and Abelard and Aquinas on the other simply as an opposition between "affective piety" and "theology."

But Augustine's approach is the way of *immediacy,* the retirement of the self into itself in reflection aimed at recovering within the depths of the self the Uncreated Light, or the very presence of God. This path is meditative and not in the strict sense dialectical or argumentative. It does not start with the world or with the things of sense, but with the self and with the self's own awareness of its existence and its powers. For Augustine, the man who has been illuminated by faith and who seeks sincerely for God may, through reflection, be led to the grasp of that Uncreated Light in his own soul. The crucial modification of this approach, as Paul Tillich has shown, was made when Aquinas and others, aiming at the dissolution of the approach through immediacy, maintained that, in retiring into the self, the self can at best attain only to the first principles of the created light. Or another way of stating this is to say that for them the first principles of thought which the self can recover through reflection are no longer to be regarded as the presence of the *Uncreated* Light, but simply of *created* light and nothing more. This shift means that God is no longer to be recovered directly. Along with this development went a turning away from the self as a starting point in religion and a shift of attention from immediacy to the world of objects (the "cosmological arguments" come to the fore) and to dialectical or discursive mediation. More fundamental than any contrast between "emotion" and "thought" was the contrast between *immediacy* and the retirement into the self in meditation on the one hand, and speculative or dialectical *mediation* on the other.

This shift in emphasis carried with it a consequence of great importance for the poetic sensibility. Not only did the Augustinian tradition have a certain mistrust of the sensible world as a possible source of distraction of the self from God, but, following its Platonic heritage, it regarded its own reflective approach to God as a purely intelligible affair in which sense knowledge plays almost no part at all. Along with criticism and rejection of this reflective approach went a new concern for the world of sense, for the cosmos in all of its beauty of quality and of form. The Aristotelian Christianity which gradually replaced the Augustinian tradition at the end of the Middle Ages is characterized by a sense-bound epistemology, by a regard for the visible world, and by a mistrust of the purely intelligible thought so dear to the Platonic tradition in Christianity.

The task facing the poets of meditation was, therefore,

not so much the synthesis of "thought" and "emotion," as Martz suggests, but a much more complex one. On the one hand, they had to strike a fruitful balance between the reflective approach through immediacy and the discursive approach with its analysis, comparison, and contrast. And on the other, they had to work with the wealth of material made available by the new regard for the world of sense without losing the self at the center, for, according to Martz's own account of the meditative style, the self and its unification remained a matter of prime importance to the poets of meditation.

Throughout his treatment, Martz makes comments about Protestantism which are less than complimentary; it seems that he is under the illusion that Protestantism is all predestination and "omnipotence," while Roman Christianity is all "charity" and good works. And he seems unaware that whereas Aquinas clearly and unambiguously states that some men are predestined to perdition by God, Luther, for example, always condemned those who speculated about their election or that of others instead of trusting the biblical promises of salvation.

Martz's brief account of Puritan meditation, particularly his idea of what the search for "evidence of election" meant, though it is undoubtedly included for completeness and to show that Puritanism also tried to introduce religious meditation, is not prefaced by a sufficient treatment of Protestant thought to enable the reader to understand the problems. Protestantism made the Bible central and this meant, among other things, that the Christian content must come from that source, not from the tradition within the church and still less from the demands of aesthetic theory. Martz makes no attempt whatsoever to explain why Calvin, particularly, stressed the biblical idea of predestination. In holding to the view that God alone in his providence is the determiner of the soul's ultimate destiny, Protestantism hoped to curtail the power of an ecclesiastical institution to set the conditions for salvation.

If it be objected to these complaints that literary criticism must not be expected to be theology, the edge of the reply is easily turned. For those for whom an intimate connection exists between aesthetics and theology, there is an obligation to be as sound and critical in the theology as in the aesthetics. The chapter on Baxter serves little aesthetic or literary purpose within the whole discussion and leaves out so much of importance that it is of little value theologically.

Martz rightly stresses the fact that Puritan Protestantism had an entirely inadequate appreciation of the aesthetic dimension of life, but this is only partly due to the popular idea of the "mistrust of the senses" in Puritanism. What most needs to be made clear is that this type of Protestantism was a return to the Augustinian tradition in which the relation between the individual soul and God is all that matters. This relationship has too often been taken as a purely intelligible affair to the exclusion of the senses. In this regard Puritanism was what we might call a religion of the "ear," i.e. the *hearing* and *understanding* of the Word and of doctrine—hence the profusion of great Puritan preachers—and not a religion of the "eye," i.e. the *seeing* of the sensuous aspect of the world and the physical passion of Christ. Medieval Christianity was aesthetic, even lush, as compared with the main line of Protestantism, but this has more to do with the latter's uncompromising *religious* and *moral* emphasis than with any "puritanical" temper and all that the term connotes. Bernard, no less than Augustine, feared *adornment* in any form as distracting and unnecessary for religion, and Puritanism followed after them. Puritanism reduced poetry to rhetoric, which is precisely what must happen when poetry is denied autonomy while the imagination is left standing. And Puritanism de-

nied such autonomy to poetry because of the seriousness
with which is subordinated all to the religious question,
What is my ultimate destiny? This concern drove Protestantism either to deny the artistic aspect of life altogether,
or to reduce it to the status of a means in the service of religion and morality.

The reduction of poetry to rhetoric, however, must not
be taken to mean that Puritanism denied to the senses all
power of expressing religious insight. Haller's "The Rhetoric of the Spirit" in his *Rise of Puritanism* (a volume used
to good advantage by Martz) shows that Puritan pulpit
rhetoric was "an intensely imaginative hortatory prose,"[3]
and that what was most feared by the Puritans was "vain
rhetoric" or poetic adornment beyond what was "necessary"
for the communication of the divine word to the individual
soul in a powerful and penetrating way. Nor is it correct
to say, as Martz does quietly and Ross more polemically,
that the disparagement of sense in Puritanism is due to
rejection of the doctrine of Transubstantiation, or the Roman Catholic interpretation of the "real presence" in the
Mass. Both writers are correct in holding that Calvinistic
thought (the point does not apply to Luther) tragically underestimated the capacity of the natural world to bear or
express the signature of God, but the issue must not be
confused as it is by both Martz and Ross when they write
as if the idea of Transubstantiation were simply an extension of the theological doctrine of Incarnation. There is

3. William Haller, *The Rise of Puritanism* (New York, Columbia University Press, 1938), p. 129. Compare the following from Haller: "Whatever
contributed to edification was but a means of preaching naked Christ. Whatever did not was vanity. The primary objection to metaphysical wit, learned
allusions, tags of Greek and Latin, snatches from the heathen poets and
philosophers, and all figures of speech depending upon recondite knowledge
was that many members of the audience were sure to miss the point. The
Puritan preacher was quite prepared to use anything he knew as a means
to his end, but the end was to make everybody feel the force and reality of
what he was saying." See Martz, p. 283.

no necessary connection between the doctrine of Incarnation and the particular interpretation placed by the Roman church upon the "presence" of Christ in the Eucharist. Both Luther and Calvin, for example, maintained the doctrine of Incarnation, Christ's appearance in history, but they rejected the metaphysical theory known as Transubstantiation purporting to explain *how* Christ is "present" in the continuing religious community.

There is a further aspect of the Puritan attitude toward the aesthetic which is not touched upon by Martz, and it is very important. The exclusively biblical orientation of Protestantism led the Puritans to attempt the derivation of everything from the Bible. This meant, among other things, that they took the poetic and rhetorical form of the biblical writings as normative. A sharp distinction was drawn between "human" symbolism and the symbolism "of God" as expressed in the word of the Holy Spirit. Calvin brings this out very clearly when he defends himself against the charge of being a "mere Tropologist"; he distinguishes between the "symbols invented by man" and the "symbols instituted by God,"[4] and he rests his own case upon the validity of the latter. Sometimes this opposition between the two types of symbols and the elevation of the divine over the human poetic and rhetoric has been interpreted to mean that Puritanism rejected art and the aesthetic generally. What Puritanism did was to adopt a too narrowly biblical perspective and from this standpoint judge all human attempts at creativity as superfluous, as an arrogant attempt to improve upon the divine form of communication. What need is there, they argued, for human adornment of the Word, when the Holy Spirit has already made plain in the Bible itself the type and extent of metaphorical expression appropriate to the divine revelation?

4. *Institutes*, IV.17.21.

Behind this exaltation of the Scriptures at the expense of everything human was a much deeper motive in Protestantism, and it is one which affected the further development of English poetry, not only in the later seventeenth century but in the two succeeding centuries as well. Along with suspicion of human wit and ingenuity Protestantism had a certain suspicion of secular *culture* itself. Culture, it was thought, tends to the glory of man; the development of the fine arts may distract men from what should be their chief concern—the divine *gloria* and the salvation of the soul. Such an outlook forbids an autonomous aesthetic; what aesthetic there is must be wholly in the service of religion. This point of view explains why poetry and theology are virtually indistinguishable in Milton, for example, and why critics are "pro" or "con" in his case mostly upon the basis of their convictions about his theology; this is something which is not true for Donne. For Puritanism the images and signs of religion and the doctrines of theology are no longer "material" for the poetic sensibility; on the contrary, poetry and rhetoric become means for the communication of theology.

As was indicated above, the present discussion of *The Poetry of Meditation* represents an oblique treatment, directing attention to certain underlying issues and away from the main historical thesis. This has been done in the conviction that these issues are not likely to receive the emphasis they deserve at the hands of literary critics and historians. The strength of Martz's monumental study lies in the detailed analysis of the poetry itself and particularly in the success with which he makes metaphysical poetry intelligible by setting it against the background of religious meditation. No one else has probed so deeply or done so sustained a piece of work along these lines. Unfortunately the work also exhibits an inadequate grasp of basic theological conceptions and too complete a confidence in the interpretative power of simple contrasts. It will no doubt be some time before the full impact of this exhaustive volume becomes apparent, but it is certain that study of these poets and of the issues raised by their works will be permanently affected by Martz's work.

In *Poetry and Dogma,* Ross attempts to attack more directly the theological issues between Roman, Anglican, and Protestant as they bear upon the poetic situation in England during much the same period as that treated by Martz. Consequently, Ross's work is long on theological and philosophical interpretation and somewhat short on poetic criticism. In this regard his work exactly reverses the emphasis in Martz, and, it must be added, it has none of the firsthand documentation which makes Martz's study significant.

The central thesis of *Poetry and Dogma* is that poetry, particularly that written within a Christian framework, can be successful as poetry only to the extent to which it can presuppose what the author calls a certain "firmament of symbol," i.e. a theological standpoint in accordance with which the finite and created things can be taken as valid symbols of the uncreated God. Ross's main contention is that English religious poetry suffered a mortal blow when Protestant theology rejected the doctrine of Transubstantiation, denied the "real presence," and allegedly cut off the created world so that it could no longer be a valid bearer of the divine meaning. In his view Roman (or Anglican?) Christianity maintains a theology in which symbols have an "ontological reach" (p. 16), whereas Protestantism is all "subjective" in its interpretation; it is this subjectivism which led to the decline of significant Christian poetry in the period following Herbert.

Ross starts with the position that every defensible aesthetic must include the view that the world of sense, of symbol and metaphor, must have a foundation in reality, i.e. that it must validly express a reality beyond itself. He then asks what particular dogmas must be maintained and emphasized in order than an aesthetic may be possible within which poetry of Christian stature can be written. Ross does not expound his thesis in exactly this way because he seems unaware of the extent to which the content of Christianity is made by him to depend upon the demands of aesthetic. He does not ask what aesthetic standpoint is possible within the basic Christian world view, but asks instead what Christian doctrines must be singled out and what interpretation must be placed upon them in order that the poetic symbol may be guaranteed ontological standing. As compared with the position he accepts, Ross finds the Puritan or Protestant position so filled with an unqualified individualism, subjectivism, and psychologism that the ultimate referents of the symbols disappear and genuine Christian poetry is made an impossibility.

Ross's ingenious method of refutation by comparison leaves his thesis dependent for success upon the accuracy with which the non-Anglican position is stated. And this is precisely where the book is weakest. Instead of considering in detail the pronouncements of Luther and Calvin on the nature of the Sacrament and the status of symbols, Ross chooses to rely upon two Anglican interpreters, Dix and Messenger, for the presentation of the Reformation position. The dubiousness of reliance upon Messenger's *The Reformation, the Mass and the Priesthood* can be seen from the fact that in his exposition of the meaning of the Mass no more than 15 pages out of a total exceeding 500 in the first volume alone are given over to what the Bible has to say on the institution of the Lord's Supper.[5] Considering

---

5. Ross specifically acknowledges (p. xi) his indebtedness to Messenger, and the extent of the dependence can be seen in that he reproduces slips made by Messenger as well; on p. 29, n. 5, the Irenaeus citation is *Adv. Haeres.* IV.18.5, not IV.8.5 as in the text and in Messenger. Incidentally, note 2 on the same page should be "I Cor.," etc.

that the whole of Calvin's long seventeenth chapter, the *locus classicus* of Puritan doctrine on the subject of the Lord's Supper, is based upon the Bible alone, except for a few quotations from the writings of Augustine, it is not difficult to see that Ross's presentation of the Protestant position is inadequate.

The whole subject of the Eucharist and the controversies about it are entirely too involved to be considered here, but several points of importance can be raised. In the first place, Ross does not discuss the all-important issue whether the "real presence," whatever that is finally to mean, must mean "attached to the bread" in the sense asserted in the Transubstantiation formula. This is precisely the point raised by Calvin and it is crucial.[6] Ross, following a great many others to be sure, simply assumes dogmatically that there is no "real" participation of Christ in the Supper unless such participation is in this form. But this is precisely the point at issue and it is surely a poor way to argue to assume a position and then condemn as erroneous another position merely on the ground that it differs from the position dogmatically asserted. The problem, as Calvin was well aware, is to grasp exactly *how* Christ can be "represented"[7]

---

6. *Institutes*, IV.17.31.

7. A thorough treatment would, of course, deal with the question of the meaning of "repraesentio" and its distinction from "praesentio" (see pp. 30 ff.). Ross seems not to understand that, whatever the two terms mean, they *cannot* have the *same* connotation, i.e. "praesentio" in this context means the appearance of Christ in the spatio-temporal world in his earthly life. "Repraesentio" means some later manifestation, for example in the Communion, of Christ, such that at any time later than the earthly life Christ can be said to be "represented." The important point is that the sense attached to "praesentio" in the compound "repraesentio" cannot be the same sense which "praesentio" has when it means the earthly, historical appearance of the Christ. Nothing can be represented unless it has first appeared, i.e. been presented. If the sense of "praesentio" were the same in both cases, there would be no need for "elements" of representation, indeed there would be no need for representation at all, for in that case represen-

in the Supper, and it will not do simply to assume that the theory of substance and accidents is the only solution to that problem.

Unfortunately, I cannot give the attention I should like to the dubious distinction, maintained by Ross throughout his discussion, between the "dogmatic" and "conceptual" levels of the sacramental symbol (see pp. 31 f.; cf. p. 232). This distinction is dubious because the initial dogmatic formulation is itself already a conceptualization, and, moreover, the idea that there is some unformulated view on a given theological topic called "dogma," such that when a given theologian discusses this "dogma" his assertion simply represents a "conceptualization" of it, is a myth. There can be no doubt that there are theological *themes* upon which there can certainly be variations, e.g. topics like creation, eternal life, atonement, etc., but these themes can be considered only when they have been conceptualized or formulated; there is no such thing as a pure dogma to be distinguished from its interpretations or formulations. The distinction, like that in Aquinas between implicit and explicit, is intended to make it possible for two thinkers to mean different things while at the same time continuing to exist validly within one and the same "dogmatic" tradition. The difference between the Augustinian formulation offered by Ross on p. 32 and the formulation from the *Catholic En-*

---

tation would simply mean "is present," and Christ would still be living his earthly life, which is absurd. Moreover, the issue between the Roman church and the Reformation position is not *whether* Christ "participates" in the Supper (the term "really" adds nothing here which is not question begging), but *how* and in what form the participation takes place. The Roman and Anglican contention is that unless the participation is of the form they describe in Transubstantiation, there is no "real" participation. This, of course, is exactly what begs the question. I very much doubt that Ross is correct in interpreting the obscure passage from Tertullian's *Ad Marc.* IV.25 (ANF, *3*, 390b) so as to make "repraesentio" mean "physical presence" when the term always has the connotation of "be a surrogate for" or "stand for."

cyclopedia with which he compares it is not merely a difference in "conceptualization." To be sure, both statements concern the same theological topic, but what and where is the "dogma" of which both are supposed to be "conceptualizations"?

If, of course, Ross means by "dogma" an ecclesiastical formula such as those contained in the Canons of Trent, this would be a legitimate usage, as long as it is recognized that such dogma is itself a conceptualization and differs from a pronouncement by Augustine, for example, not in any logical sense but only in the sense that as a dogma it represents the result of ecclesiastical decision and is normative for the whole church, whereas the views of Augustine are simply those of a single individual. The situation is further confused when we are told (p. 33) that the Fourth Lateran Council formulation of Transubstantiation—surely a dogma if there are any dogmas at all—is a "synthesis" of the Augustinian and "realist" formulations or "conceptualizations." I find this all very puzzling.

Central to Ross's whole attack upon Protestant thought for contributing to the dissolution of the symbolic cosmos is the charge of "subjectivism" and "individualism" (Ross uses the two terms virtually as synonyms); he thinks that when Protestantism speaks of the Holy Spirit and of faith as dwelling in the heart of the individual that this must be understood in a purely "psychological," i.e. subjective, sense. No argument whatever is offered to support his contention that the Protestant doctrine of Holy Spirit reduces everything to individual states of mind. Time and again Ross simply assumes that faith, a cornerstone of the biblical picture of the Christian life, is "merely psychological" in contrast to the "real" objective transactions presumably taking place within the firmament of the Anglican communion. The chief error of those who believe they are defending a return to "ontological foundations" is to suppose that to be ontological is the same as being "realistic" in the metaphysical sense of the term, whereas realism is only one ontological position among others. It apparently never occurred to Ross to ask this question: What is the evidence for the belief that when Augustine or Bonaventura retired into the "inner chambers of their minds" to recover the presence of the Uncreated Light, they found something "objective," whereas when Calvin or Baxter (who are both Augustinians in this regard) do the same thing, they are simply engaged in a thorough subjectivism? Unfortunately, all the arguments which might convict Protestantism of subjectivism will also destroy the validity of the Augustinian position itself. Nor will it do to say that Augustine was thinking within the "Catholic" symbolic firmament which we know to be *bene fundata* while Calvin and the other reformers were not, for once again this is just the point at issue. One thing is clear: The ultimate status of symbols in a comprehensive view of reality is a question which requires a thoroughly analytical and metaphysical treatment; it cannot be settled by appeal to historical authorities.

The central issue for a religiously oriented aesthetic concerns the status accorded to the religious symbol and its precise relation to what it symbolizes. Ross's view is that in the Roman tradition the symbol allows for the "real presence" of what is symbolized, while Protestantism denies this and makes the meaning of the symbol dependent upon the psychological constitution of the participating individual. This view, as I have suggested, is entirely too simple and its inadequacy can best be seen if we examine more carefully the conditions of the sacramental situation.

The only sound basis for a symbol is the *structural identity* between the material of the symbol *in its intrinsic nature* and the meaning to be expressed. Thus the water is used in the sacrament of Baptism because of its own inherent structure in virtue of which it functions as a cleansing agent. This position we may call "high" symbolic ground because it places all the emphasis upon structures which transcend the interpreting mind. But this position is exceedingly difficult to maintain because, among other reasons, all religious symbols stand in need of "institution," i.e. they must be fixed in relation to a community of individual believers at a definite historical time. The institution of a symbol, however, modifies the relation between the symbol and what it symbolizes, making it *dependent to a certain extent upon* the conditions of institution, whether in the form of the particular time at which it is done, the particular polity of a church, or the disposition of the individual believer. Regardless of the particular condition in question, the actual institution of a religious symbol causes the symbol to depend, at least in part, upon something *other than* the intrinsic nature of the symbolic material.

The Roman and Protestant traditions are not so far apart as regards the conditioning of the symbol, whereas they are poles apart as regards the particular condition emphasized. In the Roman Mass, the connection between Christ and the elements is ultimately dependent upon *ecclesiastical fiat* in the sense that, without the miraculous act of the priest as an official member of the sacred hierarchy, no "transubstantiation" takes place. Thus it is not solely in virtue of the intrinsic nature of the material and its capacity to function as a symbol that the "real presence" is communicated; on the contrary, the material object must receive its capacity to be a symbol, its sacramental power, from the consecration by the priest. The ecclesiastical institution thus becomes a condition which guarantees the "ontological reach" of the symbol. It is as if the bell which tolls in the Mass tolls for God, as an announcement that once again the church, through an official representative, summons Him to ex-

change the substance while leaving the accidents un-
changed.

In Calvin, it is the response of the individual in faith
to the hearing of the word which furnishes the circumstan-
tial condition over and above the symbolic capacity inherent in the nature of the symbolic material itself. Calvin,[8]
no less than Augustine, believed in the capacity of the physical elements to bear the divine. For him the corporeal elements, in virtue of their own intrinsic natures, have symbolic capacity, but this alone is not sufficient for the sacrament.
The *faith* of the individual is necessary for the apprehension
and appropriation of Christ in the Supper. "If the language
of Augustine be preferred," says Calvin, "I deny that men
carry away from the sacrament any more than they collect
in the vessel of faith."[9] This means that *faith* is a *necessary*
condition for participation in the Supper, but it is not a
sufficient condition, nor is it faith but rather Christ present
as the Holy Spirit that is the reality of the sacrament. The
physical elements of *themselves alone* are not adequate, but
something more is required; here, instead of the instituting
condition being a function of the church, it is a function
of the response of the individual believer. The "real presence" of the object signified by the symbol is effected by
the Spirit, and neither Augustine nor Calvin had any speculative theory intended to explain what occurs in the so-
called "objective" situation apart from the believing individual. For Calvin there is, as he says, no "kind of magical
incantation" which produces the referent of the symbol
quite apart from the faithful response of the believer.

Both Catholic and Protestant positions are forced to in-
terpolate a human condition between the intrinsic nature
of the material element and its capacity to function as a

8. *Institutes,* IV.17.3.
9. *Institutes,* IV.17.33.

valid symbol with "ontological reach." In the Roman tradition it is the authority of the ecclesiastical institution; in Protestantism it is the hearing of the Word and the response in faith to the divine promises. The fact remains, however, that with Protestantism the doctrine of the Spirit comes into the foreground and gives to religion an inward reflective turn and to theology a rationalistic emphasis. The result is the directing of attention away from the objects of sense and the denial of aesthetic autonomy. The Roman tradition, in contrast, retains greater respect for the independence of the sensible world and for the aesthetic aspect of life and experience.

What is called for is an analysis of the effect on English poetry (and of poetic symbolism in general) of the introduction into the religious consciousness of the intensely personal response characteristic of Protestantism. What happens to poetry when the aesthetic or dramatic display intended to stimulate sight, taste, and smell is forced out of the center of religion and is replaced by the hearing and comprehending of the Word and by the interior response in faith? This question brings us back again to the contrast between the "ear" and the "eye." What influence did the shift over to the "ear" in Protestantism have upon the poetic sensibility of the seventeenth century? Serious discussion of this question cannot be carried on successfully by those who refuse to set forth with equal care both strains of spirituality. Ross's treatment serves to call attention to the problems to be faced, but it is too one-sided to be finally successful.

The most comprehensive framework within which the general themes of these books can be placed is a theory of the relation between religion and culture. When we ask for the connection between religion and any of the creative arts, we at the same time involve ourselves in the wider question of the attitude adopted by the religious tradition toward human culture and the development of man's creative capacity. Two opposed interpretations of this relationship have maintained themselves throughout the history of Christianity. At one pole stands a general suspicion of culture and the development of human artistic and aesthetic capacities. This attitude can be traced back to the Old Testament period when Hebraic religion expressed its distrust of human artifice as a dangerous prelude to the undue exaltation of man and the consequent diminution of the divine majesty. Moreover, this general cast of mind sees art as an unnecessary distraction, or at least as a temptation, causing man to forget that he is a stranger and a pilgrim on the earth, and that his main concern should be for the salvation of his soul and the glory of God. When unqualified and unchecked, this type of religion leads to an extreme moralism which virtually eliminates the aesthetic.

At the opposite pole stands the view that the development of human capacities to form that complex of individuals, institutions, and their relations which we call culture is *not* opposed to the glory of God or to the salvation of man. The culture-affirming type of religion is anxious that the arts should flourish, although it frequently attempts to minimize the risks accompanying any development of man's artistic nature, not by destroying the aesthetic but by seeking to bring it wholly within the influence of the church. In a sense this results in a loss of autonomy, but it does not mean either the complete suppression or total elimination of art.

Whereas medieval Christianity stood in what we may call the culture-affirming tradition, Protestantism has tended to be more moralistic in its emphasis and to stress the possibilities of human pride inherent in high human cultivation. Both positions are, however, paradoxical in the sense that the Roman tradition has maintained in its official theology a sharp distinction between "natural" and "supernatural," while Protestantism, in the works of the reformers, denied the separating off of any part or aspect of life from other parts as "holy" or "supernatural," on the ground that the *whole* creation stands *equally* under the judgment of God. To be "religious" in the medieval period meant being a member of a religious order and not being engaged in "secular" activity after the fashion of the "world." The Protestant reformers, on the other hand, vigorously maintained the doctrine of *vocation* in which religion is a matter of the consecration with which "worldly" tasks are seen as the "call" of God and discharged in a worshipful manner. Despite these respective backgrounds, Protestantism has most often denied the continuity between religion and culture, thus forcing art out of religion, while the Roman tradition has kept the aesthetic dimension alive and nurtured it. Behind the entire discussion stands the most important and perplexing problem in the philosophy of religion—the relation of religion to culture.

12. The Individual, the Religious Community, and the Symbol

THE MAIN SUBJECT to be considered here is the place of symbolism in religion. A completely adequate treatment of this topic would require a great deal of analysis—logical, epistemological, and metaphysical—and even if it were possible to complete such an analysis, the wider social implications of the symbolic element in religion would remain untouched. While it is of the utmost importance for us to have a clear account of the logical structure of symbols and signs in religion, and especially of the knowledge claim to which the symbols of religion are entitled, it is also important to touch upon another and different aspect of religious symbolism. This aspect may be summed up as the role of religious symbols in sustaining religious community and in making possible a form of human togetherness without which no individual would understand either himself, his neighbor, or the basic religious faith of the tradition to which he belongs. The main body of this study will be given over to a consideration of this function performed by religious symbols.

DEFINITION OF TERMS

Sign

A sign is literally *anything* which serves as a medium of communicating meaning. As such, a sign may be a written or spoken word in a natural language, a wholly convention-

al mark in an artificial language, an overt act, a facial expression, etc. In this broad sense a sign is anything which
does or can "stand for" or mean something and as such, it
needs to be interpreted or read because it points beyond
itself to something else. It is useful to start with this broad
usage and then go on to distinguish a variety of different
kinds of signs: for example, symbols, icons, indices, etc.
These types all share the distinguishing characteristic of
"sign" in the broad sense, but they are differentiated among
themselves by reference to (a) the precise way in which they
"mean" or "stand for," and (b) the type of meaning which
is being communicated or expressed. According to this
broad usage, all symbols are signs but not all signs are
symbols. There is likely to be some confusion because some
writers have used the term "sign" in a narrow sense, according to which it is distinct from and opposed to the symbol.
In this narrow sense "sign" is not a generic term but a
name for a specific type of meaning device. In this sense a
sign is purely arbitrary and conventional in that there is
no internal or necessary connection between the sign and
what it signifies. Its function is simply to designate and in
itself it has no expressive value. The algebraic sign "x,"
for example, may be used to "stand for" an unknown but
determinate quantity, but there is absolutely nothing about
the nature of that sign which is expressive of what it means
or points to. It is on this account that signs, in the narrow
sense of the term, do not play a very large part in religious
faith and expression.

Symbol

"The religious symbol," says Urban, "shares of course
in the general characters of all symbols. Images are taken
from the narrower and more intuitable relations and used
as expressions for more universal and ideal relations which,

because of their pervasiveness and ideality, cannot be directly expressed."[1]

This expresses well enough the main function of the religious symbol. In contrast to the sign, the symbol is expressive just because the images employed are not arbitrary nor do they exist out of all relation to what they symbolize. The symbol is expressive because it is itself of the nature of what it expresses. It should be said in passing that the distinction between symbol *(to symbolon)* and sign *(to semēion)* cannot be made, as has been suggested, on etymological grounds, for while there may be some difference of meaning between them, connotations virtually coincide. "Symbol," in the sense in which it is important to religion and theology, has the following distinctive features:

1. Its ultimate referent is "supersensible," because it refers either to God or to some other aspect of faith which falls beyond the spatial and temporal limits of our experience as, for example, creation, eschatology, etc.

2. It is not conventional in the sense that the choice of symbols is not based on deliberate decision for theoretical purposes (as is the case with signs), but it is organically related to an historical situation, and this means, at the same time, to a community.

3. It employs concrete, empirical experience, without restriction, as a medium of expression—any aspect of "natural" or "secular" can become symbolic religiously under a certain set of conditions.

4. It "participates" in that to which it points and thus possesses "power" to produce effects in the lives of men.

5. It cannot be changed by fiat and its life is not wholly at the command of human will. It can change and develop only in relation to the needs and demands of the historical situation; change and development in religious symbolism

1. Wilbur M. Urban, *Language and Reality* (London, Allen and Unwin, 1939), p. 580.

is a function of a dialectic between historical situations and human decisions.

Sign Event

In his discussion of the symbolic character of religion, Paul Tillich[2] has suggested the use of the expression, "sign event," for the term "sign," often used in the New Testament in relation to the miracles. According to his view, we should not use the term "sign" alone here because it leaves out of account the symbolic character of these events. Hence he proposes "sign event" in order to keep touch with New Testament usage, and at the same time he adds a necessary qualification. If, of course, sign is used in the broad sense indicated above, there is no problem, but at present, at least, the more common usage among philosophers is the narrow sense, and this is clearly inadequate. The historical context of biblical faith means that many of the entities which are regarded as pointing to God are historical events; hence a sign event may be understood as a concrete historical event which has revelatory significance and is expressive of the nature and purpose of God. An adequate interpretation of the prophet's function in "discerning the signs of the times" could be made only by reference to such sign events.

MAN NEVER escapes concern over the tensions and contrasts which stem from the fact that he is both an individual and a social being. Of all the beings in existence, man is alone in his capacity to distinguish himself both from his world and his neighbors, to refer to himself in his unique individuality as "I," and it is on this account that his equally natural capacity for social relations takes on a new aspect. Man is not together with others of his kind as

2. See Paul J. Tillich, *Systematic Theology* (Chicago, University of Chicago Press, 1951), *1*, 115 ff., 238 ff.

the lower animals are together in a herd or colony, where there is surely no personality and virtually no individuality. Man is capable, just because of his unique individuality, of a form of togetherness which exists both beyond and alongside that individuality or "privacy." We may borrow a term from Whitehead[3] and refer to the social nature of man as an instance of *togetherness* and to his individual nature as an instance of *apartness* (this is not Whitehead's word but I suggest it as a convenient counterpart). One of the most important truths about man is that he exhibits both of these natures, a fact which should never be overlooked.

In all aspects and at all levels of existence—social, political, economic, moral, religious—there are to be found ramifications of this dual nature of man. More often than not it has manifested itself historically in the form of extremes which are at the same time distortions of the truth: The distorted form of togetherness is *collectivism* and the distorted form of apartness is *individualism*. At the present time, as is well known, it is at the political level that this topic is in the foreground of discussion, and on all sides there is concern over possible loss of the individual person and his rights in the face of mass society and totalitarian government. It is not, however, only in this sphere that concern is expressed; no small amount of the current appeal which certain types of existential philosophy have is due to their emphasis upon individual personality, individual responsibility, and individual moral and religious commitment, in opposition to the homogeneity of the mass man and the meaningless life of a predominantly technical so-

3. The term I intend to use here is "togetherness," although I do not use it in the full sense it has in Whitehead's system but to denote actual relations between distinct entities. See Alfred North Whitehead, *Process and Reality* (New York, Macmillan, 1930), p. 29. "Actual entities involve each other by reason of their prehensions of each other. There are thus real individual facts of the togetherness of actual entities."

ciety. What makes the issue more pressing is that the more surely the mass man takes possession of modern life, the more vigorous is the protest in the name of an unrestrained individualism. In this respect Hegel was right when he called attention to the mutual dependence of the opposites in every sphere of existence—neither collectivism nor individualism is autonomous and independent, simply because both find their nature and structure in large measure dependent on their mutual relations and antagonisms. They thrive on each other at the same time that each makes the existence of the other possible.

The basic problem is to find a form of human existence which can do justice to both aspects of human nature and, at the same time, avoid the two distorted forms which deny either one aspect or the other. Individualism denies togetherness and emphasizes the isolated individual, atomic in character and complete in himself; collectivism denies apartness and emphasizes the corporate body as the only reality, thus leaving no room for individual personality. Both contain an element of truth because each seizes upon a genuine aspect of man's nature, but at the same time both are distortions and therefore false because of what they deny. In what follows it will be shown that religious community, combining as it does the togetherness of man as well as his apartness, can express the dual nature of man. Such community has togetherness but avoids collectivism; it requires distinct individuals but it excludes individualism. Religious community falls beyond the two distortions, preserving what is valid in them but overcoming their one-sidedness and error.

Thus far the main problem has been stated in such a way that its main relevance to religion has not been stressed. It is necessary at this point to call attention to that relevance and consider the relation of apartness and togetherness to religious faith.

Of all the aspects of experience, religion has faced the problems of togetherness and apartness to a greater extent than any other. And this has been true for a variety of reasons, some internal and some external. On the one hand, both Judaism and Christianity have sought to provide man with an archetype of true community by reference to which all "secular" community may be judged, and on the other, as forms of human experience and expression beside others, these communities have had to face within themselves the very problems which it is their aim to overcome. Theologians and philosophers have often dwelt at length upon the distinction and even opposition between "individual" and "corporate" forms of piety. William James, for example, went far in the direction of exalting individual piety over corporate expressions of religious faith, leaving behind the impression that personal religion alone is "real" and the religion of a church something of a "secondhand" affair. Durkheim, on the other hand, was equally insistent on the primacy of the social aspect of religion and he marshaled all the evidence of the newborn science of religious origins and institutions to prove his thesis. More recently, in this regard, it has become popular to draw the contrast as one between "personal religion" and "organized religion," usually with the implication that the former has a genuine character which the latter can never possess.

No one can study the history of religion, and especially the development of the Old and New Testament communities, without feeling a deep dissatisfaction with all simple distinctions between individual and social in which it is supposed that one is genuine while the other is not, or that it is necessary to make a choice between the two. The truth of the matter is that religion is intensely personal and individual as well as necessarily social and corporate. Any attempt to deny this duality not only goes against the facts of actual religion but it also involves an explicit denial of the dual nature of man. One of the most fruitful contributions to be made by the philosophy of religion is an account of the nature of religious community in relation to the individual believer. It is at this point that the symbolic character of religion assumes the greatest importance, for it will be seen that it is essentially bound up both with the problem and such resolution as is possible.

Religion is intensely personal and individual, and yet one of the most universal characteristics of religion as we know it in all times and places is its almost exclusive expression in the form of a community or church. We must now attempt to understand what is involved in this duality. There can be no doubt that religion is an affair of the individual in the sense that each person must raise the religious question of his own ultimate destiny and commit himself to a specific faith for himself and nobody else. No man, or group of men, can have faith for another man, nor can they choose to lead in accord with the will of God any lives but their own. This much is clear: in religion man is, like Jacob before the field of Edom, "left there alone," and it is thus that he stands before God. "We are," said Royce, "beings, each of whom has a soul of his own, a destiny of his own, rights of his own, worth of his own, ideals of his own, and an individual life in which this soul, this destiny, these rights, these ideals, get their expression."[4] The truth of the foregoing is nowhere more evident than in religion where the individual as such stands in relation to God; religious faith is personal or it is nothing.

As soon, however, as this is said, there comes to mind an equal and seemingly opposite truth, the omnipresent fact of religious community. In speaking of the social element in religion, Urban says, "There is doubtless a sense in which faith is a matter of man's own solitude, but," he adds

4. Josiah Royce, *The Problem of Christianity* (New York, Macmillan, 1914), 2, 24.

significantly, "it does not follow that faith needs no other witness."[5] The religious man is always in touch with the "cloud of witnesses" and is never merely alone. Religion invariably proves itself to be a matter of history, of common tradition, and of human togetherness. If we are asked whether there is any one generic trait manifested by the history of religion, the answer is to be given by referring to the presence of the corporate religious body whether in the form of tribal units, church, or monastic order. How very often do we find in religious literature the powerful symbol of the "household of faith" expressing the fact of human togetherness before God! Neither Hebraic religion and its continuation in Judaism, nor Christianity, is intelligible apart from its corporate expressions. The God of Abraham, Isaac, and Jacob is the very same God Who is supreme for the "house of Israel," and the God of Jesus and of Paul is the same God Who manifests Himself in the church or the "body of Christ." Whatever, then, may be said on behalf of a purely personal piety, the fact remains that the great living religions of mankind, Judaism and Christianity in particular, stand out in their corporate or community form as expressions of an enduring common faith held in common by individual believers.

Nevertheless, the presence of both these tendencies is bound to lead to tension and one-sidedness following from the need for each side to present itself in exaggerated form in order that it may not be done away with. Concern for individual piety easily leads to an individualism which disrupts the household of faith. On the other side, the ecclesiastical body will inevitably seek to preserve order and tradition by setting limits to individual piety and thus will tend to approximate a form of collectivism. How are the two aspects of religion and of human nature to be expressed

5. Wilbur M. Urban, *Humanity and Deity* (London, Allen and Unwin, 1951), p. 316.

and brought together in fruitful harmony? What is the nature of genuine community and how are individual believers related to it? These are the problems now to be pursued and in doing so we shall be led to a consideration of the function of religious symbols in communication. We shall see that it is the religious symbol which stands as the basis of the community and provides the link between it and the individual believer.

In order to keep the following discussion as clear as possible, it will be helpful to set forth, in telescoped fashion, the points to be made. Within the confines of the present study no full or detailed argument is possible, and on this account it is necessary to have the main points clearly stated. First, I shall point out the necessarily symbolic character of religious faith, both in its initial grasp and its articulation; secondly, I shall suggest the necessity of such symbolic form for the foundation and continued growth of the religious community embracing a multiplicity of diverse and distinct individual believers; and thirdly, I shall show that religious community can unite the dual tendencies in man and overcome the distortions of individualism and collectivism. In each case the role played by the symbol will be of decisive importance.

Much has been written, both past and present, about symbolism and the symbolic character of religion. It is a subject that is likely to be attended by misunderstanding and confusion, because it is elusive and has been interpreted in diverse ways. The first point to be noticed is that it will not do to call religion "symbolic" if all that is intended is a fairly loose and perhaps even arbitrary characterization of religious faith and its object as "poetical" or "figurative." It is not in this loose and usually derogatory sense that the term "symbolic" is to be understood. Religious faith is symbolic as is its systematic articulation in theology, because both have to do with a type of meaning which, though related in a determinate way to the visible world, points beyond that world to an ultimate meaning and purpose which is both its ground and its goal. But although, in biblical faith, God transcends the world, He is, nevertheless, thought to manifest Himself through various aspects of it and certain events in it. Thus there are various media—persons, places, natural objects, times, events— which may be called the bearers of the divine.

These media are regarded as symbols and signs of God and as they *are not* God but *mean* God, they must be interpreted or read by those to whom is given the power to understand. Therefore, when it is said that the inspired man of God, the prophet, has the task of "discerning the signs of the times" (see "sign event" on page 230), this is a statement which may be taken as, in a sense, literally true. The prophet experiences God via the medium of such symbols and, at least for biblical faith, if God is not grasped in this way, He is not grasped at all.

Those original communications between God and man upon which biblical religion is based are analogous in themselves to the situation where two individual persons seek to communicate with each other.[6] When I intend or mean something and want to express that meaning to another, I can do so only through the use of a medium symbolic in nature. The mind of my neighbor is not open to direct inspection nor can it be known simply by conceiving of him in his general characteristics. As an individual person distinct from myself, but, as I believe, similarly seeking for meaning and purpose in life, he is an active intelligence who can only express himself to me through a medium or language which I must be able to read if I am to enter into

6. There is, of course, one absolutely fundamental difference between the two situations: the experience of human selves is localized through our bodies, whereas God as Spirit or Life has no body.

his consciousness and understand who he is and what he intends. This medium may be varied in character and may be in the form of words, gestures, deeds, etc., but whatever its form, it is essential and cannot be done away with if the chasm which exists between two selves, in virtue of the fact that they are really two selves, is to be bridged. This can be done only through a dialectical process lasting through time in which each self attempts to understand the meanings and intentions of others by reading their symbolic expressions. It is not any illegitimate narrowing of the gulf between God and man to think of God's manifesting of Himself as analogous to this process of communication. The Bible, seen from this vantage point, is a vast structure of symbols and sign events which are expressive of the nature and purpose of God; it represents as well a record of man's attempt to grasp and to express the divine nature and purpose as it appears in the constitution of nature and the turning points of human history. God and man are engaged in a cosmic dialogue and in it man is attempting to understand the divine intentions through the symbols which are expressive of Him. It is not simply the literal or physical description of these symbols that is of importance, but the *meaning* which is being expressed through them.[7] In writing about the great "events" of revelation, Urban says, "whatever literal character may be ascribed to these 'events' in time, they are . . . revelatory of that which is before all time and before all worlds."[8] These events can be revelatory only when taken as symbols or sign events of a meaning which is expressed through them. This ultimate

7. If, for example, a man makes a "wry face" which I understand as an attempt to communicate a meaning to me, my ability to perceive or to conceive that face will avail nothing for purposes of communication unless I understand it as a sign and know how to "read" its meaning. Signs are to be read; a mere description is not enough, because it is not what they are or look like but what they mean that is of importance.

8. Urban, *Humanity and Deity*, p. 245.

meaning which is before all time is, at least in part, what is meant by God.

A few technical points about signs and symbols are necessary at this juncture. Gradually it has come to be understood that man is the "meaning-seeking" animal and that, in the process of seeking what all things mean, he discovers his capacity to express what he has learned about himself and his world in a form which is relatively permanent and can be communicated from self to self. It is thus that man comes to be called the sign-reading or symbolic animal. It has become customary to distinguish between sign and symbol in order to show that man alone is capable of having a symbolic response and of grasping and expressing symbolic meaning as distinct from the sign or signal response. There can be no doubt that this distinction, or one like it, must be made and kept.[9] There is, however, a problem of usage, which though verbal, is liable to cause confusion and should be cleared up. The term "sign" is often used in at least two senses, a broad and a narrow one. In the broad sense, "sign" means literally *anything* (words, sounds, events, etc.) which "stands for" or conveys a meaning or needs to be read.[10] In this usage sign is a class name embracing many different types of signs like icons, symbols, etc. These types are all said to share the general characteristics of signs but may be distinguished by reference to the precise way in which they mean and the type of meaning

9. Much evidence could be brought forward to support this distinction but, in this connection, mention need only be made of Cassirer's work. His analysis showing the difference between signs or signals as *operators* and symbols as *designators* is convincing. See Ernst Cassirer, *An Essay on Man* (New Haven, Yale University Press, 1947), pp. 31 ff. Other illustrations are to be found in his *Language and Myth* (New York, Harper, 1946), and in *Die Begriffsform im mythischen Denken* (Leipzig, Berlin, B. G. Teubner, 1922).

10. See, for example, the broad meaning of sign in Peirce, *Collected Papers* (Cambridge, Mass., Harvard University Press, 1931), 1.540. Cf. Royce, pp. 281 ff.

which is involved. When sign is used in this broad sense, all symbols are called signs. There is, however, a narrow sense of the term "sign," according to which it means either "signal" like a bell in a stimulus-response situation or a conventional, arbitrary mark to be assigned meaning for some technical purpose and having no intrinsic or internal relation to what it stands for. It is mainly with symbols that we are concerned in religion and not with signs in the narrow sense (except in the case of biblical "signs" which are, as Paul Tillich has pointed out, more properly called *sign events*). For symbols are expressive of what they mean in their own nature and are thus neither arbitrary nor accidental, whereas an algebraic sign, for example, is arbitrary in the sense that there is no necessary connection between the sign and the meaning assigned to it.

Religious faith in seeking to lay hold on God is necessarily symbolic in its expression. It seeks what is beyond all literal seeing,[11] and to achieve its goal it must avail itself of symbolic media. On this account religion is not bound up with symbolic meaning by accident or by human choice or preference; it is symbolic by its very nature. Many attempts have been made, through the disciplines of theology and metaphysics, to "break through" religious symbolism and translate the language of religion with its image and its myth into conceptual language. An appraisal of the final success or failure of such ventures falls beyond our purpose, but it is doubtful whether the affirmations of religion can ever be cast in a wholly nonsymbolic form such as a rationalistic theology proposes to do. At any rate the point to be stressed is that the conditions surrounding the self-manifestation of God require that every grasp and articulation of God's nature and purpose be effected via the symbolic medium.

11. The "seeing" which is involved in religion is closer to the "seeing" involved in "seeing the point" than to that involved in "seeing the table."

Religion is symbolic not only because God is beyond the confines of our sense experience but because its grasp of God must be articulated in order to be preserved through time. The only way in which the revelatory experience of an Amos, an Isaiah, a Peter, or a Paul can be preserved is via a symbolic medium. Apart from this it would vanish as soon as it was born. The medium of such preservation is the sacred literature, customs, institutions, etc., of the community together with the body of commentary and interpretation which grows up around it. This literature is itself a body of symbols and signs which need to be interpreted both by the members for the community and by the community for the members.[12] Thus the Bible is not only a record of the attempt on the part of the "men of God" to read and understand through their own experience the symbols of the divine plan, but it is itself set forth in symbolic form and thus requires further interpretation. This accounts for the perennial difficulties over interpretation, for man is always, in a sense, at a second remove from the mystery which is God: first, the symbols and sign events themselves, and secondly, the normative attempt to read and record them found in the sacred literature which, in turn, needs to be read and interpreted, and so on to the end of time. Full justice to both of these aspects of religious symbolism cannot be done here, but they should not be overlooked, nor should they be merged into each other; both have played an important role in the history of Judaism and Christianity.

At this point it may reasonably be asked what bearing the symbolic character of religion has on the founding and

---

12. This two-way process of interpretation is one feature serving to distinguish true community from collectivism. In the latter none but official interpretation of the tradition of the community for the members is allowed; "private" interpreting is rejected.

sustaining of the religious community. The present section will address itself to this question.

All experience, including that experience which points specifically to God as its source, is individual, is somebody's experience, and is localized in a finite center or individual personality. Only a distinct person capable of distinguishing himself and designating himself as "I" is able to have experience in the full sense in which it passes beyond both sensation and response to a stimulus from outside. For a man to grasp and understand an experience of God, it is not enough for him simply to be receptive or aware, as is so often thought; in addition, he must be able to cast what has confronted him in a form which will endure beyond the present fleeting moment. In order to make its experience articulate for itself (to say nothing, for the moment, about other selves), the self must express that experience in a symbolic form. A fuller analysis of experience would show that this is true whatever object is involved; it is true *a fortiori* in religion because no man lays hold upon God directly but only through a process of interpreting the symbols of God in the world. Experience is not a clear-cut, static content which is "had" at an instant and remains just what it is, but it is a process which takes time, as both Charles Peirce and Royce pointed out so convincingly. For an individual to carry on the process of comparing, contrasting, inferring, and interpreting, without which there is no experience at all, he must have expressed what he apprehends in symbolic form. For this is the only form in which past experience can be brought into the present and carried over into the future. Otherwise man is unable to carry on that inner dialogue with himself and with God without which there can be no meaningful life at all. Religion thus may be said to employ symbols in a twofold sense: one which it shares with other types of experience and one which is peculiar to itself. On the one hand, no meaningful experience at all is possible without symbolic elements, and on the other, the very nature of the reality which religion seeks requires a symbolic understanding.

If an individual is thus led to employ symbols in his own experience, what are we to say about the attempt of one self to communicate his experience to another? While it may be true that all religion starts with individual experience, the fact is that such experience is never merely individual. The Old Testament prophet, even if he be, like Amos, a lonely herdsman, is not an isolated consciousness. He already stands in a certain tradition, and in communicating his experience to others, he revises and extends that tradition. How, then, is he to make known what he has apprehended of the nature and will of God? He must first grasp it for himself and, in so doing, cast it in a form which can be addressed to another consciousness, who in turn seeks to grasp and understand it by reference to his own experience of himself, his world, and God. Amos cannot point to his experience and simply bid another self see what he has seen—or hear what he has heard. He can only attempt to express in symbolic form as much as he has apprehended and understood. Hence, Amos, as well as many other biblical writers, employs a variety of images and symbolic devices in the attempt to communicate his message. Apart from such symbolic expression, individual experience must forever remain isolated and wholly private.

It is this necessity of communicating and sharing experience which leads to the foundation of community. In order to save space I shall condense the following account of the conditions which are necessary for community, relying largely on the precise analysis set forth by Royce in *The Problem of Christianity*.[13] He has shown there better than anyone else, the exact way in which many selves can be

13. See pp. 57 ff.

linked together in a supertemporal community, while at the same time retaining the apartness without which they would cease to be individual personalities.

According to Royce the satisfaction of certain conditions entitles us to say that a community of a certain type exists.[14] These conditions are as follows:

1. There must be distinct individuals aware of themselves as such, capable of remembering the past and hoping for the future with which they can freely identify themselves.

2. These selves must be able and willing to communicate with each other in order to discover and preserve what is in common between them, i.e. those remembered past events and anticipated future events which each can conscientiously and devotedly regard as belonging to his own past and future.

3. A group of such selves constitute a community with respect to a common past or a common future (both are present in the case of Judaism and Christianity) when the individuals involved are prepared to recognize and accept those common elements as being at the same time part of their own actual selves.

The Old and New Testament communities fulfill these requirements to the letter. Isaiah, no less than Paul, can review the past of his community as a great structure of persons, deeds, and events which are, symbolically, the mighty acts and promises of God. As such, they belong to the past of all members of the community, and in referring to them, members at all times and places can say not "they" but "we" did this or that. Similarly, they can look forward to the fulfillment of life, again symbolically represented as the "last things," the end of all creation, as the hope common to all members. Only insofar as each self accepts this

14. See my extended account of this in *Royce's Social Infinite* (New York, Liberal Arts Press, 1950), pp. 64 ff.

common basis and attempts to understand it as part of his own self, do we have a new structure, a set of relations which defines a new being—the religious community or church.

Because it is what is held in common that is of crucial significance here, it will be wise to consider that further. If we ask what forms the basis of the Judeo–Christian tradition, we must answer: a body of beliefs concerning God, man, and sentient creation, ultimately mediated through certain historical persons and events taken as symbols and signs of God and His purpose. It is not primarily with the philosophical description or causal explanation of these symbols that the community is concerned, but instead with their meaning, in the sense of purpose and pattern. The members of the community seek an interpretation of God and of His existence, and this they can achieve only by reading the meaning of the symbols of God and of creation. The creed which forms the basis of Christianity is a body of interpretation, a body which expresses the nature of God, the purpose of man, and his determinate place in the wider scheme of things. It is not primarily a description of things to be *seen,* or a set of explanations to be *conceived,* but rather a set of symbolic expressions which must be read and *interpreted.*[15] Only he who knows how to read the symbols in which the faith is expressed is in a position to grasp what the tradition stands for and the common faith which sustains it.

The original experiences, sign events, crucial occurrences out of which biblical religion emerged, were, to be sure, individual experiences, experiences of the great men of faith, but they did not and could not remain merely individual. The selves for whom these experiences were first real had to recognize them as symbols and signs of God and

15. Precepts are to be *seen,* concepts to be *conceived,* but symbols and signs are to be *read* or *interpreted,* something which requires more than either seeing or conceiving.

to interpret them for themselves through that inner reflective dialogue which is of the very nature of self-conscious life. Furthermore, not only did these individuals seek to interpret their own experiences for themselves and in so doing express them in symbolic form, but their experience, in becoming the basis for a community, came to be interpreted by others who in turn sought to interpret it for still others and so on without end. In this process there was a continual grasping of symbols and signs and a continual attempt to read or interpret them through further symbols and signs. It is this long process of interpretation, as preserved in the sacred literature of the tradition together with commentary upon it, which forms the *common basis* of the community.

We must now turn to our final consideration: the role of religious community in expressing the dual nature of man and in overcoming the distortions of individualism and collectivism. Religious community requires both what is individual and distinct and what is common or together. There is no mystical blending of individuals, no matter how closely knit the community; on the other hand, there are no isolated individuals who are complete in themselves and able to make their way entirely alone. What keeps the close and fruitful harmony of the two factors is the symbolic tradition of the community and the capacity of the members to understand, interpret, and appropriate it for themselves. The religious congregation is not a herd of mass men overpowered by "group" symbols, but a working and living whole of distinct individuals, actively and freely relating themselves to the common faith of their tradition and, at the same time, entering into that knowledge and understanding of each other which is possible only through the sharing of a memory and a hope which each has in common. Mr. A and Mr. B are drawn together by an indissoluble bond existing beyond all the spatial and temporal distinctions which may separate them when each knows that the other believes and trusts in the same God and hopes for the same fulfillment of life. Both features, however, the symbolic tradition in common and individual interpretation, must be present; should either one of these be absent or should one take precedence over the other, the result will be the breakdown of the community and the triumph of either individualism or collectivism. Collectivism (togetherness without apartness) employs mass symbols, operates with an official interpreter who is not questioned, and eliminates individual interpretation and understanding; individualism (apartness without togetherness) rejects what is common to all, denies the power of symbols to unite men, and finally, ends with isolated and lonely individuals. Against the evils of collectivism, individualism looks like a sure solution, and in the face of individualism (particularly in its "rugged" form), collectivism appears to be a valid corrective. The truth is that both are wrong because they are based on a false view of the nature of man. As an individual able to refer to himself as "I," man is *apart;* as a social animal going out to those he loves and needs, man is *together;* to deny either of these facets of his life is to fall into error. It is religious community alone which can do justice to both. And such community can endure and develop only so long as the symbols of its faith continue to be grasped and understood, only so long as they have power to bind the members together in a unity which transcends time, place, and circumstance, just because this unity is the unity of God, the one Reality all the distinct selves have in their common past and future.

13. The Permanent Truth in the Idea of Natural Religion

THE IDEA OF NATURAL RELIGION is one of those arresting ideas which never get fully defined but which nevertheless excite reflection and even controversy whenever they appear. The history of its life within the Christian tradition is a case in point: The idea has been taken as a foundation to be built upon, and it has been rejected as a combination of concepts involving the same sort of contradiction to be found in the notion of a round square. Natural religion has been appealed to as a touchstone of rationality, and it has been attacked as illegitimate if not actually blasphemous. An idea capable of producing such reactions cannot be ignored.

A realistic approach to our topic bids us begin with two acknowledgments. First, natural religion has been understood in many senses and this has often led to confusion and discussion at cross purposes. Secondly, in the current revival of Protestant theology any idea of natural religion is anathema. Even more, there are those for whom religion itself is regarded as a merely "human" phenomenon which belongs to culture, having nothing to do with God as understood in the Christian tradition. Such a beginning may not seem very promising, but it has the merit at least of being in touch with the facts, and as F. H. Bradley reminded us in his own ironic way, "Where all is bad it must be good to know the worst."

My chief aim is to set forth what I shall call the permanent truth in the idea of natural religion. The problems leading to the proposal of the idea are perennial in character. They do not appear only under this or that historical circumstance, merely to disappear like Palinurus beneath fresh waves of historical change. They belong instead to the nature and essential structure of religion in human life and history. Whenever the idea of natural religion is suggested, familiar problems are not far behind: the place of knowledge in religion, the relation between theology and philosophy, the bearing of pervasive experience and secular knowledge upon the claims of historically rooted religious doctrine. These problems confront us at present, and they take on a new urgency because of the exciting developments witnessed by recent years in religious thought. The impact, for example, of the philosophy of existence and of the attempted recovery of the Reformation theology and ethos serves to raise anew ancient issues concerning religion, faith, and understanding. It is clear that in the present state of philosophical, scientific, and religious thinking, there stands above all others the perplexing question of the place of reason in religion and the extent to which theological doctrine can be maintained in isolation from both philosophical dialectic and the appeal to general experience and scientific knowledge. It would be a great mistake indeed if we should suppose that the present revival of theology entitles us to avoid the continuing problems involved. Before it is possible, however, to make clear what I take to be the permanent contribution in the idea of natural religion, its background must be explored.

The idea of natural religion is, as we all know, a very old one and, as we should expect, it has been subject to considerable reinterpretation in the course of its extensive history. It seems clear enough that the meaning it bore in the period of Enlightenment has been the decisive meaning for developments of the past two hundred years. Let us call the Enlightenment conception the classical conception of natural religion. The clue to that conception is found in the contrast which it implies; that is to say, the meaning of natural religion must be sought in the nature of the religious form it was intended to exclude. As far back as Herbert of Cherbury in the seventeenth century, natural religion, sometimes called Deism, was understood as a body of beliefs based upon human reason and taken as independent of a special mode of disclosure commonly called revelation. Although these beliefs were regarded as forming a unity distinct from any of the so-called positive religions, the claim was frequently made that the beliefs of natural religion represented what was common to all the positive religions. The implication was that the points in which the positive religions differed from each other are unimportant, belonging only to the particularity of historical circumstances as over against the universality of reason.

This conception of a natural religion was to suffer at least two crushing blows in the centuries to follow. On the one hand, the criticism of human reason at the hands of Hume no less than of Kant led to a denial of the ability of theoretical understanding to reach any transcendent reality in a cognitive way. When Kant declared that he had found it necessary to deny knowledge of God and freedom to make way for rational faith, he was striking deep at the heart of the Deistic natural religion. He was in fact seeking to base religion on something other than either metaphysics or a general science of nature. Though he continued to speak of a rational or natural religion, he meant a religion based upon what he called the practical side of things. The upshot of the entire discussion was that for some all discourse about the things of religion was said to be beyond human cognitive powers, while for others it seemed imperative that we have done with the dialectic of natural religion altogether and return to the idea of revelation. Still others sought to find a new foundation in experience, such as morality or art, in order to preserve the connection between religion and human experience without at the same time running afoul of the criticism which held that God cannot be an object of theoretical knowledge.

The second major blow fell in the nineteenth century when the historical consciousness and the historical dimension of life were thrust into the foreground. The idea of a universal human reason capable of working independently of historical circumstances and conditions became suspect. From various sides and for various reasons it was claimed that a universal human reason, if it is not itself an abstraction with no real existence, can at any rate reach nothing more than highly abstract truth. Not only was it held that reason cannot operate in a vacuum apart from historical circumstances and special interests—economic, political, social—but it was claimed that reason cannot provide any content for itself unless immersed in historical action and decision. Here the situation of the previous century was reversed: Instead of the distinctive features of religions being set aside as belonging to what is merely historically particular, these same features became decisive, and the supposedly universal or common core of natural religious belief was itself rejected as abstract. The latter trend has continued into our own day and it is signalized by the current conviction that religion in the sense in which it is a pervasive phenomenon in human life belongs merely to culture and has no essential connection with the divine. According to this view we should cease talking about religion and confine attention instead to historical revelation as experience and record established by God alone and discontinuous with all human, finite, and natural experience. Stated in its most extreme form, this view contends that Christianity is not a religion—since to classify it thus is to subordinate it to a general category—but revelation itself, opposed to all religion. To a consideration of the implications of this view, we must return.

There are several lessons to be learned from the historical development we have briefly sketched. Most pertinent to our present purpose is the discovery that the reality to which natural religion points cannot be adequately described after the fashion of the eighteenth century. The belief that a clear and unambiguous distinction can be drawn between a purely rational, and in this sense natural, religion on the one hand and a purely historical or revelational religion on the other, is based on an error. This is not to say that there is no distinction at all required, for we shall attempt to formulate one shortly, but rather to point out that the facts of the situation will not support the total separation which the older distinction required. Systematic, rational constructions purporting to be true of the real world are never self-contained expressions of reason; they always depend upon encounter with existing reality taking place under historical conditions. On the other hand, the revealed content, which in the older theory stood in total separation from natural religion, could never have been received by the human mind without being expressed, interpreted, and judged through forms and canons of human reason. The revealed content, moreover, in order to assume its rightful status as religious truth, could not have been left in the form of historical record but it had to be formulated in rational concepts and endowed with such form as is appropriate to a truth making a universal claim. It appears that each side interpenetrates the other; reason is always dependent upon a reality encountered, and revealed or historical religion is dependent upon attaining to rational form. The inescapable presence of one side of an antithesis in the other suggests the illegitimacy of any attempt to present the two sides as totally disconnected.

Leaving to one side, for the time being, whatever difficulties are involved in the distinction expressed in the classical conception of natural religion, we must seek the reasons prompting it in the first place. What exactly were these earlier thinkers trying to express? What significant insights lay behind their strong conviction that the religious situation cannot be adequately summed up in the so-called positive religions alone? With answers to these questions in hand, we may return to our present situation and show how they bear on current Christian thinking.

There were in point of fact three main ideas that sought expression in and through the classical doctrine. All three were elaborated under the guidance of a more or less basic purpose largely political and even ethical in its import: the purpose of overcoming disputes based on theological differences. The insistence upon doctrinal uniformity, so it was generally believed, meant persecution and wars of religion. Natural religion was invoked as furnishing a set of general truths known to all or capable of being so known and transcending special, historically founded religious claims and interests. The selection of these common truths, moreover, was made in accordance with the idea that religion is primarily a practical affair whose main contributions are the molding of good citizens and the preservation of society. Important, however, as this motivating purpose has been in the development of religion since that time, more serious problems are contained in the three ideas at the heart of the classical conception.

First, there was the idea of a universal religion stripped of all particularity or provincial ties such as would serve to confine it to some particular group or class of human beings. Secondly, there was the idea that personal, individual experience and understanding are essential to genuine religious faith and that these are threatened by institutional forms of mediation. Thirdly, there was the idea that reason as a trustworthy guide finds its proper locus in the universal or pervasive traits of human experience and consequently that differences in experience and doctrine derivative from particular, historical circumstances are to be disregarded as unimportant. Let us consider each idea in turn.

As regards the concept of a universal religion representing a distillation from particular religions of certain doctrines such as the existence of God and human immortality, two considerations are essential. A rational or natural religion so derived would, of course, be dependent upon the historical religions and their distinctive disclosures of God. The mark of rationality or the sign that we have here to do with a universal religion would be found in the doctrines held to be in common; rationality and universality, in the sense of the common core of belief, coincide. Such a religion could be said to be completely independent of the historical traditions only if its defining beliefs were formulated in concepts not themselves derived from or even in part constituted by beliefs peculiar to any one historical tradition alone. Thus, for example, to make good the claim it was necessary to hold that neither the concept of God nor the idea of divine worship was uniquely derived from Christianity. And yet from the historical facts, we know that this was not the case; the common core of rational religion was in fact based largely upon corresponding Christian beliefs. It even happened in some cases that Christianity was openly identified as the natural religion and attempts were made to show that it was "as old as creation." The conclusion to be drawn is that the position was unable to sustain its own dichotomy between the natural and the historically revealed.

The natural religion, moreover, could have no separate existence as an identifiable *cultus* or religious community, a fact which casts suspicion upon its right to be called a religion at all. A religious community and tradition are not created merely by a convocation of individuals ready to sign a creed or charter. Common experience and life are necessary and these cannot be supplied by intellectual agreements alone. Criticism and reinterpretation of an already existing tradition are possible, but such criticism by itself does not constitute a religion. The natural religion of Enlightenment was either a philosophical doctrine unconnected with religious observance and functioning, or it was a special way of regarding the doctrines of the special historical religion in which the individual happened to stand. In the latter case the natural religion was not determined independently of the historical religion and the hoped-for separation of the two does not stand.

The second of the three ideas behind what we have been calling the classical conception concerns the protest against institutional religion and its mediating function. In maintaining that religious meaning and truth must be apprehended by the individual through his own reason, the proponents of natural religion were in fact underlining the necessity of individual participation and personal involvement in the religious relationship. In many cases this meant a call, not for further separation from traditional religious doctrines, but rather for a closer association with them. Appropriation through reason and experience was thought superior to acceptance of religious truths at secondhand mediated by the "credit" or authority of the proposer. Curiously enough, Herbert of Cherbury did not hesitate to refer to such appropriation or apprehension by the individual through his own reason as a form of revelation or disclosure of God.

The possibility of such individual appropriation, however, points up the need for continuity between the experience and reason of the individual on one side and the proposed religious truth on the other. If a doctrine of God is to command the assent and allegiance of the person, it must not appear to him as infinitely strange to his own experience and it must be cast in intelligible form. The nature of a rational being demands that whatever is proposed for acceptance by that being should be continuous with a rational nature. Kant expressed the point best in his doctrine of autonomy and heteronomy. Whereas heteronomy signifies that the human self is subjected to conditions that deny its own distinctive rational nature so that it is reduced to the status of a thing, autonomy requires that a rational being be treated in accordance with his own rationality and not in a subhuman way. Religion is possible only for rational beings; it would be a paradox beyond any of those which so delight the contemporary theologian if, in the sphere of religious faith, man should be required to abandon his rationality. The classical conception of natural religion made provision against such a result through the doctrine of individual apprehension of religious truth.

The third idea underlying the classical doctrine is the most important of the three: It concerns the metaphysical basis of the entire contrast between natural and historical or revealed religion. It contains as well the main idea behind what I have been calling the permanent truth in the idea of natural religion. Natural religion, in virtue of its roots in reason, appealed to general experience of both the natural world and man; it did not confine itself to special experiences associated with historical personages or traditions. By contrast, revealed religion was taken as essentially historical and was thus seen as drawing upon events neither capable of repetition nor of exemplification in experience generally accessible across cultural lines. We are now in a position to state more precisely the meaning of the fundamental contrast in question. It concerns two different channels or approaches to God: the approach through repeatable experience and public knowledge and the approach through historical events and their records as preserved and interpreted by a continuing community or church. I propose to call the former channel the approach through *general occa-*

sions and the latter the approach through *special occasions.*
The natural religion was identified with general occasions
and the historical or revealed with what I am calling special
occasions. We must not, however, identify general occasions
with nature understood as the physical cosmos in contrast
to man, nor will it do to characterize special occasions as
having to do with human experience alone as if these occasions were not permeated by natural structures and did not
take place under the constraint of the general conditions
surrounding all existence of whatever variety. The reason
for this cautionary word points back again to the impossibility of sustaining an absolute separation between the
natural and the historical after the fashion of the classical
view. For the two interpenetrate each other as we have
pointed out in several ways. General occasions must include
all experience and this means that distinctively human experience cannot be excluded; a religion remaining in touch
with general occasions will not be one based on the nature
of the physical world alone, but it will have as part of its
resources pervasive human experience as well. Special occasions, on the other hand, though they belong to the dimension of human history, take place within a natural setting
and they do not escape the conditions of natural existence.

The proponents of natural religion had the true insight
that it is man as man who is the religious animal and that
the religious question arises out of man's situation in the
world. This is not to say that religion is by any means a
wholly human affair; there is no positive religion at all
without a transcending religious object. But the essential
point remains: man is the one being who has both the need
of and the capacity for religious faith and insight. There are
many aspects or dimensions to life in the world; man alone
raises the religious question and reveals that concern for
the ground and goal of his being which shows that life has a
religious dimension. In supposing that man could answer

the religious question and complete the religious quest merely through the exercise of his reason, the advocates of natural religion went too far. But in their demand that religious truth be intelligible, they saw that if the unity and integrity of the human self is to be preserved, the doctrines of religion cannot be left in a sphere totally foreign to human reason and general experience. We cannot be religious animals by parts and we cannot seal off the knowledge we gain from our participation in general experience from religious truths which we receive through an historical tradition. The two must interpret each other.

The full import of this latter point was not seen by the thinkers of Enlightenment because of their express aim of separating the natural from the historical. On the one hand they did not see that reason is but one of the sources of religious insight and therefore they tried to make it accomplish too much; they underestimated the resources of history and the religious insights derived from special occasions. On the other hand they did see that reason and general experience are not only relevant to the grasping and appropriating of an historical faith, but that both are required for its interpretation and for continuing criticism. This point is absolutely basic and it forms one of the major issues in the revival of theological thought that has taken place in the past decade. Are we to understand man's relation to God solely by reference to an historically instituted divine disclosure or revelation which is wholly discontinuous with human reason and general experience? Or, putting the question in another way, shall we declare that man's general experience and his reflection upon it are so radically set apart from the Christian conception of God that there is no bridge or point of contact between the two? There are those today, and the number seems to be increasing, who hold that Christianity is in no sense a faith which answers to a question and a predicament presented by man as a natural and rational being in the universe. They say that it has nothing to do with religion as a generic form of life, being instead a disclosure of God wholly from beyond man and his experience. As a result, Christianity is made to appear wholly disconnected with reality as experienced and known through what we have been calling general occasions. Revelation, in this view, belongs in a realm apart from that constituted by general experience. Revelation, moreover, although it comes as an alien body of ideas to a being who does not and cannot seek it of himself, is to provide the norm for all of our thinking. And, in addition, it is claimed that such revelation is not dependent either in its reception or for its interpretation upon human reason and knowledge. The divorce is effectively accomplished: Not only is the revealed totally severed from the natural, but religion as a pervasive aspect of human life is set aside as a purely human or cultural phenomenon. The Christian faith is not then a religion beside others, and it is not essentially related to any predicament or religious concern which man as natural creature exhibits. Human knowledge and experience have no essential role in interpreting and certainly no competence for questioning the validity of the revealed content. The final outcome is, as it must ever be with such scepticism, that Christianity is forced to rest on a purely fideistic basis and to make large use of the command to believe. It abandons, as apologetic beneath the dignity of revealed truth, all efforts at expressing itself intelligibly in terms borrowed from general experience and it refuses to allow any external criticism. Its appeal is the wholly positive one of appeal to revealed fact, excluding the relevance of science and philosophy and refusing the possibility of justification from external sources. Such theology is the exact counterpart of a positivistic philosophy seeking to base itself upon either scientific fact or common sense alone to the exclusion of metaphysical analysis and criticism. Further reflection on this outcome would prove instructive to certain theologians and perhaps even to some philosophers.

The bifurcation in man's spiritual life implied in the foregoing position is a direct consequence of the attempt to sustain an absolute distinction between natural and revealed religion, between the special occasions of historical revelation and man's own nature and general experience. If the men of Enlightenment went too far in their attempt to base religion on reason and general experience, the dogmatic reaction to that attempt is no less one-sided. It seals off the Christian heritage from the very historical life and thought to which it was meant to be so intimately related. And indeed the situation would be less tragic were it not so obvious that the proposed bifurcation of our spiritual life is not and indeed cannot be sustained. No sooner do we propose to seal off a portion of our life from outside influence than we discover that the very attempt must be made by a mind that cannot function by parts nor can it will to set aside as irrelevant its own rational canons and cumulative knowledge. To think at all is to make use of natural and secular knowledge, so-called, not to be derived from Christian sources or indeed from any one religious tradition. To ask that the human mind operate as if it neither possessed nor required what it patently does have and need is akin to invoking an ancient recipe for dispelling a headache in which the sufferer is required to go about the house three times *without* thinking of a fox. But, again, if the dichotomy in question cannot in fact be sustained and the two sides continually interpenetrate each other, why may they not supplement each other and at the same time provide mutual criticism and clarification?

Recent years have witnessed concerted efforts to recover the classical content of the Judeo–Christian tradition and to set aside apologetic formulations. In this process of recovery, primary emphasis has been placed upon what is unique in the tradition and it has come to be accepted as a principle by many that the revelation of God is most clearly established at those points where the ideas stand in the sharpest opposition to so-called natural or rational thought and expectation. It is this principle, firmly fixed as a criterion, that leads to the discontinuity already mentioned and to the consequent rejection as irrelevant to revelation of any appeal to general experience and knowledge. We must now show the inadequacy of this conception and at the same time show the inescapability of appeal to general experience, to man as the religious animal, and to the fact that man's own nature in the universe requires that life have a religious dimension built into it.

The evidence of anthropology and the well-known fact that no form of human society has ever been found which does not have a religious community in some form, can only lead to the conclusion that man is by nature a religious animal. That is to say, he is the being who asks the question of the ground and goal of his life and exhibits a concern which betrays his radical need for some answer to his question and the overcoming or fulfilling of his concern. This means that there belongs to human life in the world as we encounter it, a religious dimension; above all the special aims and activities of life, there is a concern for our ultimate purpose in the scheme of things. This purpose is, as Van der Leeuw has expressed it, the "final word" because it bestows significance upon all of our finite concerns and does not itself need to be illuminated from beyond itself. No specific accomplishment is ultimately satisfying if life itself is regarded as without an essential purpose. Every man participates in the religious dimension of life and it belongs to the structure of human life as such. It is a pervasive feature exhibiting itself in every cultural form. Our knowledge of human experience shows that man does not wait for some special historical occasion of revelation before raising the

question of God or before exhibiting that concern for ultimate destiny which is the hallmark of the religious consciousness. On the contrary, the raising of the religious
question and the having of the concern are prior conditions
of man's quest for a disclosure of God and a necessary background against which any such historical disclosure can be
received and understood. Since the religious dimension
belongs to life itself, it must stand in essential relation to
whatever positive religious faith is proposed for our acceptance. If the quest for God belongs to human nature as such
and manifests itself in general experience, then the fulfillment of that quest cannot be received and understood
apart from our nature and experience. The religious insights belonging to the special occasions forming the basis
of Christianity must be received and interpreted by us
through the medium of our reason and the knowledge we
have derived from general occasions. We must now seek
to determine more precisely the connection between general and special occasions.

There are four ways in which general experience and
man's constitution as a religious animal have contributed
and still contribute to the dominant religious tradition in
which we stand. First, there is manifested in human life
universally that question concerning ultimate purpose and
destiny and that concern for resolving the question which
defines the religious dimension of life. We betray our own
incompleteness by our drive toward a final purpose. The
religious question, as has been already emphasized, is not
initially posed in the face of special occasions or revelatory
events; it is rather a precondition of the quest for these occasions. Every fulfillment stands related to an expectation,
and to speak as though a given fulfillment could generate
its own expectation is either to confuse us or to put the cart
before the horse. Those who try to disconnect the revelatory
events of Christianity from the conditions in human life

which lead us to ask for the meaning which those same events are meant to convey, betray the very historical approach to faith which they would defend. If, for example, we are confronted by a doctrine such as atonement and our attention is directed toward the life and death of Christ as the historical basis for that doctrine, we cannot make one step in the direction of comprehending such a notion unless we understand through our own experience what guilt is and unless we can grasp, again through our own experience as human persons, what vicarious suffering might mean. We may not know the full proportions of our failures, nor the total potentialities we may possess apart from some insight into the divine nature, but it is surely folly to suppose that such disclosure simply breaks in upon us in a manner which totally ignores and negates our own reason and being. The religion of special occasions is always dependent upon interpretation through the experience and knowledge of general occasions. Were man not by nature the religious animal, such interpretation would be impossible.

Secondly, the mind and self which are to receive a disclosure of God in a special occasion have already been informed by general knowledge of the world and man. The figure of the *tabula rasa* or blank wax tablet so cherished by later philosophers as a description of the receiving apparatus of the human mind was just as erroneous a representation of things in the first century as it has been shown to be through the criticism of Kant and Leibniz. There is in fact no such blank tablet; there may be empty heads, but there are no empty minds. The natural conditions for all knowledge and experience determine that every encounter of reality by man is conditioned by the one who receives it. Such conditioning does not in any sense imply reduction of religious meaning to something other than itself, nor does it make its validity rest on irrelevant considerations. On the contrary, experience—including all the decisive

and normative experiences that have served as media of
revelation in the Judeo–Christian tradition—needs expression for the realization and continued contemplation of its
meaning. Expression, in turn, requires a language, thought
forms, and categories; these essential elements are never
uniquely supplied by the experience itself. They belong to
the more or less perennial structure of the human mind and
to the special features of the actual situation in which it
finds itself at a given time. It was no accident, therefore,
that those writers who first set out to express the true religious meaning of the set of events constituting the life of
Jesus, should have employed concepts such as *logos* and
symbols such as *light* in order to set forth the meaning of
what they had experienced. These elements plus a great
many others, including the assumed logic and common
sense beliefs about the universe current in their time (e.g.
that the world would soon come to a physical end), belong
to the conditions under which human beings received disclosure of God through special occasions. Just as revelatory
events are not self-interpreting, so they also do not carry
with them the language and categories in which they are
to be expressed. This is not to say that the use of the logos
concept, for example, is no more than a repetition within
the Christian context of a meaning to be found current
among, let us say, the Stoics. It was, of course, special to
Christian insight that the logos became identified with a
life and indeed with a death; there was through this fact
a transforming and reshaping of the idea. This fact, however, does not obscure the equally important fact that the
concept had its own meaning when it was taken over and
that meaning could not have been purged away in the new
context. There were reasons behind the selection of the
concept as the Alexandrian theologians began to make explicit; it pointed to the intrinsic connection between a
universal logos implicit in general experience—a logos of

being—and its peculiar manifestation in the one who is received as the Christ. This connection, as we shall point out, not only allows but even demands that there be continuity of thought between general experience and the interpretation of special occasions taken as the bearers of religious revelation. Whatever novelty may be delivered to us through special occasions cannot be wholly foreign to and destructive of general experience and the knowledge derived from it.

There is a third point at which the positive or historical religious tradition is dependent upon our rational powers and knowledge. A living religious tradition requires not only a repeated interpretation and reinterpretation, but, insofar as it cannot remain insensitive to historical change, it finds itself confronting new knowledge and novel historical situations. Such novelty presents both a challenge and a guide. When, for example, Augustine wrote *Concerning the Literal Interpretation of Genesis*, he could not foresee the situation which would confront a Christian standing in his own tradition trying to compose a work on the same theme in the nineteenth century after 1859. This is not to say that the theory of evolution uniquely determines what the content of theology shall be, but rather that advances in knowledge change our conceptions both of ourselves and of the universe in which we think and live, thus redirecting thought and refocusing issues. Insofar as these changes present a challenge to older interpretations, it becomes necessary to respond. And in so doing we are led on to new interpretations of ancient doctrines and to discover in them possibilities of meaning and implications that could not have been detected at an earlier time.

The medieval Christian thinker, to take another example, was not yet confronted with problems posed by historical or so-called higher criticism. He was also not confronted with the Marxian or Freudian man and, of course, he had no opportunity for responding to such challenges. But a living tradition must respond to such challenges and in so doing it probes more deeply into itself, discovering further implications of its doctrine and setting forth new interpretations of traditional ideas. All great religious thought, though it appears, when well established, as the settled expression of a comfortable orthodoxy, was in its own time a constructive and creative response to a new situation and advancing knowledge.

Discoveries and novel developments in history do not always present challenges to religious truth. It has often been the case that new intellectual achievements have aided in the understanding of ancient religious wisdom. For example, despite difficulties and problems, the extension of critical historical methods to the interpretation of sacred literature has made a more subtle grasp of this literature possible. It has even laid the foundations for recovery of the idea that history is the medium of revelation. It is clear, moreover, that the development of German classical philosophy from Kant to Hegel and ultimately to the philosophy of existence has left an indelible mark upon Protestant theology in the present century. The claim sometimes expressed according to which theology is supposed to develop in a completely internal way and quite apart from dependence upon either reason or secular knowledge, is a claim that cannot be sustained. Secular knowledge, moreover, is often of the first importance in bringing us to a clearer understanding of what is implied in religious truth.

The fourth way in which reason and general experience contribute to religious life and thought is by far the most fundamental. It introduces the thorny but ubiquitous problem of critical validation—the problem of religious knowledge. Ever since the beginning of critical reflection both in and about religion, men have faced the question: Have we knowledge of God or independent being and, if so, what are the critical tests of knowledge? Many different answers to this question have been given. One of the curious features of the present state of opinion is that from two quite divergent viewpoints, such knowledge is denied. A denial is defended not only by those who would confine knowledge to the natural sciences and hand religion, along with ethics and politics, over to the essentially irrational, but also by dogmatic theologians of revelation for whom there can be no "natural" knowledge of God. If we may paraphrase the famous expression of Kant, the former find it necessary to deny knowledge of God and immortality to make way for science, while the latter find it necessary to do so in order to make way for revelation.

We cannot consistently maintain a total rejection or scepticism concerning human reason and man's natural religious concern, without incurring unwelcome consequences for theology itself. The more the power of human reason is impugned, the less possible does it become to defend the validity of religious knowledge. We cannot successfully establish revelation in a special sphere of its own, safe from critical attack, while at the same time joining with the secular mind in the thorough rejection of a reason which has metaphysical depth in it. If Christianity is to be more than a cosmic mythology, however important, an attempt must be made to express it in terms intelligible to our general experience so that we can understand how it might be taken as true and not merely useful. If it is the case, as indeed many signs seem to indicate, that the modern man has lost God, surely one of the major reasons for this loss stems from the increasing strangeness of the Christian ideas in a world dominated by highly abstract and technological modes of thought. The concepts of original sin, for example, or atonement, originating in events of a distant past, seem increasingly strange to a mind schooled in the belief that we know nothing except what can be discovered through manipulating things under strictly controlled and therefore artificial conditions. Is a solution to be sought in accepting a complete divorce and in retiring the religious ideas into a domain apart in which their truth is inviolate except that they no longer have any logical connection with our general experience and scientific knowledge? This solution presents itself as a happy one to many minds at present. And yet as we contemplate it, we should see at once that it is no solution. It is too easy; we cannot suppose that the perennial and much debated problem concerning the relations between religion, scientific knowledge, and philosophy can be resolved merely by supposing that the three are all irrelevant to each other. Must we not seek instead to overcome the gap between the modern mind and the classical Christian ideas by seeking to recover that dialogue between reason and faith which began with the Alexandrian theologians and ceased only when men acquiesced in that departmentalization of life and thought which has been among the major blights of modern times?

Here is the point at which we can see most vividly the contribution to be made by what I have been calling the permanent truth in the idea of natural religion. All claims to religious truth must be related to the fact that man is by nature the religious animal, the one who has the religious concern and who asks the religious question. We ask who we are, why we are, and what the whole thing means. This *is* the question of God, and man, just because he is the one being who asks what it means to be, is the one being equipped to receive the religious answer. But question and answer cannot be located in two entirely different orders of being. If a religious answer represents the truth about man, the world, and God, then it cannot exist in a realm apart—it must show itself in the nature of the world in which we live and it must be connectible with our experience and our knowledge. A religion purporting to be true of our cosmos and of human history cannot carve out for itself a special private world in which alone it appears true, while leaving the common world in which we all live to its own devices. This would be, as Kierkegaard vividly expressed the point in criticism of Hegel, to abscond to the realm of pure being while leaving the rest of us to face the worst!

Let us attempt a brief summary of our conclusions. In the first instance the classical distinction and separation between natural and historical religion cannot be sustained. One consequence is that there is no natural religion in the sense of our constructing a system of theology, an ethic, and a liturgical system from our knowledge of the world and ourselves. But there is a *religious dimension of experience* which belongs to human life as such in the universe. It belongs to life itself to ask the question of God and to experience the need for that ultimate power and purpose which unifies the self and preserves it from the destructiveness of self-indulgence and the chaos of many competing possibilities when they are without the constraint of an ultimate purpose. No claim in behalf of revelation can be made in disregard of these facts. For in the face of such a claim we cannot avoid asking for the connection between our natural religious concern and the interpretation we are to give to the religious intuitions derived from what we have called special occasions. Since, moreover, man is capable of attaining natural knowledge through general experience in which all participate, the question of the bearing of that knowledge upon religious truth becomes inescapable. Whenever the proponents of natural religion understood their claim in this sense, they were right.

The second consequence is that there is no purely historical or revelational religion either. The truths about God and man delivered through special occasions must be received and interpreted by man under the conditions that govern the reception of all experience and the attainment of all knowledge. This means that the language, the thought forms, and the secular knowledge possessed by the interpreting mind will enter essentially into the expression and development of the religious truth.

A profound understanding suggests that when we entertain the concept of natural religion, we think not of how much can be attained through reason alone and how much is derived from other sources, but rather of the *religious dimension of experience* and of the relevance of our natural knowledge for the interpretation and validation of the traditional faith in which we stand. A religious tradition which seeks to insulate itself from all connection with man's general experience and knowledge on the supposition that God is not to be measured by the wisdom of this world, not only shows impiety toward the divine creation but also runs the risk of losing its very life. The history of religion is filled with examples of causes lost because their proponents believed it possible to preserve their ancient wisdom free from all contaminating contact with insights derived from general experience and secular knowledge. A rational religion cannot afford to make that mistake.

Index